James Monroe, John Marshall and 'The Excellence of Our Institutions', 1817–1825

When James Monroe became president in 1817, the United States urgently needed a national transportation system to connect new states and territories in the west with older states facing the Atlantic Ocean. In 1824, the Supreme Court declared that Congress had the power to regulate traffic on all navigable rivers and lakes in the United States. Congress began clearing obstructions from rivers and these projects enabled steamboats to transform cross-country travel in the United States. This book explains how building a nationwide economic market was essential to secure the loyalty of geographically remote regions to the new republic. Aschenbrenner defends the activist role of President James Monroe (1817–1825) and Chief Justice John Marshall (1801–1835). Under their leadership the federal government made national prosperity its 'Job One'. The market revolution transformed the daily lives of households and businesses in the United States and proved to Americans that they shared a common social and economic destiny. As Monroe declared at the conclusion of his Presidency: 'We find abundant cause to felicitate ourselves in the excellence of our institutions'.

Peter J. Aschenbrenner is the National Convenor (US) for the International Commission for the History of Representative and Parliamentary Institutions and a Fellow of the Royal Historical Society.

Routledge Advances in American History

16 **Education and the Racial Dynamics of Settler Colonialism in Early America**
Georgia and South Carolina, ca. 1700–ca. 1820
James O'Neil Spady

17 **The Overseers of Early American Slavery**
Supervisors, Enslaved Labourers, and the Plantation Enterprise
Laura R. Sandy

18 **An Unfamiliar America**
Essays in American Studies
Edited by Ari Helo and Mikko Saikku

19 **George W Bush Administration Propaganda for an Invasion of Iraq**
The Absence of Evidence
Larry Hartenian

20 **Redefining Irishness in a Coastal Maine City, 1770–1870**
Bridget's Belfast
Kay Retzlaff

21 **James Monroe, John Marshall and 'The Excellence of Our Institutions', 1817–1825**
How Monroe's Presidency Became 'An Important Epoch in the History of the Civilized World'
Peter J. Aschenbrenner

For more information about this series, please visit: https://www.routledge.com/Routledge-Advances-in-American-History/book-series/RAAH

James Monroe, John Marshall and 'The Excellence of Our Institutions', 1817–1825

How Monroe's Presidency Became 'An Important Epoch in the History of the Civilized World'

Peter J. Aschenbrenner

Routledge
Taylor & Francis Group
NEW YORK AND LONDON

First published 2022
by Routledge
605 Third Avenue, New York, NY 10158

and by Routledge
4 Park Square, Milton Park, Abingdon, Oxon, OX14 4RN

Routledge is an imprint of the Taylor & Francis Group, an informa business

Library of Congress Cataloging-in-Publication Data
A catalog record for this title has been requested

ISBN: 978-0-367-89473-3 (hbk)
ISBN: 978-1-032-25107-3 (pbk)
ISBN: 978-1-003-01938-1 (ebk)

DOI: 10.4324/9781003019381

Typeset in Sabon
by KnowledgeWorks Global Ltd.

For Teresa, Aaron, Nathanael
and Benjamin

Nature, in the main, vindicates her law.
Skill to do comes of doing; knowledge
comes by eyes always open, and working
hands and there is no knowledge that
is not power ... the men who fear
no city, but by whom cities stand

Ralph Waldo Emerson, *Complete
Works*, 'Old Age', 7:321 (1862)

Contents

Foreword ix
Acknowledgments xiii

Introduction: 'Destinies Beyond the Reach of Mortal Eye' 1

1 'Westward the Course of Empire Takes Its Way' 18

2 'To Adopt a System of Internal Improvement' 38

3 'Powers to Create and to Preserve' 59

4 'Captivating Improvements to Seduce Their Constituents' 82

5 'There Is More Than One Mode of Accomplishing the End' 107

6 'To Protect the Public Industry from Parasite Institutions' 129

7 'An Important Epoch in the History of the Civilized World' 152

Appendix A: Survey of 1,147 Improvement Projects 170
Appendix B: Railroads Subsidized via Federal Land Grants 172
Appendix C: The Political Governance and Resource Exploitation Clauses 174

Appendix D: The Cumberland Road 177
Appendix E: The 'Two Governments' Formula 179
Appendix F: Technical Appendix and Editorial Practices 181
Appendix G: Public History, Practice and Purpose 183
Appendix H: James W. McCulloch, John Marshall and the US Sinking Fund 185
Appendix I: Comparing and Contrasting Nations and Cultures in The Federalist 187
Appendix J: Marshall and Monroe Discuss the 'Views' 189
Appendix K: The Bonus Bill (1817) and the 1818 House Resolution. 190
Appendix L: Unravelling the Northwest Ordinance 192
Index 195

Foreword

'Why create the American republic?' With this sentence I opened my own inquiry into the problem of internal improvements in the early United States. Was the purpose to do good things for the people, or was it simply to prevent the intrusion of government on private liberty? In this new study of political reasoning in the early United States, Peter J. Aschenbrenner shows that the answer is 'both'.

My original goal was to call attention to the dissonance that abounded in the institutions of the early republic as a result of the blending of optimistic and pessimistic assumptions that informed revolutionary republicanism. On the optimistic side, Americans embraced a truly utopian ideal of virtuous citizens electing 'disinterested' statesmen to gather and deliberate in their behalf, empowered to deliver the governance 'the people' wanted and needed – no more, no less. On the pessimistic side, revolutionary Americans had persuaded themselves that cynical corruption and abuse of power had eaten the heart out of the English constitution, delivering sovereign power into the hands of selfish and immoral agents of a corrupt polity and society.

There never was a solid consensus among our so-called founding generation, but the process of institution-building took place within the bounds of four assumptions: (1) governance is necessary; (2) power corrupts; (3) liberty requires protection; and (4) the citizen *is* the sovereign. Several pre-existing facts complicated this founding exercise. First, the American colonies never had been, close siblings, and they lacked confidence in each other's motives and interests. Second, colonial governance was strongest at the local level, where structural similarities suggested a commonality of experience that fostered the illusion of unity. Third, the revolutionary movement condemned central imperial governance as alien, sinister, and contrary to liberty. As a result, revolutionary Americans clung ardently to their post-colonial state governments and jealously resisted any flow of power toward the national center.

By 1787 friends of the national union felt compelled to re-energize the central government, but they found it useful to mask their intentions and manipulate political discourse to win consent of the governed for a 'more perfect Union'. In other words, in the construction of our utopian 'excellent institutions', America's founders projected a pristine universe of civic virtue while engaging in practical behavior that was neither disinterested nor ideal. New life springs from indulgences that 'parents' rarely confess to the children.

One of the enduring questions coming out of the American revolutionary settlement lay in the peculiar 'two governments' formula that made ratification possible. Late-eighteenth century speculative philosophers believed that right institutions could guide human behavior toward benevolent ends, but in practice local American governments appeared to reward narrow, licentious purposes. Unwilling (or unable) to ask the states to surrender sovereignty to a strong central authority, the founders built the new constitution directly on the backs of the people, laying a unitary government over the top of the several states. Critics declared it absurd – *imperium in imperio* (a sovereignty within a sovereignty) – but the theory of popular sovereignty made it possible to locate indivisible authority not in one or the other but in the whole people out-of-doors. Whether a brilliant innovation or a desperate improvisation, the two governments formula evolved into one of the central pillars of America's 'excellent institutions'.

Aschenbrenner's new study, *The Excellence of Our Institutions,* picks up the story of implementation that follows the creation of the American Republic. With the new Constitution in hand, its friends (Aschenbrenner calls them 'Majoritarians') set about activating this awkward structure while trying to incorporate lingering opponents ('Superminoritarians') within a workable praxis of politics. All parties had to learn to finesse the divisions of power and conflicts of interest, build trust in the framework, regulate the process, modulate expectations, all without triggering the revolutionary urge that had produced the Constitution itself. One could argue that for several decades implementation of the system stood as the most important work of the new American government.

Many historians – myself included – struggle to understand the complex calculus that goes into political reasoning and statecraft. Jefferson's Manichean distinction between 'honest men and rogues' tempts us always to look for elegance and principle when we scrutinize the work of public servants. Equally mischievous is the naïve assertion that 'the people' at large are innocent and unstained. In reality, political service requires that agents process dozens of incoming facts, juggle conflicting demands, assess probable outcomes, calculate the strength of voter support, fortify strategic alliances, and *take action.* The historian may appreciate the irony, complexity, or gravity of a situation, but it is the lawmaker who is called upon to vote and get on with it. This is what Aschenbrenner calls 'parliamentary science' or 'legislative competence', and in this fascinating study Aschenbrenner tries to expose for us a rational, analytical approach to the reasoning process that real politicians cannot avoid.

In this book Aschenbrenner zeroes in on what he calls a 'data set' of events that support propositions laid down by two key players in early nineteenth-century American politics: James Monroe and John Marshall. Their writings wrestled with two closely-related gaps in what was meant to be a clear delineation of power between state and national authorities. The role of the central government in providing and controlling networks of transportation and communication vexed the members of the First Federal Congress and continued to do so through the interstate highway initiatives of the Eisenhower administration 160 years later. Likewise, the power to create a national bank was neither affirmed nor denied in the Constitution of 1787, setting the stage for an equally long struggle over control of the money system. Both of these issues promised to integrate far-flung American communities through social and commercial intercourse. Both appeared to be 'necessary and proper' to the goals of the national government and the interests of the whole people. But each could be used to pit interest against interest, locale against locale, public against private initiative, and state against federal authority. Even worse, over time, each emerged as a proxy for making moves on the established balance of federalism and the unholy national agreement to tolerate slavery in some states.

In my interpretation there are no greater examples of the tragic ambivalence of governance in the early republic than banking and internal improvements. Obstructionist coalitions weaved and bobbed to distort nearly every discussion of these two concerns, producing what Aschenbrenner calls 'organic paralysis'. Historians have faulted either the resulting policy stalemates or the damage done to electoral games that otherwise kept things like slavery at bay. Yet Aschenbrenner, quoting James Monroe, titles his study 'The Excellence of Our Institutions'. A long career on the federal bench – as United States Magistrate Judge – has impressed him that politics is 'the art of the possible' and that pristine, uncomplicated choices do not obtain in the real world. Well versed in both modern and classic treatises on jurisprudence, government, decision-making, and rhetoric, Aschenbrenner here develops a unique set of methods for trying to analyze rigorously the building blocks with which Monroe, Marshall, and their contemporaries built arguments to facilitate the business of governing without pulling down the house (as Jefferson so rudely prescribed) whenever the regime failed to serve the 'happiness' of the people.

Methodologically unique and intellectually challenging, Aschenbrenner's new book forces us to meditate on the gradual accretion of ideas, principles, and precedents that finally impressed upon the American political community the virtues of their somewhat ungainly experiment. Confidence in the kind of reasoning laid down by Monroe and Marshall sustained the republic through sixty years of raucous expansion and development, until the festering grievances of certain 'Superminoritiarians' coalesced into a sectional 'Majoritarian' movement that pulled the trigger on the right of revolution. Although the Union victory in the Civil War did salvage the structures of the old constitutional settlement, the fabric of national goodwill had been rent and the complex practice of politics would have to be invented anew.

John Lauritz Larson
Professor, Purdue University
Department of History
March, 2021

Acknowledgments

David Currie's series *The Constitution in Congress* inspired me to read the Public Statutes at Large, starting with 1 Stat 1. I narrowed my lens to transportation and communication projects (with additional attention to national banking and financial affairs). Regrettably Prof. Currie is no longer with us. One can only imagine what he would think of page-turning as a lesser methodology.

Colleagues at the Universität Wien, Rechtswissenschaftliche Fakultät made suggestions during the early development of this paper. In September 2018, Dr Markus Lampe, Wirtschaftsuniversität Wien, Institut für Wirtschafts- und Sozialgeschichte, graciously consulted with me on the Smithian productivity analytics. Dr Jurgen Honig (Purdue University, West Lafayette) and Dott Rocco Giurato (Università di Calabria, Cosenza/Rende, Italy) offered comments which I found very useful. All errors are mine.

I also acknowledge inspiration from Prof. Dan Carpenter *The Forging of Bureaucratic Autonomy* (Princeton, 2001) and Prof. Dan Preston (editor-in-chief, *The Papers of James Monroe*) both of whom afforded me interviews. These enlightened me on the subject of bureaucratic agenda and bureaucratic autonomy.

Bonnie Litschewski Paulson and Stanley L. Paulson – interpreters and translators of Hans Kelsen's *Reine Rechtslehre/Pure Theory of Law* – met me in Kiel (March 2018). The evening introduced me to the inner mysteries of Kelsen scholarship and inspired the paper I gave at the International Commission conference in September of that year.

Scholars at the National Archives (US) and Library of Congress unraveled many technical difficulties in obtaining access to material.

Editors at Routledge offered unfailing courtesy and prompt responses. Since this is my second monograph that Routledge has published, this was no surprise. I extend my sincere gratitude to my managing editor Max Novick for his gracious attention to the project. I especially wish to thank Alison Kirk without whose encouragement the project would not have matured into this study.

Introduction

'Destinies Beyond the Reach of Mortal Eye'

'Thus had the campaign progressed, without any visible steps towards works of defence, either permanent or temporary'

The Second War for American Independence (1812–1815) visited entirely foreseeable near-death consequences on the United States. Very welcome news, however, crossed the North Atlantic from Ghent (in the United Netherlands). The Senate promptly ratified the Treaty of Ghent upon its arrival in Washington (16 February 1815). On the next day Secretary of State James Monroe hand-delivered the Senate's ratification to the British envoy in Washington.[1]

James Monroe and John Marshall are the principal figures in my study. I concentrate my attention on 15 compositions datable to 1819 and 1822. Marshall composed and published 12 essays in 1819. The best known of these compositions is an opinion Marshall wrote for the Supreme Court on the subject of national banking arrangements,[2] along with 11 lesser-known essays supplementing his opinion.[3] Marshall published these essays under the pseudonyms 'A Friend to the Union' (2) and 'A Friend of the Constitution' (9). I refer to these as his 'Friend' essays. In 1822 Monroe penned a short veto message disapproving a bill installing tollgates on a national road.[4] Monroe also composed a lengthy essay which he titled 'Views of the President of the United States on the Subject of Internal Improvements'.[5] I treat the 'Views' as comprising two essays. Monroe composed most of this text in 1819, with the remaining text datable to 1822. Monroe arranged his materials in an awkward fashion. Monroe divided his 1819 text and sandwiched the newly-composed 1822 text between opening and closing tranches of his 1819 text.

My study concentrates on the interval 1817–1825. On occasion I turn back to the founding of the Second Republic (1787–1789). I also draw on events from the early days of the (first) Washington administration (1789–1793) as well as events from the presidency of Andrew Jackson (1829–1837). James Madison and Thomas Jefferson made notable contributions to the methods that I expose in the compositions of Monroe

DOI: 10.4324/9781003019381-1

and Marshall. In general, my interest is drawn to technical achievements. I also refer to the work of Adam Smith, Wm. Blackstone, Matthew Hale and Francis Bacon. Their investigations are historically relevant to the 15 essays that Monroe and Marshall composed. Other authors in Great Britain/United Kingdom, France, Germany, Italy and ancient Greece and Rome play walk-on roles.

John Marshall (1755–1835) served in the First War for American Independence (1775–1783), set himself up as a lawyer in Richmond, was elected to the Confederation Congress (1782), served as a delegate to the Virginia ratifying convention (1788) and also served in the 6th Congress (1799–1800). When President Adams dispatched envoys to Paris – the Quasi-War with France roiled trans-Atlantic trade – Adams appointed Marshall to the delegation. Although the mission was a failure, it showcased Marshall's considerable talents as a team player and negotiator. Adams appointed Marshall – at the time a Virginia Congressman – as his Secretary of State, a post he held for nine months (1800–1801). Adams then appointed Marshall to the Supreme Court. Marshall became the nation's fourth Chief Justice, serving from 1801 until his death in 1835.[6]

James Monroe (1758–1831) also served in the First War for American Independence. Monroe sustained a severe wound in street fighting at Trenton (26 December 1776). Monroe was elected to the Virginia House of Delegates (1782), the Confederation Congress (1783) and served as a delegate to the Virginia ratifying convention at Richmond (1788). Elected to serve in the United States Senate (1790–1794) and twice elected Governor of Virginia (1799–1802, 1811), Monroe also held posts as Ambassador to France and to the United Kingdom. James Madison appointed him Secretary of State (1811), a position he held to the end of Madison's presidency (1817).[7] I note that Monroe and Marshall crossed swords at the Virginia ratifying convention (June 1788). Monroe opposed unconditional ratification of *Constitution II*, while Marshall made two major speeches in favor of ratification. They were acquaintances from boyhood in Virginia.

Monroe's political career was marked by two episodes in which his pride overwhelmed his better judgment. Monroe published a rebuke to President George Washington after Washington recalled Monroe from Paris where he was serving as Ambassador to France.[8] This was followed by a dustup with President Jefferson after an unsuccessful round of negotiations with the British empire.[9] While Marshall glided upward to higher office, Monroe struck many as a man in a hurry to satisfy his ambition for the nation's highest office. Present at the Battle of Bladensburg debacle on the afternoon of 24 August 1814, Monroe drew criticism for orders he gave repositioning troops on the Eastern Branch of the Potomac. The House of Representatives conducted an investigation. Its report blamed the American defeat on lack of earthworks.[10] Today one can visualize the line that US troops could have held, if their commanders had ordered 'works of defence' to be constructed. It runs along 38th Avenue and crosses highway US Alt 1 near Hope's Laundramat, situated at 3631 Bladensburg Road, MD 20722. The earthworks would have provided a second line of defense for Americans to reform and defend Washington after the British crossed the bridge over the Eastern Branch of the Potomac. I refer to the statement of General Van Ness (that he made to the committee investigating the disaster). 'Thus had the campaign progressed, without any visible steps towards works of defence, either permanent or temporary, either on the land, or the water side (I never heard of a spade or an axe being struck in any such operation)'.[11] After sacking his defense minister, James Madison appointed James Monroe as his Secretary of War. This was another appointment that Monroe added to his glittering roster of non-presidential offices.

In the interval 1801 to 1817 Thomas Jefferson and his hand-picked successor, James Madison, made good their prior claims to the nation's highest office. After Monroe cooled his heels – through four presidential elections – it seemed that voters in the presidential election of 1816 resolved to reward Monroe for his dogged determination to survive political, military and diplomatic shoot outs. When the reader reaches the upper floor of the Metropolitan Museum of Art (Fifth Avenue, New York City), she may admire Emanuel Leutze's *Washington Crossing the Delaware* (1851). The officer who has covered himself in the Stars and Stripes is James Monroe.[12]

'Two governments, completely distinct and independent of each other'

The theme that unites the 15 compositions (referenced in the previous section) is the 'two governments' formula.[13] My Appendix E: The 'Two Governments' Formula includes representative passages that illustrate the employment of this formula. Marshall employed the formula in a passage that he recycled (for a total of three mentions) in essays published in 1819. Monroe employed the phrase eight times in his 'Views' (1822). Monroe assigned 'great principles' to the relationship between the unitary (national) government and the parochial (state) governments.[14] Monroe based his exposition of the 'two governments' formula on the representative nature of both governments.

> It is impossible to speak too highly of this system taken in its twofold character and in its great principles of two governments, completely distinct from and independent of each other, each constitutional, founded by and acting directly on the people, each competent to all its purposes, administering all the blessings for which it was instituted, without even the most remote danger of exercising any of its powers in a way to oppress the people.[15]

Both the unitary and parochial governments acted 'directly on the people'. Each government, Monroe explained, was designed to be 'completely distinct from and independent of each other'.[16] Inhabitants were assured, on this account, that the national government would not be 'exercising any of its powers' to accumulate power for the sake of power. Each of two governments (occupying the same political society) would be expected to stabilize themselves by delivering benefits to inhabitants. That's what governments do; they deliver benefits to inhabitants to maintain or enhance their stability or they go out of business. If two governments engage in parallel efforts to deliver benefits, Monroe and Marshall argued, these efforts do not necessarily bring the governments into conflict. For its part, the national government would find that economies of scale cautioned against spending national dollars on projects of local importance.

There was a downside to organizing a political society around two governments, however. As the reader will have guessed, competing demands on the allegiance of inhabitants invited organic paralysis. That was not the only challenge that the task of building a national government in North America faced. On many occasions, charters (establishing provinces in British North America) ignored mountains, rivers or lakes as natural borders or, even worse, employed lines of latitude and longitude that were untethered to geophysical reality. The result was that many provincial boundaries overlapped tracts assigned to other provinces. Parochial governments could not effectively unify a nation divided by such a crazy-quilt pattern of geopolitical surfaces. State cessions of overlapping tracts were designed to make sense of the provincial boundaries that states inherited when they declared independence in 1776. A further step towards unifying the nation occurred when the Second Republic designated postal routes throughout the nation as a means of uniting the nation's sprawling and diverse landscapes (1792).[17] In 1806 Congress took the next logical step, launching four national road projects in two Acts of Congress; only 23 days separated final passage on these two bills.[18] These legislative acts invite attention to the Second Republic's commitment to deliver communication and transportation services throughout the new nation.

'Persons having the highest numbers not exceeding three on the list of those voted for as President'

This brings me to the role that the Philadelphia convention played in framing arrangements that encouraged organic paralysis. I begin with transportation projects. Congress might enact laws for the purpose of 'opening roads and navigations [and] facilitating communications through the United States'. In line with a proposal brought up at the Philadelphia convention (20 August 1787), the convention considered assigning these duties to a Secretary of domestic affairs.[19] No vote was recorded on the proposal, however. The convention did ballot on a proposal to vest Congress with the power to incorporate canal companies (14 September). Of the 11 states considering the question only three supported the proposal. The Philadelphia convention postponed the inevitable. Once Congress was organized and began to do business it was entirely foreseeable, for example, that Congress would consider bills to open 'roads and navigations' and facilitate 'communications through the United States'.

It was also foreseeable that some states would demand that changes to constitutional text precede programmatic action. If Congress considered a bill to launch a project within the subject matter area 'XYZ', a search for words and phrases (lexically) associated with 'XYZ' would return a null result. (a) Accordingly, the Philadelphia convention wagered that a minority would concede the change in constitutional text necessary to authorize a given program *if and only if* the parties arrived at a mutually acceptable price. (b) The convention also wagered that states would not refuse to negotiate changes. Refusal to negotiate changes in *Constitution I* brought about repeated crises of governance in the First Republic (1781, 1783, 1784).[20] The Philadelphia convention assumed that the Second Republic would not suffer the same fate. (c) I turn to Article I, Section 8, Clauses 2 through 17. The fact that *Constitution II* listed some powers, the assumption ran, would inspire a majority to restrain itself from considering other projects, such as projects designed to establish a network of national roads. *Constitution II* did not include the phrase 'national road' in its text. Based on these three wagers – outlined above – the Philadelphia convention assumed that (a) those seeking authorization for new service missions would open negotiations for constitutional text to authorize projects fulfilling such service missions, (b) proponents would also signal their willingness to pay a suitable price for the minority's acquiescence and (c) successful negotiations would follow. The political science of the foregoing wagers can be templated via the well-formed formula 'if x, then x, else z'. *If* a majority sought to build a road of national importance, *then* the minority would concede new constitutional text (at a mutually acceptable price), *else* the road could/would not be built.

Propositions of the type – 'if x, then y, else z' – are fact-testable.[21] Was the minority's acquiescence in granting authority for new service missions for sale? I turn to prices exacted at the Philadelphia convention. (a) Some states demanded a malapportioned second house of Congress. This arrangement boosted the political leverage of states with less than average populations. (b) Some states demanded and got additional Congressmen assigned to their states based on the number of African-Americans that the state disenfranchised. (c) Moving to a higher level of abstraction, Article V rewarded future coalitions of quarrelsome states if they were minded to resist organic change. Thus, Article V institutionalized superminority extortion, since only 'Amendments ratified by the Legislatures of three fourths of the several States, or by Conventions in three fourths thereof ... shall be valid to all Intents and Purposes, as Part of this Constitution'. In the interval 1803–1812, the threshold for such leverage numbered 5 of 17 states. The 'three forths' formula granted superminority blocking power to five states. The arithmetic follows. The fraction 12/17 reduces to 70.5% which is less than the 75% approval (of state legislatures) required to amend the constitution. Accordingly, the truculence of five states could defeat the will of 12 states. In 1824 Congressman John Randolph of Virginia identified the superminority states. In a speech in the House of Representatives, he referred to the region including Maryland, Virginia, North Carolina, South Carolina, Georgia and Alabama.[22]

How would a minority of states price their acquiescence to new constitutional text after the Louisiana Purchase was concluded, that is, post-1803? There is no need to speculate on this point. The text of the Twelfth Amendment discloses the price the superminority demanded and got for their acquiescence to that change in organic arrangements. If no candidate received a majority of electoral college votes, Article II, Section 1 of *Constitution II* sent all candidates to the House of Representatives where a wild west ballot-off would take place. Assuming a host of 'favorite son' candidates garnered at least a single electoral college vote from their respective home states, *Constitution II* – before the Twelfth Amendment – diluted the power of a few states to form coalitions when a presidential election moved into the House of Representative. 'In chusing the President, the Votes shall be taken by States, the Representation from each State having one Vote'. Article II, Section 1, Clause 3. The Twelfth Amendment, however, restricted the consideration of that body to 'the persons having the highest numbers not exceeding three on the list of those voted for as President'. It's one thing to make 17 presidential candidates (one 'favorite son' candidate per state, as of 1804) bid against one another for the support of a majority of state delegations in Congress. It's another thing for one or two coalitions of states (acting through their Congressmen) to force three candidates to bid against one another. A presidential election would turn on willingness of each candidate to wheel and deal his path to the presidency. Congressmen from states with few members would hold the whip hand, since each state had one vote to cast in the proceedings. The lesson of the Twelfth Amendment follows. Those opposing constitutional amendments – as the keystone of their strategy – were tempted to make the rest of the nation pay dearly for changes that majoritarians sought. I underscore the asymmetry at work. The majoritarians were obliged to bargain for constitutional amendments to get bills passed that launched transportation projects. The superminoritarians sought changes in the nation's organic arrangements to shore up their power to block the majoritarians from building a national government with powers of continental proportions.

It seemed that another opportunity to leverage this asymmetry to the superminoritarians' advantage presented itself in 1805–1806. The 9th Congress took up bills to construct four national roads. Congress planned the initial segment of the first project to run from Cumberland MD to Wheeling VA. Congress obliged President Jefferson to shop the Cumberland Road project to four state legislatures and obtain the consents of Maryland, Pennsylvania, Virginia and Ohio. Called upon to say 'yes' or 'no' to Act of March 29, 1806, state lawmakers could also condition their consent.[23] I refer to the long and sordid history of conditional ratifications and conditional consents in the United States.[24] Maryland's long-awaited ratification of *Constitution I* (2 February 1781) arrived in such a fashion and followed on the heels of Virginia's conditional cession of lands north and west of the Ohio River.[25] The nation required a network of roads to achieve basic efficiencies in moving people and products across the 17 existing states along with the three bulk territories that Congress controlled as of 1803.[26] The Louisiana Purchase (1803) doubled the extent of frontier lands that the United States claimed. If a minority of states were minded to 'sell' a constitutional amendment to Congress – authorizing a road from Athens GA to New Orleans, for example – negotiations might tempt the minority to exact more political power from the majority.

And then, quite suddenly, this state of affairs took a dramatic turn. While Congress required the President to seek state consents for the Cumberland Road (29 March 1806),[27] 23 days later (21 April 1806) Congress launched three more national roads into western lands without instructing the president to shop these projects to state legislatures.[28] (a) Congress designated a route for a national road to run from Athens GA to New Orleans (in the Orleans Territory). (b) Congress also authorized 'a road or roads through the territory lately ceded by the Indians to the United States, from the river Mississippi to the Ohio, and to the former Indian boundary line which was established by Treaty of Grenville', roughly through northern Ohio to the Mississippi River. (c) Congress designated the third project to run from Nashville TN and into the Mississippi Territory terminating at Natchez.

Congressmen gained the support of voters for an aggressive program of national road construction. Voters' thirst to move better, faster, cheaper throughout the United States and its territories motivated their acceptance of the leadership role that Congressmen and Senators advocated. But this is not just a story about roads, canals and rivers cleared of snags and sandbars enabling paddle-wheel steamboats to foam the waters. Marshall and Monroe took the opportunity gifted them – in the interval 1817–1825 – to refound the Second Republic. As leaders, they advocated an expansive role for the national government. If it required bribery or extortion or browbeating, Congress would brandish the whip hand in demanding state participation or (at least) acquiescence in infrastructure programs that federal leadership launched.

'Devising and causing to be surveyed under captivating disguises the thousand local improvements'

I surveyed acts of Congress from the 1st Congress, 1st Session (1789) through the 24th Congress, 2nd Session (1837). I draw on details presented in Appendix A: Survey of 1,147 Improvement Projects. My purpose was to locate all enactments launching or curating improvement projects. When Congress initially devoted attention to a project in a statute or resolution, I refer to this legislative effort as 'launching' a project. When Congress modified the features of a project (already written into law) I use the term 'curating'. Two Acts of Congress bracket the improvement projects that I located in statutes and resolutions. On 3 March 1791 the 1st Congress, 3rd Session designated a postal route from Albany NY to Bennington VT. The Act of March 3, 1837 concluded my survey. In that measure the 24th Congress, 2nd Session subsidized the New Orleans and Carrolton Railroad with a grant of public land. In launching or curating projects, Congress (a) designated project routes (typically by naming beginning and end points), (b) selected funding vehicles for projects, (c) directed the participation of federal, state and private agents in these projects, (d) constructed the project, (e) managed claims (for additional compensation) that contractors and employees asserted and (f) disposed of project assets at the end of the project's useful life.

During the 46-year interval (1791–1837), Congress enacted 190 different statutes and resolutions that devoted attention to transportation and communication projects. These texts appeared in the first four volumes and ran into the fifth volume of the US Public Statutes at Large. I counted 1,147 mentions of improvement projects in these 190 statutes and resolutions. By casting out duplicates I arrived at a subtotal of 243 provisions of text (in statutes or resolutions) addressing distinct projects in the interval 1791–1837. In counting projects, I gathered all postal route designations within a single state, for example, as one project. My justification follows: when Congress built out transportation and communication infrastructure it was required to allocate resources *among* states and *within* states. In other words, Congress obliged itself to resolve *intra*state competition for federal benefits as well as *inter*-state competition. When a state's congressional delegation was unable to resolve intrastate disagreements (for example, competing claims to postal services advanced by seaboard vs. back country regions), the House of Representatives would be compelled to step in. I cross-reference an example of *intra*state competition for postal services in North Carolina (1792).[29]

I divided these 1,147 mentions of improvement projects into three intervals. Through the Presidencies of Washington, Adams, Jefferson and Madison (28 years) Congress launched or curated 284 projects. During Monroe's eight-year presidency Congress launched or curated another 194 projects. During the presidencies of J.Q. Adams and Jackson, Congress launched or curated 669 projects.[30] The rates at which Congress passed improvement bills during these intervals were, approximately, 10 projects per year, 25 projects per year and 55 projects per year. It did not escape notice that Congress was – over time – increasingly eager to launch improvement projects. If one credits Martin Van Buren's memoir (1854), Congressmen were proposing improvement projects in a 'wild spirit of speculation'.[31]

> The wits of Congressmen were severely tasked in devising and causing to be surveyed and brought forward under captivating disguises the thousand local improvements with which they designed to dazzle and seduce their constituents.[32]

My total of 1,147 projects approximates Van Buren's 'thousand local improvements'. My survey included postal routes, national roads, canals, railroads, navigation improvements (such as construction of docks and piers or removal of snags, sandbars and other obstructions from rivers), bridges, beach restorations and coastal surveys. I also included Congress's approval of state projects improving access to navigable waterways or ports. I didn't count federal lighthouses. These numbered 24 by 1800.[33] Lighthouses struck me as too blue water for inclusion in my survey.

Congress designated postal routes by naming towns and villages; these served as nodes that marked out routes over which the US mail would travel. Proceeding in this manner, Congress learned how to batch-process multiple projects in a single bill. In its first attempt to gather communities into a national postal system, Congress named 206 places in the Act of February 20, 1792, Section 1.[34] In enacting this legislation, Congress served as the national broker of benefits and burdens. Brokering benefits may be regarded as the core function of Congress. Successful benefit distribution demonstrates legislative competence. Later in this study I will dissect brokerage into auction, bargaining and deferred satisfaction.[35]

Appendix A: Survey of 1,147 Improvement Projects explains how I coded funding vehicles that Congress created and employed. The list follows:

- user fees,
- land sales (from statehood grants),
- direct funding via Congressional appropriation,

- federal equity investment in the project and
- permanent land grants or grants of access to navigable waters.

I also coded four types of institution agents.

- Congress might name the President as the actor responsible for fulfilling its mission specific instructions and then name generic 'commissioners' as his subagents; these officials would carry out Congress's instructions, *or*
- Congress might name an existing federal agency (like the Post Office Department) as its agent, *or*
- Congress might name a state or local government agency (such as the Wardens of the Port of Philadelphia). Congress would task this body to fulfill a specific mission *or*
- Congress might name a private company (such as the New Orleans and Carrolton Railroad Company) as its agent.

After a project was launched, Congress might change the type of project (from canal to railroad) *or* change the type of funding (from direct appropriation to fee-for-service). I sidebar that the 21st, 22nd, 23rd and 24th Congresses (1829–1837) made land grants to 16 private railroads. Appendix B: Railroads Subsidized via Federal Land Grants details the subsidies Congress enacted during the Jackson administration. As I explain in this study, Andrew Jackson vehemently opposed investment of federal cash in road projects while approving federal land grants to promote railroad construction.[36] The appetites of state, local and private actors for federal benefits – cash, land, project leadership, claims management – enabled Congress to remodel the federal government on the fly. As to the employment of the phrase 'laissez faire' in the early years of the Second Republic, private actors who received public benefits consistently claimed that maximizing private choice was a sublime motto and ennobled the age.

'Let us conquer space with a perfect system of roads and canals'

Chapter 1 concentrates on the role that postal services played in the early years of the Second Republic. The Act of February 20, 1792 served as the founding charter for the Second Republic's Post Office Department. For three years, Congress had postponed the hard work of naming the places that would mark out the nation's postal network, leaving the task to President Washington. In the Act of February 20, 1792 Congress found itself obliged to resolve both *inter*state contests over postal routes, along with *intra*state disagreements on that score. A North Carolina Congressman noted that President Washington's postal routes favored seaside communities at the expense of the interior regions of that state. The 1792 Act that Congress composed did not, however, run postal routes through Congressman John Steele's hometown of Salisbury NC.

In this chapter, I give the floor to Postmaster General W.T. Barry and his 1830 report to Congress. On the heels of a 42-fold increase in the number of post offices (over the interval 1792–1830), Barry's report exuded bureaucratic exuberance. By 1830, as Barry reported, the 'whole yearly transportation in coaches, steamboats, sulkeys, and on horse-back, amounted to about 14,500,000 miles'.[37] The Postmaster General confidently predicted that, beginning 1 January 1831, 'the mail will run from this city [Washington, D.C.] to New Orleans in thirteen days'.[38]

In Chapter 2 I turn to James Monroe's message 'Views of the President of the United States on the Subject of Internal Improvements' (4 May 1822).[39] This reached Congress in unusual circumstances. When Congress passed a bill to charge tolls to Cumberland Road travelers – Congress dedicated the anticipated toll revenue to road repairs – Monroe vetoed the bill (4 May 1822). On the same day Monroe sent Congress a lengthy message on the subject of internal improvements. In his 'Views' Monroe declared that 'the powers of the General Government are believed to be utterly incompetent [to] the establishment of turnpikes and tolls'.[40]

At the mid-point of his 'Views', however, Monroe informed his readers that 'my mind has undergone a change'.[41] In the passages following, Monroe explained that he approved Congressional spending on physical infrastructure, provided that the federal government did not acquire a footprint for the project. In other words, it was the construction of toll houses and toll gates that triggered his veto. In arranging the text of his 'Views', Monroe did not discard the material he composed in 1819.[42] Monroe preserved (more or less intact) his 1819 text and sandwiched his 1822 argument (Congress can spend money) into the middle (more or less) of his 1819 argument (Congress can't spend money, absent a prior constitutional amendment). Monroe's 1822 argument was in sync with the temper of the times. In the House of Representatives (4 February 1817) Rep. John Calhoun declared, 'let us bind the republic together with a perfect system of roads and canals. Let us conquer space', he concluded.[43] A few days later Sen. Martin Hardin of Kentucky summed up the national mood. 'The national sentiment is in favor of internal improvements', the Senator assured his colleagues.[44]

Monroe's 'Views' won high praise from Justice Joseph Story. 'But perhaps the most thorough and elaborate view, which perhaps has ever been taken of the subject, will be found in the exposition of President Monroe, which accompanied his message respecting the bill for the repairs of the Cumberland Road, (4th of May 1822)'.[45] Monroe's survey of 13 improvement projects enacted in nine statutes owed significant inspiration to John Marshall's opinion in *McCulloch v. Maryland,* 17 US (4 Wheat.) 400 (1819).

In Chapter 3 I dissect Chief Justice John Marshall's opinion for the Supreme Court in *McCulloch*. Marshall supplemented the opinion he composed in that case (announced 6 March 1819) with 11 essays he published in Pennsylvania and Virginia newspaper (April through June/July 1819). The 'prosperity of the American people', he declared, is 'inseparable from the preservation of this government'.[46] Marshall highlighted the significance of this observation by placing it in the opening paragraph of one of his essays defending the *McCulloch* decision.[47] If government's 'Job One' was to promote prosperity, then successful programs, he argued, stabilized the current form of civil government.

In Chapter 4 I turn to steam-powered transport projects on America's waterways. These projects radically transformed the Second Republic's future. In the case of *Gibbons v. Ogden*, 22 US (9 Wheat.) 186 (1824), Marshall, speaking for the Supreme Court, Johnson J concurring, upheld exclusive federal management of traffic on the nation's navigable waterways (1824).[48] *Constitution II* was silent on that subject. Days after the Supreme Court banned state regulation of traffic on navigable waterways, Congress launched a construction project designed to open the Ohio River to steamboat traffic (1824). New state-making and transportation projects – the latter concentrating on clearing snags and sandbars from rivers – were interdependent processes. If bulk territories were to be sliced into nascent states – that is, prepared for admission into the Union – people and products would need improved access to remote regions. Better, faster, cheaper means of moving people and products tempted Americans of European origin to settle new territories located in the northwest, west and south. Preparing nascent states for admission to the Union gave Congress a credible reason to stabilize US frontiers by launching and curating a national transport network on navigable rivers and lakes. In 1824 Congress designed a network of waterways – rivers made safe for steamboats – to link up with the five-road national road system planned or under construction.

In Chapter 5 I build on the methodological accomplishments of the Second Republic in improvement projects. I begin with a case study in which Marshall dissects the 'bounty-draft' paradox. What happens when a parliamentary assembly is faced with two (or more) candidates for programmatic action, but each proposal appears – during the assembly's consideration – to be as viable as its competitor?

> Undoubtedly there are other means for raising an army. Men may enlist without a bounty; and if they will not, they may be drafted. A bounty, then, according to Amphictyon, is unconstitutional, because the power may be executed by a draft; and a draft is unconstitutional, because the power may be executed by a bounty.[49]

In his 'Friend' essays Marshall argued that the Second Republic vested tie-breaking power in its inhabitants.[50]

> The people are as much interested, their liberty is as deeply concerned, in preventing encroachments on that government, in arresting the hands which would tear from it the powers they have conferred upon it, as in restraining it within its constitutional limits.[51]

This sets up a larger question. What would happen if voters launched a challenge to federal programmatic action? More generally, federal, state, local and private actors and bodies might declare that Congress had engaged in 'abuse' of its powers? 'Surely nothing can be more obvious, nothing better established, than that the right to canvass the measures of government, or to remonstrate against the abuse of power, must reside in all who are affected by those measures, or over whom that power is exercised, whether it was delegated by them or not'.[52] Following Marshall's lead, I surveyed 'measures of government' in the nine-year interval 1815–1824. In each case an actor or body exercised its 'right to canvass' programmatic action that it might regard as an 'abuse of power'. In each of these seven instances federal officials faced serious challenges to their leadership. I then recast these challenges into methodological terms.[53] According to Marshall, it is for the American people to assess how programmatic action affected their 'public happiness' and 'public liberty'. Based on their collective assessment, they grant or withhold 'powers of the government'.

> The equipoise thus established is as much disturbed by taking weights out of the scale containing the powers of the government, as by putting weights into it.[54]

At the close of Chapter 5, I give the floor to Virginia Congressman John Randolph. Randolph attacked the growing power of Congress in a speech to the House of Representatives (1824). It was a deadly binary that Randolph had in mind. *Either* Monroe's 'unite and conquer' strategy would be successful *or* his 'divide and conquer' strategy would prevail. On the first prong, remote regions would be crushed under the 'accumulated pressure' that the center exerted. In the alternative, the federal government might apply its overwhelming powers to 'divide and conquer', in which case it might legislate emancipation of human beings forced to labor without reparations paid to their so-called owners.

In Chapter 6 my focus moves from considerations of efficiency and inefficiency to productivity. This brings the reader face-to-face with the deliverables of the Second Republic. The overarching performance standard, from voters' point of view, was better, faster, cheaper transportation. The consumers' perspective on the travel/transportation experience invited Second Republic leadership to whole-heartedly embrace technical achievement for its own sake.

At mid-chapter, I shift my attention from distribution of benefits to distribution of burdens. Monroe and Marshall assumed that a government able to manage distribution of benefits – as well as the leaders of the Second Republic were doing post-Ghent – would have little difficulty managing distribution of burdens. If a Congressman were to 'betray his trust', Monroe declared, such a legislator would be 'sure to lose' the confidence of his constituents and 'be removed and otherwise censured according to his deserts'.[55] Policing trust violations, on this account, could be off-loaded to the voters in Congressional constituencies. Management of trust violations was no more challenging than calling on voters to disapprove programmatic action that disturbed the 'harmonious' equilibrium that should prevail between the two governments. 'In the case of any disagreement', Monroe argued in 1824, 'a calm appeal be made to the people [and] their voice [will] be heard and promptly obeyed'.[56] At the next Congressional election voters would settle the matter. In contrast to Monroe's optimism, I expose doubts that Thomas Jefferson, David Ricardo and Antoine Destutt de Tracy raised when it came to the ease with which 'just and regular' distribution of burdens could be achieved.

Building on these points Chapter 6 concludes by touching on the concept of victimhood. If remote communities resented the center's pressure to bring them into communion with other regions of the country, they might redirect their allegiance to demagogues. Demagogues channeled grievances – both real and imagined – into centrifugal pathways intended to destabilize the unitary government. Monroe's optimistic engagement with American political history, on the other hand, minimized destabilizing threats to the systems, structures and institutions of American political society.

In Chapter 7 I employ the running chapter head 'An Important Epoch in the History of the Civilized World'. The chapter evaluates the legacy of Marshall and Monroe. In Monroe's First Inaugural Address (4 March 1817) he employed the phrase 'the excellence of our institutions'.

> From the commencement of our Revolution to the present day almost forty years have elapsed, and from the establishment of this Constitution twenty-eight. Through this whole term the Government has been what may emphatically be called self-government [and] we find abundant cause to felicitate ourselves in the excellence of our institutions. During a period fraught with difficulties and marked by very extraordinary events the United States have flourished beyond example. Their citizens individually have been happy and the nation prosperous.[57]

The First and Second Republics survived three separate entanglements in a 40-year world war – the Wars of the Coalitions – that began at Lexington and Concord (1775) and concluded at Waterloo (1815).[58] After the arrival of peace (1814/1815), two leaders set about dealing with challenges that previous generations have been unable to solve or (at least) wrestle into a semblance of manageability. These two leaders helmed different offices. As it happened, they were from the same region of the nation. From boyhood they were more than mere acquaintances. Each understood how the other thought. They tried their hands at almost all species of technical accomplishment in statecraft. Thanks to their efforts, the refounding of the Second Republic is exposed for our mature – and technical – consideration.

To their way of thinking, the nation that Monroe and Marshall guided into the future was 'rising ... spread over a wide and fruitful land'. Just as Jefferson had declared, the nation was 'advancing rapidly to destinies beyond the reach of mortal eye'.[59] Our two leaders were determined to bring the nation's destiny into very intimate contact with the personal destinies of the inhabitants themselves.

Notes

1. See senate.gov/about/powers-procedures/treaties/senate-approves-treaty-of-ghent.htm [last retrieved 3 November 2020].
2. *McCulloch v. Maryland*, 17 US (4 Wheat.) 400 (1819). See Appendix F: Technical Appendix and Editorial Practices for an explanation of my citations to Supreme Court decisions.
3. Marshall, *Defense*.
4. See www.presidency.ucsb.edu/documents/veto-message
5. See presidency.ucsb.edu/documents/special-message-the-house-representatives-containing-the-views-the-president-the-united
6. See bioguideretro.congress.gov
7. *Ibid.*
8. Ammon, *Monroe*, 150-151, 168-169.
9. *Ibid.*, 262, 264-269.
10. See memory.loc.gov/ammem/amlaw/lwsp.html; *American State Papers, Military Affairs*, 524-599; Doc. No. 137; 29 November 1814; at 580 [statement of General Van Ness].
11. *Ibid.*
12. See Washington_Crossing_the_Delaware_(1851_painting) [last retrieved 22 February 2021].
13. See text at 66-71.
14. See presidency.ucsb.edu/documents/special-message-the-house-representatives-containing-the-views-the-president-the-united. See Appendix F: Technical Appendix and Editorial Practices for an explanation of the paragraph numbering system (employed herein) which supplies inline citations to text in Monroe's 'Views'. 'Views' ¶27.
15. *Ibid.*
16. *Ibid.*
17. See text at 10-11, 20-21.
18. See text at 27-28.

19. Farrand, *Records*, 2:342-343.
20. *Continental Congress Journals*, 19:109 at 110-113, 3 February 1781 [Congress recommended that states lay 'an impost of 5 pr. Cent ... on all goods... imported into them' and 'to vest Congress with full power to collect and appropriate the same ...'.]; *Ibid*., 24:256-262, 18 April 1783 [Congress asked states to grant Congress the power to 'levy for the use of the United States' certain duties.]; *Ibid*., 26:317 at 318-322, 30 April 1784 [blue water shipping restricted to vessels 'belonging to and navigated by citizens of the United States'; 'unless Congress for this purpose shall be vested with powers competent to the protection of Commerce, they can never command reciprocal advantages in trade and without such reciprocity our foreign Commerce must decline and eventually be annihilated'.]. For discussion of the relevant events see Burnett, *Continental Congress,* 483, 570 and 603.
21. A bit more precisely: I refer to propositions whose variables can be aligned with the well-formed formula 'If x, then y, else z'.
22. See text at 122-123.
23. 2 Stat 357, c. 19.
24. McDonald, *E Pluribus Unum*, 48.
25. For details of Virginia's conditional cession, see virginiaplaces.org/boundaries/cessions.html; for details of Maryland's conditional ratification see Aschenbrenner, *Foundings*, 56-57.
26. As of 1803, the three territories were (a) the Indiana Territory, organized in anticipation of Ohio joining the Union, (b) the bulk territory known as the Louisiana Purchase before the Orleans Territory (more or less the present state of Louisiana) was split off and (c) the Mississippi Territory.
27. 2 Stat 357, c. 19.
28. 2 Stat 396, c. 41, Sec. 7.
29. See text at 20-21.
30. Appendix A: Survey of 1,147 Improvement Projects.
31. Van Buren, 'Autobiography', 182.
32. *Ibid.*
33. See uslhs.org/history-administration-lighthouses-america; last retrieved 11 November 2020.
34. 1 Stat 232, c. 7.
35. See text at 134.
36. See text at 130, 172-173.
37. See memory.loc.gov/cgi-bin/ampage; *ASP/Post Office*, 256, 257; Doc. No. 60.
38. *Ibid.*
39. See presidency.ucsb.edu/documents/special-message-the-house-representatives-containing-the-views-the-president-the-united.
40. 'Views', ¶109.
41. 'Views', ¶101.
42. See text at 39-40.
43. See memory.loc.gov/ammem/amlaw/lwac.html *Annals*, 14th Congress, 2nd Session, 851, 853-854.
44. *Annals*, 14th Congress, 2nd Session, 176, 26 February 1817. Sen. Hardin served from 1816 to the end of the 14th Congress, 3 March 1817. He is now buried in the State Cemetery at Frankfort.
45. Story, *Commentaries*, Sec. 976.
46. See text at 117, 147.
47. See text at 117.
48. Johnson J concurring in the result.

49. Marshall, *Defense*, 95.
50. Marshall, *Defense* ['A Friend to the Union', 91-105; 'A Friend of the Constitution', 155-161]. See text at 115.
51. *Ibid.*, 159-160.
52. *Ibid.*, 83.
53. See text at 108-109.
54. Marshall, *Defense*, 160.
55. 'Views', ¶102.
56. See millercenter.org/the-presidency/presidential-speeches/december-7-1824-eighth-annual-message
57. See millercenter.org/the-presidency/presidential-speeches/march-4-1817-first-inaugural-address
58. I refer to the First War for American Independence (1775-1783), the Quasi-War with France (1798-1800) and the Second War for American Independence (1812-1815).
59. Jefferson, 'First Inaugural Address'. See millercenter.org/the-presidency/presidential-speeches/march-4-1801-first-inaugural-address

References

Primary Sources

Marshall, John, 'A Friend to the Union' *and* 'A Friend of the Constitution' *in John Marshall's Defense of McCulloch v. Maryland* (Stanford, CA, 1969; Gerald Gunther, ed.).

Records of the Federal Convention of 1787 (New Haven, CT, 1911, 3 vols; Max Farrand, ed.; rev. ed. 1937, 4 vols.).

Story, Joseph, *Commentaries on the Constitution* (Boston, MA, 1833; 1st ed.).

Van Buren, Martin, 'The Autobiography of Martin Van Buren' (Washington, DC, 1918; ed. John C. Fitzpatrick) [published in *The Annual Report of the American Historical Association*, vol. II.].

Secondary Sources

Ammon, Harry, *James Monroe, The Quest for National Identity* (Charlottesville, VA, 1990).

Aschenbrenner, Peter, *British and American Foundings of Parliamentary Science, 1774-1801* (Abingdon-on-Thames, Oxfordshire, UK, 2017).

Burnett, Edmund Cody, *The Continental Congress, A definitive history of the Continental Congress from its inception in 1774 to March, 1789* (New York, NY, 1941, 1964).

McDonald, Forrest, *E Pluribus Unum, The Formation of the American Republic 1776-1790* (Indianapolis, IN, 1965).

1 'Westward the Course of Empire Takes Its Way'

'A hut in the midst of the forest was a post-office'

Edmund Burke (1729–1797) was long dead by the time that Alexis de Tocqueville (1805–1859) and Gustave de Beaumont (1802–1866) toured the United States. The French government dispatched de Tocqueville and Beaumont across the North Atlantic to investigate prison conditions. Arriving in 1831, these two social scientists spent nine months touring the country. The American fascination for speed and novelty distracted de Tocqueville and Beaumont from their original purpose. De Tocqueville's resulting travelogue and commentary *De La Démocratie en Amérique/Democracy in America* appeared in Paris in two volumes (1835, 1840). English translations followed in London and New York.[1] De Tocqueville recorded the following anecdote. Traveling the back country of North Carolina, he reported that 'from time to time we came to a hut in the midst of the forest; this was a post-office. The mail dropped an enormous bundle of letters at the door of this isolated dwelling, and we pursued our way at full gallop, leaving the inhabitants of the neighboring log houses to send for their share of the treasure'.[2] De Tocqueville equated the incoming letters and newspapers that residents might collect as their 'treasure'.

In December 1830, Postmaster General W.T. Barry reported to Congress on the operations of the Post Office Department. Barry assured Senators and Representatives that the financial condition of the Post Office was sound. The Department's books reflected a surplus of $148,724.22. The Department had, as Barry declared, 'fulfilled all anticipations of its efficiency'.[3] Moreover, the Post Office stood ready to take on more projects. 'In the several States, improvements in mail facilities have been loudly called for'.[4] On Barry's account Americans needed more than the 8,401 post offices that his department was operating throughout the United States. One of these was De Tocqueville's 'hut in the midst of the forest'. Such a 'hut' satisfied a remote community's need for basic services. The 'growing population and extending settlements of the country', Barry informed Congress, 'have absolutely required them'.

DOI: 10.4324/9781003019381-2

Americans were 'loudly' demanding postal services, Barry reported. This clamor, he judged, proved that Americans were underserved.[5] Barry was adept at dabbing the canvas with a nationwide brush. Beginning in 1831, the Postmaster General promised Congress, 'the mail will run from this city [Washington, D.C.] to New Orleans in thirteen days'.[6] The 'whole yearly transportation in coaches, steamboats, sulkeys, and on horse-back, amounted to about 14,500,000 miles'.[7] Edmund Burke, however, warned governments with republican tendencies that unleashing consumer demand for their services would be the first step on the road to anarchy (1790). 'By having a right to every thing they want every thing'.[8] If your neighbors were enjoying postal services, why should you sacrifice your appetite for government offerings on the altar of Burkean thunderings? Barry took full credit for his department's accomplishments, while also disclosing operational details that readers could employ to assess his department's administrative competence. There are 'rules that have been adopted in relation to the conduct of postmasters'. These norms guided and governed the behavior of official in the Post Office Department; their purpose was to root out 'official delinquencies' and correct 'losses' caused by such misbehavior. What was required was the 'unremitted and undivided attention of a competent officer'.[9]

'Bureaucratic agenda' is my term for the official face that a department exhibits to Congress. In this regard the institution's purpose is to secure 'a degree of confidence in the fidelity of its officers', as Barry put the matter. Barry's 'officers' are the federal officials that a department (agency) tasks to fulfill the will of Congress.

'Bureaucratic autonomy' is my term for the human face that an institution agent exhibits to consumers of its goods and services. Barry assured his readers that his department achieved 'increased expedition of the mails on many routes of great interest'. Barry referred to the introduction in North Carolina of 'a line of stages from Edenton to Washington' and a 'steamboat line from Wilmington to Smithville ... to run twice a week each way'. Touching a note of interest to modern and post-modern readers, Barry assured Congress that the price of postage would remain the same. 'The current revenue of the Department for the succeeding year will be sufficient for its disbursements'.[10]

'The sea-coast exclusively enjoyed the benefit of speedy conveyance'

As the 1st Congress, 3rd Session reached the midpoint of its legislative life, John Steele – a Federalist Congressman from North Carolina – rose to speak in the House of Representatives. As of 31 January 1791, the House was – for the third and final time – postponing action on postal route designations. Congress bobbled its obligation to legislate programmatic action and Steele was not happy about it. The Congressman argued that Congress should settle the matter by naming towns and villages to serve as beginning, middle and end points in a national postal network. On three occasions, however, the 1st Congress surrendered to President Washington the power to designate postal routes.[11] Rep. Steele also observed that, 'upon the president's establishment of the principal post-road, a considerable and populous part of North Carolina derived no advantage from the establishment, and the sea-coast exclusively enjoyed the benefit of regular and speedy conveyance for their correspondences, and thus the agricultural interest was sacrificed to the commercial'.[12] I will return to this *intra*state dispute over postal routes shortly.

It was not until February 1792 – during the 2nd Congress, 1st Session – that the House of Representatives resolved the delegation issue. I refer to the Act of February 20, 1792.[13] That statute chartered the modern Post Office Department, the predecessor to the United States Postal Service. In so doing, Congress anticipated Postmaster Gen. Barry's declaration that the 'growing population and extending settlements of the country have absolutely required' delivery of postal services on a nationwide scale (1830).[14] Lessons learned in 1792: if the country 'absolutely required' programmatic action, Congress would get its hands dirty with the necessary details.

Congress crafted the Act of February 20, 1792 as an exercise in batch-processing. Accordingly, the members of the House of Representatives named 206 places in Section 1 of the Act of February 20, 1792. Congress designated the postal route from Wilmington DE to Dover DE, for example, to run from 'Newcastle [to] Cantwell's Bridge and Duck Creek'. This route offered scenic views of the Delaware River. Steele drew attention to another facet of batch-processing. It is one thing for a parliamentary assembly to resolve competition for post office facilities between Rhode Island and Georgia. *Intra*state allocation was also an issue. Steele noted that North Carolina's 'sea-coast exclusively enjoyed the benefit [of postal services] and thus the agricultural interest was sacrificed to the commercial'.[15] *Constitution II* assigned North Carolina five Representatives.[16] Presumably the five North Carolina Congressmen serving in the 2nd Congress, 1st Session were unable to settle conflicting *intra*state demands for postal services. If North Carolina's Congressmen could not settle these disputes, their colleagues in the House would be obliged to do it for them.

Congress pointedly refused to fund the post office with funds appropriated from Treasury revenues. Section 28 of the Act of February 20, 1792 made this clear by dedicating a 'surplus' from any calendar year to the purpose of 'defraying any deficiency' carried over from the prior year.[17] Delivery of postal services expanded from 200 locations (1792) to over 8,400 (1830), a 42-fold increase. Consumers of postal services funded this expansion. Efficiency in delivering services was therefore a paramount goal. Only by encouraging consumers to accept their collective role as a funding vehicle for future expansion could unserved communities get their mail at de Tocqueville's hut in the back country.[18] Congress was well aware that achieving efficiencies called for energy-saving measures. In one case Congress assigned a fixed value to time wasted. 'And if any ferryman shall, by willful negligence, or by refusal to transport the mail across any ferry, delay the same, he shall forfeit and pay for each half hour that the same shall be so delayed, a sum not exceeding ten dollars'.[19]

There were alternatives to batch-processing. Congress designated a single postal route to run 'from Albany [NY] to Bennington [VT]',[20] on 3 March 1791, the day before Vermont joined the Union.[21] In the interval 1792 to 1837, however, Congress rarely employed a one-off approach.[22] The term 'brokerage' requires further attention. 'It required an extraordinary degree of resolution in a public man', Van Buren declares, 'to attempt to resist a passion that had become so rampant'. It became the task of Congressional legislators to transform Van Buren's lust for a 'thousand local improvements' into batches of semi-regimented sentences.[23] This is the chokepoint through which policy must be filtered to achieve its formal (and final) expression. Statutory text – on this or the other side of the pond – need not be composed by lawyers. If read aloud, however, statutes must *sound* like lawyers wrote them.

'The Yeas and Nays shall be entered on the Journal'

The *House Journal* for the 2nd Congress, 1st Session discloses that members did not take a roll call vote on the bill that became the Act of February 20, 1792. When the 2nd Congress convened, the membership of that body numbered 67 members.[24] 'One fifth of those Present [on a given vote]' enjoyed the right to demand that 'the Yeas and Nays ... be entered on the Journal'. A member of Congress who allied with a minority of 19% (or fewer) of 'Members ... Present' would have a significant hurdle to overcome if he were minded to take his case to the voters. In the House of Commons, however, a single member could demand that the House divide on a question.[25] *Constitution II*'s Article I, Section 5, Clause 3 provided that:

> Each House shall keep a Journal of its Proceedings, and from time to time publish the same, excepting such Parts as may in their Judgment require Secrecy; and the Yeas and Nays of the Members of either House on any question shall, at the Desire of one fifth of those Present, be entered on the Journal.

A second provision of *Constitution II* must be taken into account when the success of the House of Representatives is considered, functionally speaking. The House of Commons did business under a 40-member quorum requirement; this is still the rule today.[26] (Until 1801 the membership of the House of Commons numbered 558.) Each House of Congress in the US operates under a majority rule, requiring one more than 50% of its members to be present in the chamber. A 'majority of each [House] shall constitute a Quorum to do Business'. Article I, Section 5, Clause 1. With the admission of Kentucky (1 June 1792), the number of representatives in the House was fixed at 69. Therefore, the presence of at least 35 members was required before the House of Representatives could conduct business.

To put this another way, the low quorum and low roll call thresholds in the House of Commons were logically paired. In the US House of Representatives, the higher quorum requirement stimulated more bargaining among more members. Combined with the 20% roll call requirement, US arrangements tempted the majority to bulk up its numbers and shrink the percentage of opponents below 19%. This threshold applied, as noted above, only to those members who constituted 'one fifth [or more] of those Present'. The arrangement that prevailed in the US House of Representatives was not a logical pairing of low quorum and roll call requirements but a functional coupling that stimulated expenditure of wheeler dealer energy. In line with the foregoing, majoritarians' tactics in the House of Representatives called for a bill's managers to solicit members to pass a bill (or survive a procedural vote) with an 81% majority.[27]

'An annual appropriation of two million of dollars would accomplish great objects in ten years'

On 2 March 1807, the Senate of the United States requested that Secretary of the Treasury Albert Gallatin report on 'the means and prospects of their being completed'. Gallatin assured his readers that his suggested 'undertakings' – he referred to 'opening roads, and making canals' – were 'within the power of Congress'. Having nodded to orthodoxy, Gallatin took the brief entrusted to him and ran with it. Gallatin's report listed 'undertakings' that he proposed to Congress as 'objects of public improvement'.[28] Gallatin did not trouble himself to detail conflicting views on the constitutionality of these projects.

What Gallatin proposed was nothing less than a transportation network designed to connect all regions of the United States and its territorial possessions. Gallatin's roads would run along the Atlantic seaboard from the District of Maine to Georgia.[29] Gallatin anticipated that travelers would seek the shortest route to travel up or down the Atlantic seaboard. Gallatin's canal system would enable year-round intercoastal waterborne transport from New York City to South Carolina. Gallatin also proposed that the federal government clear obstructions to navigation in the Susquehanna River, the James River and other major waterways.

Running inland from the Atlantic, a second network of canals would afford access to the near hinterlands and from there to the back country of the United States. Gallatin argued that his proposal for 'great canals'[30] and a 'great turnpike extending from Maine to Georgia'[31] was affordable. The sum of $20 million 'would accomplish all those great objects in ten years'.[32]

Gallatin also touched on the nineteenth century's one-word motto 'efficiency' when he suggested that movement of people and products could be made 'efficient' throughout the United States and its territories. 'The early and efficient aid of the *federal* government is recommended by still more important considerations'. Gallatin also addressed the threat of frontier instability. 'The inconveniencies, complaints, and perhaps dangers, which may result from a vast extent of territory, can not otherwise be radically removed, or prevented, than by opening speedy and easy communications through all its parts'.[33] In Gallatin's opinion, North America was a splendid continent. However, the 'great geographical features of the country'[34] could be materially improved – tidied up, so to speak – if Congress spent money to enable better, faster, cheaper transportation and communication. From a traveler's point of view, mountains and rivers frequently posed hurdles, thereby inconveniencing the nation's inhabitants. Gallatin's 'most important ... improvements' offered 'great links' as upgrades to the reality that nature provided.[35]

Gallatin could not assign 'arithmetic precision' to the figures he presented to Congress. Nevertheless, he poured out his assurances, promising to address 'all the great interests of the Union'.[36] Gallatin compared his ambitions with the Louisiana Purchase (1803). Congress funded the $15 million purchase price, cashing out French and Spanish claims to a third of a continent. The federal government could, Gallatin argued, increase the attractiveness of tracts of land in the new territories to settlers. Land sales would replenish Gallatin's fund for internal improvements. 'The fund created by those improvements, would afterwards become itself a perpetual resource for further improvements'.[37] Gallatin did not neglect bondholders' thirst for government debt instruments. He proposed that 'stock might be sold to individuals or companies, and the proceeds applied to a new improvement'.[38] Gallatin offered something to everyone. I note that the Secretary acquired his legislative arts via service in the 4th, 5th and 6th Congresses as a Congressman from Pennsylvania.

Albert Gallatin must be accounted a solid and even a fervent Smithian. Productivity gains could be assessed in two perspectives. (a) Those who moved into less settled regions were planting European style civilization in these new communities and regions. They were creating something from nothing. These settlers were not taking anything away from anyone. (b) On this account, the government should assess proposed programmatic action in the light of (projected) productivity gains. Today's land sales, for example, would fund tomorrow's national transportation and communication networks. Over time, these sales would reliably increase the value of private land and private business operations in these newly settled regions. George Berkeley's famous line 'Westward the course of empire takes its way'[39] did not satisfy the Secretary of the Treasury. Gallatin was not content with any humdrum vision of families driving their Conestoga wagons into the setting sun, pigs and cows plodding behind. All human effort in North America must be gathered as feed and fodder for a giant machine. In other words, an empire must direct a 'course' of suitably imperial dimensions. Gallatin was happy to design the gears and levers required. I note contrasting artworks in the margin.[40]

To buttress his report, Secretary Gallatin appealed to two fellow technocrats to contribute their views. Benjamin Henry Latrobe (1764–1820) and Robert Fulton (1765–1815) answered the call. These experts were well known to Congress and the public. The American engineer and inventor Robert Fulton launched the first successful steam-powered transport of passengers and cargo on the Hudson River (1807). In that year, the *North River Steamboat* (the original name for the *Clermont*) steamed up the Hudson River from New York City to Albany. The round trip covered 300 miles (480 km) in 32 hours. British inventors gave Americans serious competition in this race. John Hatsell, Clerk of the House of Commons (1768–1820), recorded progress – and failure – in such a venture (1795):

> Ld Stanhope is set off today to try his new Vessell; he is to be absent a Month. By all accounts, He would run a good chance of being drown'd in this experiment, but for the old Proverb – He told me seriously, He had no doubt, but that he should change the whole art of Navigation, & render useless, Sails, Sailors & Rudders – He will want nothing but Fuel & Storage for it.[41]

Americans should be grateful that Fulton won the race to launch waterborne steam-powered transportation. Lord Stanhope burdened his invention with an awkward title. 'Ambi-navigator comin' round the bend' doesn't convey the excitement that must have welcomed the arrival of Fulton's steamboat as it paddle-wheeled its way to the dock at Albany, New York. The success of Fulton's steamboat transformed transportation in the United States. In his contribution to Gallatin's report, Fulton offered effusive praise for Gallatin's endeavor. Such 'right thinking', he declared, 'does great honor to our nation, and leads forward to the highest possible state of civilization'.[42] Latrobe also contributed to Gallatin's report. His essay ran nearly 10,000 words. (Latrobe is best known for superintending construction of the United States Capitol.) Digressing from his brief, Latrobe commented on a new-fangled technology called the 'rail road'. Latrobe dashed cold water on rising public expectations that steam-powered transport on rails might furnish a new mode of transportation. 'The astonishing loads', he declared, 'have induced many of our citizens to hope for their early application to the use of our country'. Caution, however, was in order. 'I fear this hope is vain, excepting on a very small scale'. Latrobe immediately entertained second thoughts. Perhaps 'a rail road ... expressly constructed for the purpose' of freighting people and products – extending beyond dockyard or mining operations – might be commercially feasible, provided that there 'be a very great demand for its use'.[43] In 1821, Parliament launched the Stockton and Darlington Railway via the 'Act for making and maintaining a Railway or Tramroad from the River *Tees* at *Stockton*, to *Witton Park* Colliery, with several branches therefrom, all in the County of Durham'. George IV granted the royal assent on 19 April 1821.[44] As it turned out, there was a 'very great demand' for railway transport in the United Kingdom. Powered by steam, not horses.

'I suppose an amendment to the constitution, by consent of the States, necessary'

The Act of March 29, 1806 (launching the Cumberland Road) required the President to obtain the permission of four states – Maryland, Pennsylvania, Virginia and Ohio – to the proposed National Road. The president 'is hereby further authorized and requested', the Act of Congress ran, 'to pursue such measures, as in his opinion shall be proper, to obtain consent for making the road, of the state or states, through which the same has been laid out'. Section 3. Gallatin assumed that Article I, Section 8, Clause 17 required state approval for any improvement project within its borders. The relevant text provided that Congress may exercise the same level of authority ('like authority') granted in the District (of Columbia) 'over all Places purchased by the Consent of the Legislature of the State in which the Same shall be, for the Erection of Forts, Magazines, Arsenals, dock-Yards, and other needful Buildings'. Gallatin, in common with Jefferson (and Congress) regarded this text as an open-ended permission to build out improvement projects within a state's borders, provided that Congress solicited the state legislature's consent. This was, by any name, co-legislation thanks to the condition subsequent Gallatin teased from constitutional text.[45]

The planning and design phase of improvement projects furnished a suitable opportunity to induce state legislatures to buy into the project. Engineers must first survey the route – including alternatives – and then price competing proposals. In the case of the Cumberland Road this effort consumed four years. Construction did not begin until 1811; in that year Congress authorized the President to reroute the road provided 'that no deviation shall be made from the principal points established on said road between Cumberland [MD] and Brownsville [PA]'.[46] The interval between design and construction offered a similar opportunity for voters to weigh in on the merits of any given project. I dissect Gallatin's pricing projection and expose its votarian basics. 'An annual appropriation of two million of dollars, would accomplish all those great objects in ten years'.[47] An appropriation of $2 million per session of Congress was not peanuts. The *Statistical Abstract of the United States* records federal expenditures – excluding debt service – for 1806 at over $9.3 million. In 1811 – the last calendar year before the outbreak of war – federal outlays exceeded $8 million.[48] Federal infrastructure spending would have amounted to (approximately) one-fifth of annual federal expenditures. 'A million here, a million there, and pretty soon, you're talking real money'.[49] Gallatin's proposal required Congress to fund projects over an interval embracing five biennial elections. In addition, voters would have an opportunity to assess the work of Congress during two presidential elections. Voters would therefore enjoy multiple opportunities to make their views known at the polls via preferences sieved through the filter candidates in, candidates out and candidates back in. Keeping in mind that senatorial contests took place in state legislatures, voters could also express their views in electoral contests involving state representatives (delegates, assemblymen) and state senators. These assessments would take place as the build out of Gallatin's transportation network was underway.

Gallatin could look back on some very recent improvement projects which did *not* roil electoral politics. In 1802, Virginia sought approval for its Appomatox river improvement project; in 1804 Virginia returned to Congress for permission to improve the James River. Although *Constitution II* did not grant Congress the power to regulate the use of navigable waters, Virginia sought and Congress granted permission for both these projects.[50] The Board of Wardens of Port of Philadelphia sought federal financial assistance to improve access to the port facilities.[51] Did Congress have the power to transfer a slice of federal tax revenue to the Board of Wardens and thereby transform that state agency into a federal institution agent? The state of Pennsylvania sought permission to move forward with this scheme (1 April 1805) and Congress granted its approval via the Act of February 28, 1806.[52]

In 1806, President Jefferson called for a constitutional amendment to authorize improvement projects. I refer to his Sixth Annual Message (2 December 1806). The 'great purposes of the public education, roads, rivers, canals, such other objects of public improvement as it may be thought proper to add to the constitutional enumeration of federal powers'.[53] Jefferson concluded his remarks as follows: 'I suppose an amendment to the constitution, by consent of the States, necessary, because the objects now recommended are not among those enumerated in the constitution, and to which it permits the public moneys to be applied'.[54] The reader will note that Jefferson called for an amendment that would have retroactively authorized laws launching the

Cumberland Road and three other national roads (29 March and 21 April 1806). As to the latter enactment further discussion is in order.

On 30 December 1805, the Cumberland Road bill was introduced in the House of Representatives.[55] While that bill was moving towards final passage in the House (29 March 1806), the Senate took up a bill titled 'An Act to Regulate and Fix the Compensation of clerks, and for other purposes'. Tucked into the back of the bill, Section 7 launched a road between Athens GA and New Orleans (in the Orleans Territory), along with 'a road or roads through the territory lately ceded by the Indians to the United States, from the river Mississippi to the Ohio, and to the former Indian boundary line which was established by Treaty of Grenville'. A third project connected Nashville TN and Natchez in the Mississippi Territory.[56] This was the first occasion on which Congress launched multiple road projects via the text of a single statute.

More than a bit of mystery surrounds the enactment of 2 Stat 396, c. 41, Act of April 21, 1806. The Senate completed work on the bill on 8 April 1806.[57] The title of this bill announced that it was 'An act to regulate and fix the compensation of clerks, and for other purposes'. Final action in the House took place on Saturday 19 April 1806,[58] with proponents moving the bill forward with the title unchanged. On 21 April 1806 (Monday), the *House Journal* listed enrolled bills. The bill's title continued to lack a reference to 'public roads'.[59] On the same page, the *House Journal* recorded Jefferson's approval of the bill. The title of the bill lacked the phrase 'public roads'. Both the Bioren & Duane (1815) and the Peters (1846) editions of the Public Statutes retitled this Act of Congress 'An Act to Regulate and Fix the Compensation of clerks, and to authorize the laying out of certain public roads'.[60]

I suggest that the Acts of March 29, 1806 and April 21, 1806 should be considered the founding charter of the US national road network. I note two striking differences between the two bills. (a) Congress directed President Jefferson to obtain the consents of state legislature in the case of the Cumberland Road. However, in the bill Congress passed and the President signed – 23 days later (21 April 1806) – launching three more national roads, this step was omitted. Less than a year later – in the Act of March 3, 1807 – Congress passed a bill modifying the route of the Athens to New Orleans project. Again, Congress did not call for the consent of the Georgia legislature.[61] (b) Congress funded the $30,000 initial appropriation for the Cumberland Road from an account cumulating proceeds from land sales. The Ohio Enabling Act restricted revenue from lands to 'roads to Ohio'.[62] However, 23 days later Congress funded three more national roads from direct appropriations.[63] In the Ohio Enabling Act the 7th Congress committed any future Congress to obtain state consents when it launched road projects into the State of Ohio.[64] As soon as the 9th Congress judged itself free of the constraint imposed by the 7th Congress, it abandoned state consents and the goofy co-legislative principle that these consents imposed on the President and Congress.[65]

'The probability for the happening of an event should lie between two degrees'

Politicians find it difficult to resist the urge to attach predicates to incoming sensory experience. Snap judgments are not infrequent. However, there is a higher art to which the lawmaker might aspire. The lawmaker may take his initial belief (as to the future success of any programmatic action) and then recalibrate this judgment in light of the interaction of two variables. (a) The lawmaker may construct an error analysis that employs systemic variables of his choosing. (b) In the second variable, however, the lawmaker encounters a factor over which he has no control.

I illustrate 'Bayes Assessment Method'. This method draws its strength from 'Bayes Theorem'. The principal resource may be found in Thomas Bayes' 'Essay towards solving a Problem in the Doctrine of Chances'. Richard Price, the executor of Bayes' estate, polished Bayes' essay, supplied a short introduction and read the paper to the Royal Society in London. That body published the 'Essay' in its *Philosophical Transactions* (1763).[66] Richard Price enjoyed a lively interest in mathematical puzzles. Price was also an early and very public supporter of American independence.

I present myself at the offices of Congressman Richard Price (a distant relation to Dr. Richard Price) on a Monday. I have arranged to revisit the Congressman each of the nine following Mondays for a total of ten weekly visits. My first interview with the Congressman is well-timed. It takes place on the day he plans to introduce a bill to launch the Nasty Old River Bridge project. This project will materially improve transportation in his district. The Congressman entertains high hopes that the bill's success will mark him as an up-and-coming politician in the region.

My first question (on the first Monday) follows. 'What do you think of the chance that Congress will pass your bridge bill?' Congressman Price tells me that his guess is 40%. 'Bridge projects are like that. A bit less than a coin flip chance of passing'.

'Is that all there is to your thinking?' I ask.

'No. I'll talk you through my error analysis. Here are some of the systemic variables available for my consideration. For example,

- Is my bridge project the only project of its type in that region of the country?
- How many other bridge projects will be promoted in this session of the House of Representatives?
- How much money is required to launch my project, compared to funding that competing projects require?

- How do leaders in the House or the Senate feel about this project? Are any of them dead-set against bridges?
- Are there private actors who might oppose the bill? When any navigable waterway is bridged, the steamboat interest is always ready to raise a ruckus. They will reliably demand that the elevation of the span be raised and so forth.

'Your error analysis', I ask, 'converts all of these (and similar) facts, events, situations and so forth to produce a single figure, from .01 to .99?'

'Absolutely', he concurs. 'As the good Rev. Bayes reasoned. "The probability for the happening of an event should lie between two degrees".[67] My error analysis delivers a well-computed result of 75%. Of the bills that Congress passed, 75% of them featured provisos that managers inserted to mollify special interests and gain majority support for their legislation. I've boiled down all of my thinking – see the bullet points above – and crafted such a proviso for the bill I will introduce tomorrow'.

'Your error analysis computes the true positive?' I ask.

The Congressman continues. 'My bill is in the drafting stage. I have called on input from my colleagues in the House, Senators and private interests. General managers of steamboat companies, heavy freight haulers, those in the mercantile trade and so forth. In line with their suggestions – and cautions – I have crafted the following proviso'. The Senators reads:

> The lowest point on the underside of the bridgework must measure 125% of the height of the tallest funnel on a steamboat in regular service on the Nasty Old River in the calendar year before the bridge is finished.

The Congressman continues. 'I must be able to defend my error analysis in my exchanges with colleagues on both sides of the aisle. Thanks to my proviso, I have concluded that my bill's chances stand at 75%. Of course, the proviso will double the cost of the bridge. My thinking runs as follows: Congressmen who might balk at the project cost would vote against my project anyway. But now I'll win the support of the railroad men. There's this Congressman from Illinois – tallest fellow I ever met – and he's in with the railroad interest. I figured that getting him on my side was a smart move. He's got quite a store of funny stories and if you have time – '

'All events which happen contrary to expectation are worthy of your attention'

My meeting with Congressman Price continues.

'Haven't you overlooked the last variable?' I ask.

'The variable that celebrates Galileo's genius for experimental reasoning? Of course, I refer to doubt. And its sibling, surprise. This is stuff so pure that even a politician can't manipulate it. Managing surprise would be like herding a cat. Dead or alive *or* who knows? You've read the *Discourses*, so I don't need to cite chapter and verse from that monument to experimental procedure.[68] Obelisks and columns, horizontally raised and lowered, were the subject at hand. "I must relate a circumstance which is worthy of your attention as indeed are all events which happen contrary to expectation, especially when a precautionary measure turns out to be a cause of disaster".[69] There's a rumor buzzing around the Capitol. Apparently, the Speaker – have you heard this?'

I relate the gossip. 'The Speaker is said to have remarked: "I don't know why members think that a proviso works some kind of magic. About 90% of bills that *don't* pass Congress *do* have provisos"'.

'Imagine my surprise!' the Congressman slaps his forehead. 'I was computing what happened to bills that *did* pass Congress. But I forgot to compute what happened to bills that *did not* pass Congress. I thought I was smart to put a proviso in my bill for the Nasty Old River Bridge. To boost my chances', the Congressman sighs.

'So, your well-manicured multifactor error analysis and the incoming signal from a single factor are in conflict. Right?'

'Let's recap where we are', the Congressman relates the values attached to the relevant variables.

Independent variables:

Initial guess = 40%

Computed error, true positive = 75%

Surprise error, false positive = 90%

Dependent variable:

Recalculated guess = 38%.

'That's bad', I remark. I check the Congressman's calculations, employing an online Bayes Theorem calculator for that purpose.[70]

'And here's more sobering news', the Congressman continues. 'When you return for a second interview with me, I'll be obliged to start with the recalculated guess of 38%'.

'Allow me to put this into a larger perspective', I observe. 'In the first trial (experiment), Bayes Assessment Method operates on three variables Beginning with the second trial or experiment, there are only two independent variables at work. That is, the true positive and false positive. The principal input on the second (and later trials) will be the previous trial's output'.

The Congressman sniffles his regrets.

'I'll be compelled to trudge forward, dragging behind me the state of affairs I've made for myself in the just-completed experiment'.

'So, what will you do, Congressman?'

'There's some advice that President Van Buren gave me, way back in the day. When you think your favorite improvement project is shot to hell, instead of blaming Thomas Bayes and his celebrated Theorem, find a means to – '

'To dazzle and seduce your constituents?' I suggest.

'To dazzle and seduce *my colleagues*', Congressman Price corrects me.

Conclusion

In a letter to François-Jean de Beauvoir, Marquis de Chastellux, Gen. George Washington put pen to paper in Princeton, New Jersey (12 October 1783). The General was bored out of his mind. He was compelled to cool his heels until the 'British forces shall have taken leave of New York', as he put the matter. As soon as he could, Washington declared that he would 'quit the walks of public life, & under the shadow of my own vine, and my own Fig-tree, to seek those enjoyments, & that relaxation, which a mind that has been constantly upon the stretch for more than eight years, stands so much in need of'.[71]

In his letter to de Chastellux Gen. Washington related his impressions of a tour he had recently completed. The journey took him through upstate New York.

> I have lately made a tour through the Lakes George & Champlain as far as Crown point ... I then traversed the Country to the head of the Eastern Branch of the Susquehanna & viewed the Lake Otsego, & the portage between that lake & the Mohawk river at Canajoharie—Prompted by these actual observations, I could not help taking a more contemplative & extensive view of the vast inland navigation of these United States, from Maps and the information of others; & could not but be struck with the immense diffusion & importance of it; & with the goodness of that providence which has dealt her favors to us with so profuse a hand. Would to God we may have wisdom enough to improve them.[72]

On 26 September 1789, Washington appointed Thomas Jefferson as the nation's first Secretary of State. Jefferson returned from Paris, taking up his post on 22 March 1790. More than two years transpired (September 1789–February 1792) before Congress was able to resolve the delegation question that had roiled the establishment of the Post Office Department. As soon as Washington approved the Act of 20 February 1792,[73] Jefferson made an appointment with the President.

Jefferson recorded the meeting in his 'Memorandum of Conversations with Washington, 1 March 1792'.[74]

Jefferson was 'delayed by business, so as to have scarcely time to give him the outlines' before callers pressed their attentions on the General. It was Washington's custom to hold open house and receive callers on Tuesday at 3 o'clock. This was 'the hour & day he received visits', Jefferson noted. 'I run over them rapidly, & observed afterwards that I had hitherto never spoke to him on the subject of the post office'.[75] Jefferson suggested to Washington that postal riders record their movements (via values assigned to variables such as time, distance, weather). Jefferson's 'Memorandum' discloses that he 'opened' to the President 'a proposition for doubling the velocity of the post riders, who now travel about 50. miles a day, & might without difficulty go 100. and for taking measures (by waybills) to know where the delay is, when there is any'.[76]

I shed further light on Jefferson's proposal by reference to one of Adam Smith's best-known time-and-motion case studies. Smith highlighted his interest in manufacturing operations by placing this case study at the opening of his *Wealth of Nations* (Book I, Chapter I). Smith's case study drew attention to the energy workers expended in manufacturing pins. The worker 'could scarce, perhaps, with his utmost industry, make one pin in a day, and certainly could not make twenty'. [77] Mixing Smithian and Jeffersonian case studies, Smith might explain to his readers, for example, that the shop foreman – by 'taking measures' analogous to 'waybills' – would be able to ascertain 'where the delay is, when there is any'.[78]

Jefferson could have supported his case for waybills to Washington, by noting that Congress priced a day's delay in carrying the mail (the fault of a ferryman) at $480.00. So much for inefficiency attributable to ferrymen.[79] Efficiencies that better management could attain, Jefferson argued to Washington, should also receive their due of attention from managers of postal operations. Thomas Jefferson and Adam Smith advocated more efficient management of labor, capital and other resources in an enterprise. Their investigations opened with energy-tracking; that is, they sought to gain insight into the rate at which energy was expended in any process. This kinetic framing of process attracted the attention of Smith and Jefferson, two technocratically-inclined scholars. I recap the two dependent variables under discussion:

- the pin workers' number of pins, counted as output and
- the postal riders' speed, measured between post offices.

Dividing tasks among workers attracted Adam Smith's attention when he visited the pinmaker's factory. He assigned the number (of different tasks required to make a pin) to the variable proportionality in his analysis.[80] For Thomas Jefferson the key variable in his analysis was the time it took a 'post rider' to cover a given route from A to B. Both investigators concerned themselves with the quantum of energy that a worker/rider might expend in excess of an optimal figure. Both Jefferson and Smith were adept at avoiding what I call 'early branching error'.[81] Smith is saying – as explicitly as he can – that it is a mistake for the pin manufacturer to ask, 'If it takes one man one day to make a pin, do I need to hire 999 more workers to crank up my pin factory's production to 1,000 pins a day?' Likewise, Jefferson knew there was no point in asking postal riders to ride twice as fast. What is the technical achievement that unites the investigations of Smith and Jefferson? I begin with Jefferson's 'waybills'. After a stack of waybills had been accumulated, the data recorded would enable managers to go back and forth between data sets and any given fact-testable proposition. For example, a postal inspector might conclude that 'the most common serious delays occur at ferry crossings'. Or, 'rainy days are slow days. Better speeds are only attainable when the roads are dry'.

The back and forth between data (extracted from the material world) and a proposition (that the manager articulates) sets up a reciprocal discipline. Both the initial proposition and the initial data (drawn from waybills) are vulnerable to reconfiguration. What is called for is adjusting (reconfiguring) the proposition, on the one hand, and adjusting (reconfiguring) the data set, on the other hand. This continues until the proposition (being tested) is both verifiable and, if alternative data is gathered, falsifiable. Jefferson's suggestion amounts to the fact-testable proposition that waybills can assist post office managers when they set out to save worker energy. Smith's suggestion amounts to the fact-testable proposition that downsizing tasks saves energy. Both Jefferson and Smith suggest that productivity gains can be achieved by concentrating initial attention on energy-tracking, with Smith going farther towards energy-savings by shrinking the energy that each worker devotes to a single task. They configured their efforts to bring about energy-savings. The lesson learned? If a technocratically-inclined investigator tracks energy expended, he will reliably locate opportunities for potential energy-savings.

There is nothing really startling in what I have related, unless the reader is fascinated that two Presidents of the United States are discussing productivity gains. Both Washington and Jefferson understood the approach to energy-saving that Adam Smith recommended. Very humble and even uninteresting tasks yield opportunities for lawmakers to acquire and refine skills in institution-building. The foregoing discussion may illuminate for the reader how Senators and Representatives in the Second Republic exploited opportunities to enhance their legislative competence. Without, I hasten to add, reading their Adam Smith or Bayes-Price.[82]

Notes

1. De Tocqueville, *Democracy*. Beaumont's novel *Marie: ou l'Esclavage aux États-Unis, tableau de moeurs américaines* went through four editions by 1840. Beaumont appended various statistical and factual gatherings to his novelistic relation of slavery in America.
2. *Ibid.*, 1:317.
3. See memory.loc.gov/cgi-bin/ampage; *ASP/Post Office*, 256, 257; Doc. No. 60.
4. *Ibid.*
5. *Ibid.*
6. *Ibid.*
7. *Ibid.*
8. Burke, *Reflections*, 70.
9. *Ibid.*
10. *Ibid.,* 258.
11. See memory.loc.gov/ammem/amlaw/lwsllink.html; 1 Stat 218, c. 23, Act of March 3, 1791. The two prior statutes appear at 1 Stat 70, c. 16, Act of September 22, 1789 *and* 1 Stat 178, c. 36, Act of August 4, 1790.
12. See memory.loc.gov/ammem/amlaw/lwaclink.html *Annals,* 1st Congress, 3rd Session, 1936; 31 January 1791.
13. 1 Stat 232, c. 7.
14. See memory.loc.gov/cgi-bin/ampage; *ASP/Post Office*, 256, 257; Doc. No. 60.
15. See text at 19-20.
16. Art. I, §2, cl. 3. See also 1790_United_States_census [last retrieved 23 May 2021].
17. 1 Stat 232, c. 7, Sec. 28.
18. See text at 18.
19. *Ibid.*, Sec. 5.
20. 1 Stat 218, c. 23, Act of March 3, 1791.
21. 1 Stat 191, c. 7, Act of February 18, 1791 [admission effective 4 March 1791].
22. 2 Stat 444, c. 43, Act of March 3, 1807; 2 Stat 491, c. 56, Act of April 23, 1808.
23. See text at 8-9.
24. See United_States_congressional_apportionment [last retrieved 31 January 2021].
25. Hatsell, *Papers*, 96 n. 214 ['Sir William Young forced a division by shouting Aye, but then divided with the Noes'].
26. Hatsell, *Members/Speaker*, 113 ['for want of forty Members, the Speaker adjourned the House only till Tuesday Morning']. See also politics.co.uk/reference/voting-commons/
27. See text at 134.
28. *Ibid.*
29. *Ibid.*, 8.
30. *Ibid.*, 9.
31. *Ibid.*, 65.
32. *Ibid.*, 69.
33. *Ibid.*, 8.
34. *Ibid.*, 67
35. *Ibid.*, 11.
36. *Ibid.*, 69.
37. *Ibid.*, 72.
38. *Ibid.*, 72.

39. Berkeley, 'Verses'.
40. The mural of Emmanuel Leutze (1816-1868) 'Westward the Course of Empire Takes Its Way' (painted 1861-1862), located in a stairwell on the House side of the US Capitol, supplies a cinematic depiction of westward expansion. The mural leaves no doubt that Bishop Berkeley's lines served as the inspiration for Leutze's canvas. In contrast the imperial machinery (that underpins Gallatin's report) is reflected in the work of Giovanni Battista Piranesi (1720-1778). I refer to a dark and brooding etching titled 'Prisoners on a Projecting Platform'. This work appeared in his collection *Le Carceri d'Invenzione/Imaginary Prisons* (1st ed., 1745, 2nd ed., 1761). Leutze makes us feel that his figures are in motion – they dominate the middle third of his canvas – but it is an unknown destination that attracts Piranesi's figures. They trudge lofty, dim and forbidding walkways high above the center of the composition.
41. Letter of John Hatsell to Henry Addington; Hatsell, *Papers*, 91
42. Gallatin, *Report*, 109.
43. *Ibid.*, 107.
44. *Commons Journal*, 76:281.
45. See Appendix C: *The Political Governance and the Resource Exploitation Clauses.*
46. 2 Stat 661, c. 45, Act of March 3, 1811, Sec. 2.
47. Gallatin, *Report*, 69.
48. *Statistical Abstract*, Series P 99-108, 'Federal Government Finances ... 1789-1945'.
49. See https://www.senate.gov/artandhistory/history/minute/Senator_Everett_Mckinley_Dirksen_Dies.htm#:~:text=Cautioningthatfederalspending
50. 2 Stat 152, c. 23, Act of April 14, 1802; 2 Stat 269, c. 22, Act of March 16, 1804.
51. 2 Stat 353, c. 12, Act of February 28, 1806.
52. *Ibid.*
53. See millercenter.org/the-presidency/presidential-speeches/december-2-1806-sixth-annual-message
54. *Ibid.*
55. See memory.loc.gov/cgi-bin/ampage?collId=llhb&fileName=023/llhb023.db&recNum=49
56. 2 Stat 396, c. 41, Act of April 21, 1806, Sec. 7. The spelling 'Greeneville' for 'Grenville' seems more correct since the treaty in question employed the spelling 'Greeneville'. 7 Stat 49, August 3, 1795. However, 2 Stat 670, c. 12, Act of January 8, 1812, had 'Grenville' for 'Greeneville'. 'An Act to authorize the laying out and opening a public road from the line established by the treaty of Grenville, to the North Bend in the state of Ohio'. The Fort at which the Treaty of Greeneville was signed was named in honor of revolutionary war hero, Maj. Gen. Nathan Greene.
57. See memory.loc.gov/ammem/amlaw/lwsj.html; *Senate Journal*, 4:78.
58. See memory.loc.gov/ammem/amlaw/lwhj.html; *House Journal*, 5:410-411.
59. *House Journal*, 5:424-425.
60. Bioren & Duane, *Laws of the United States* (Washington DC, 1815); Peters, *US Public Statutes at Large* (Boston, 1846).
61. 2 Stat 444, c. 43, Act of March 3, 1807. A bit of an odd duck, the relevant provision of the Act required negotiations 'between the executive of the United States and the Spanish government' to settle details of the route. Sec. 2.
62. 2 Stat 357, c. 19, Sec. 6, Act of March 29, 1806 [Cumberland Road]; 2 Stat 173; c. 40, Act of April 30, 1802, Sec. 7 ['laying out and making public

roads, leading from navigable waters emptying into the Atlantic, to the Ohio, to the said state'].

63. 2 Stat 396, c. 41, Sec. 7, Act of April 21, 1806.
64. 2 Stat 173; c. 40, Act of April 30, 1802, Sec. 7 ['public roads ... to be laid out under the authority of Congress, with the consent of the several states through which the road shall pass'].
65. See text at 175.
66. See stat.ucla.edu/history/essay.pdf [last retrieved 5 January 2021].
67. *Ibid.*
68. Galileo, *Discourses.*
69. *Ibid.*, 53.
70. Readers can check the results using the following inputs for the independent variables: P(A) = .40, P(B|A) = .75 and P(B|1-A) = .90. A Bayes Theorem calculator will generate the answer P(A|B) = .3771. The expression P(B|1-A) may also appear as P(B|¬A) as it does in the program cited. See gigacalculator.com/calculators/bayes-theorem-calculator.php [last retrieved 2 July 2021]. I use the 'long form' of Bayes' Theorem.
71. See founders.archives.gov/documents/Washington/99-01-02-11929; 'George Washington to François-Jean de Beauvoir, marquis de Chastellux', 12 October 1783.
72. *Ibid.*
73. 1 Stat 232, c. 7, Act of February 20, 1792.
74. See founders.archives.gov/documents/Washington/05-10-02-0004; 'Thomas Jefferson's Memorandum of Conversations with Washington, 1 March 1792'.
75. *Ibid.* The original has 'run' for 'ran'.
76. *Ibid.*
77. Smith, *Wealth*, 14-15.
78. See text at 32.
79. See text at 21.
80. See text at 32.
81. See text at 28-29.
82. So much for merit-based reasoning at work in the assembly. As to procedure-based reasoning, Americans could search Jefferson's *Manual* and John Hatsell's *Precedents of Proceedings*. As to the latter work, Hatsell notes that on visiting Bath, Prince of Wales 'did me the honour to walk the Streets & converse for half an hour [in Bath, 15 January 1797]. He contriv'd, in this short space, to talk of Mr Pitt [and] paid me Complmts on The Parly Procedts, <u>which He had often look'd into</u>'. Hatsell, *Papers*, 103-104.

References

Primary Sources

Berkeley, George, 'Verses on the Prospect of Planting Arts and Learning in America' (1726), published in *A Collection of Poems in Six Volumes. By Several Hands* (London, 1763; R. Dodsley, ed.) 311-312. See berkeleyhistoricalsociety.org/history-notes/bishop-george-berkeley.html

Burke, Edmund, *Reflections on the Revolution in France* (1790), *in* oll.libertyfund.org/title/canavan-select-works-of-edmund-burke-vol-2; HTML version used; original pagination in [] single brackets.

Gallatin, Albert, 'Report of the Secretary of the Treasury on Public Roads and Canals', *in* memory.loc.gov/ammem/amlaw/lwsp.html; *American State Papers/*

Miscellaneous, 1:724–742 [with attachments at pp. 742–870] Doc. No. 250, 6 April 1808. This version includes the Senate's charge to Gallatin (2 March 1807) and preserves the Report's original pagination.

Galilei, *Galileo, Discorsi e dimostrazioni matematiche/Discourses and mathematical demonstrations ....* (Leida, 1638). Page numbering from the online edition at oll.libertyfund.org/titles/galilei-dialogues-concerning-two-new-sciences, which incorporates the National Edition (Torino, 1958) whose text is based on the 1638 edn.

The Papers of John Hatsell, Clerk of the House of Commons (Cambridge, UK, 2020; Peter J. Aschenbrenner and Colin Lee, eds.).

Hatsell, John, *Precedents of Proceedings, in the House of Commons ...* (London, 1776 and various dates through 1818). see www.precedentsofproceedings.com

Jefferson, Thomas, *Manual of Parliamentary Practice. For the Use of the Senate of the United States* (Washington City, DC, 1801; rev. ed. 1812).

Smith, Adam, *An Inquiry into the Nature and Causes of the Wealth of Nations* (Oxford, 1976; R.H. Campbell, A. S. Skinner and W.B. Todd, eds.; the 'Glasgow' edn). The prefatory essay ('The Text and Apparatus') concludes that the 3rd edition (1784) 'must be accepted as representing his final version'. At 63. My pagination matches this edition.

De Tocqueville, Alexis Charles, *Democracy in America* (London, 1835, 1840; modern English edn. 'The Henry Reeve Text'; New York, NY, 1993).

Secondary Sources

[United States] *Historical Statistics of the United States 1789-1945, A Supplement to the Statistical Abstract of the United States* (Washington, DC, 1945), available at census.gov/library/publications/time-series/statistical_abstracts.html.

2 'To Adopt a System of Internal Improvement'

'Views of the President of the United States on Internal Improvements'

On Saturday 4 May 1822 President James Monroe vetoed H.R. 50.[1] The bill's provisions placed tollgates on the Cumberland Road and directed toll collectors to charge travelers for the privilege of using that highway. Tolls would be applied to 'the repairs and preservation of said road ... and to no other purpose whatever'.[2] Over its useful life, federal funding for the Cumberland Road averaged $10,000 per mile.[3] To fund the design and construction of the Cumberland Road, Congress could draw (for that purpose) on accounts funded by land sales in Ohio, Indiana and Illinois.[4] Congress tapped these accounts for that purpose from 1806 to 1815.[5] It was not until 14 April 1818 that Congress appropriated funds from the US Treasury without drawing on these accounts. Congress signaled its intentions in this regard via the formula, 'to be paid out of any money in the treasury not otherwise appropriated'.[6] In the 1818 enactment, Congress satisfied contractor claims to the tune of $52,984.60. This was chicken feed. In the same bill, Congress directed President Monroe to throw $260,000 at 'demands which will be made under existing contracts'.[7]

Over the 50-year life of the Cumberland Road (as a federal transportation project), Congress spent close to $2.7 million on construction. Appendix D: The Cumberland Road supplies details. Repairs ran about $1.5 million. In the pre-Macadam days, contractors were challenged to lay down a surface that could bear heavy traffic.[8] For every two dollars that Congress committed to road construction, Congress would be called upon to fund another dollar in repair costs. In crafting H.R. 50 Congress drew on its experience in projects launched in the District of Columbia. In 1809, Congress incorporated a pay-to-travel canal company in the City of Washington.[9] In 1810, Congress incorporated a pay-to-travel turnpike designed to feed traffic into a Baltimore-bound highway.[10]

Monroe's Veto Message – an essay of 757 words – supplied a six-point outline of topics.[11] 'A power to establish turnpikes with gates and tolls

DOI: 10.4324/9781003019381-3

and to enforce the collection of tolls by penalties', Monroe declared, 'implies a power to adopt and execute a complete system of internal improvement'.[12] In Monroe's opinion such a 'system' was beneficial. However, an amendment to *Constitution II* was required to authorize such a project.

I turn to Monroe's composition titled 'Views of the President of the United States on the Subject of Internal Improvements'.[13] This essay exceeded 29,000 words. Monroe intended his brief Veto Message to introduce his 'Views'. Monroe frankly conceded that the results were awkward. 'The form which this exposition [Monroe's 'Views'] has assumed is not such as I should have given it had it been intended for Congress, nor is it concluded'.[14]

> Nevertheless, as it contains my views on this subject, being one which I deem of very high importance, and which in many of its bearings has now become peculiarly urgent, I will communicate it to Congress, if in my power, in the course of the day, or certainly on Monday next.[15]

In dissecting Monroe's 'Views', I teased two separate essays out of its 170 paragraphs. Some material is datable to 1819. The remaining material is datable to 1822. I refer to the former as the '1819 essay' and the latter as the '1822 essay'.

- Monroe's 1819 essay urged Congress to begin the process of amending the federal constitution. Congress should invoke the first amendatory process that Article V made available to Congress for this purpose.
- Monroe's 1822 essay concluded that the General Welfare clause – Article I, Section 8, Clause 1 – authorized federal spending on improvement projects.

Monroe's 1819 and 1822 essays arrived at very different conclusions. I supply paragraph numbers to indicate the location of passages quoted.

- In his 1819 essay, Monroe denied that *Constitution II* granted Congress 'the power to adopt and execute a system of internal improvement by roads and canals'. Congress had the 'right to appropriate the public money, and nothing more'. ¶¶65, 96.
- 'My idea', Monroe argued in his 1822 essay, 'is that Congress have an unlimited power to raise money, and that in its appropriation they have a discretionary power, restricted only by the duty to appropriate it to purposes of common defense and of general, not local, national, not State, benefit'. ¶126.

My division of the 'Views' follows:

- The opening tranche of the 1819 essay began at ¶1 and continued up through ¶101. This tranche excluded the last sentence of ¶101.
- The last sentence of ¶101 – 'my mind has undergone a change' – opened the material datable to 1822; this text ran through ¶126.
- At ¶149 Monroe returned to his 1819 reasoning. I place the final sentence of ¶149 in the margin.[16] The material from ¶149 to ¶169 is datable to his 1819 essay or is at least consistent with his thinking from that era.
- I conjecture that Monroe composed the final paragraph of his 'Views', ¶170, for the purpose of concluding both essays. The generalities Monroe offered his readers seem to align with that purpose.

However, my division (in the bullet points above) exposes the following difficulty. At ¶127 Monroe stated: 'I will now proceed to the fifth source from which the power is said to be derived …'. At ¶130 Monroe stated: 'I come now to the last source from which this power is said to be derived …'. These match up with the fifth and sixth points Monroe outlined in his Veto Message. The material from ¶127 to ¶148 is probably assignable to the 1819 essay. Monroe, however, may have revised this text before May 1822. It would be awkward for Monroe to declare that he had a 'change [of] mind' at ¶101 and then argue that a constitutional amendment must precede consideration of road and canal bills. But that is precisely how Monroe arranged his 1819 and 1822 materials. At ¶134, he called for an 'amendment to the constitution'. The effect is certainly awkward, with material from Monroe's 1819 essay – text from ¶149 to ¶169 – concluding his 'Views'.

'The most thorough and elaborate view of the subject will be found in the exposition of President Monroe'

At one level of abstraction, Monroe's 1822 essay argued that state governments should design, build and repair feeder roads and branch canals. This made Monroe's division of labor – the national government does big stuff, leaving the state governments to do smaller stuff – turn on economies of scale. In any given case, the national government should do that which is prudent to do and avoid wasting time, energy and money on projects that the states (or private companies) were well-equipped to launch.

Monroe's handling of the issues in his 1822 essay is elegant if occasionally truncated. It won serious praise from Joseph Story (1779–1845), Associate Justice on the Supreme Court (1812–1845) and John Marshall's closest colleague. 'But perhaps the most thorough and elaborate view, which perhaps has ever been taken of the subject, will be found in the exposition of President Monroe, which accompanied his message respecting the bill for the repairs of the Cumberland Road, (4th of May 1822)'. The following passage suggests what Justice Story had in mind when he praised Monroe's 'Views'.

> A State government will rarely if ever apply money to national purposes without making it a charge to the nation. The people of the State would not permit it. Nor will Congress be apt to apply money in aid of the State administrations for purposes strictly local in which the nation at large has no interest, although the State should desire it. The people of the other States would condemn it. ¶106

I employ the template 'if x, then y, else z'. *If* Congress were to 'apply money in aid of the State administrations for purposes strictly local, [then] the people of the other States would condemn it'. At this point Monroe turned to the converse argument: *If* the 'people [were not to] condemn' money voted by Congress, *then* the money must have been applied 'to national purposes'. Voter *non*-disapproval now claimed Monroe's attention.[17]

> The measures of Congress have been in strict accord with the view taken of the right of appropriation both as to its extent and limitation, as will be shown by a reference to the laws, commencing at a very early period. ¶112

Monroe took notice of the acquiescence of the nation in the 'measures of Congress' (quoted above) and 'practice of the Government' (quoted below).

> The practice of the Government, as illustrated by numerous and strong examples directly applicable, ought surely to have great weight in fixing the construction of each grant. It ought, I presume, to settle it, especially where it is acquiesced in by the nation and produces a manifest and positive good. ¶122.

As of 1822 – when the 17th Congress was at work – 16 previous Congresses had been composing public statutes of the United States. The final session of the 16th Congress met from 13 November 1820 to 3 March 1821. According to the *Statistical Abstract of the United States*, Congress adopted 2,246 bills and resolutions from 1 June 1789 through 3 March 1821.[18] The 17th Congress added 16 such enactments (before 4 May 1822) for a total of 2,262 Acts and Resolutions. A scholar of Monroe's talent should not find it difficult to gather evidence for the proposition that Congress had *in the past* has enacted improvement legislation and the voters *did not* condemn these laws by rejecting Congressmen standing for reelection. Monroe's data-set appears in his

'Views'. The survey is the centerpiece of his 1822 essay and includes 'numerous and strong examples' of programmatic action, which are 'directly applicable [and] ought surely to have great weight in fixing the construction of each grant'. ¶122.

I list the 13 projects that Monroe named in the survey that he extracted from nine Acts of Congress. In the margin, I note that Monroe cited the reader to a statute's internal page number, not the initial page number.[19]

1 Monroe began with the Cumberland Road project. Act of March 29, 1806. This bill required Jefferson to obtain state consents to the project; this requirement first appeared in the Ohio Enabling Act (1802).[20]

2, 3, 4 In this bill, Congress launched three *more* national road projects. These are (a) a road between Athens GA and New Orleans (in the Orleans Territory), (b) a road from 'the Mississippi River to the Ohio' (through northern Ohio) and (c) a road from Nashville TN to Natchez in the Mississippi Territory. Act of April 21, 1806.[21] Congress did *not* require that state legislatures give their consent to these projects.

5 This was a project re-routing and expanding the road designed to run from Athens GA to New Orleans in the Orleans Territory. Act of March 3, 1807.[22]

6, 7 These were two so-called treaty roads. One 'as contemplated by the treaty of Brownstown in the territory of Michigan', is titled 'the Miami River to Lake Erie road'. The second project is referenced as a Greenville Treaty road designed to run from Lower Sandusky to 'the boundary line established by the Treaty of Greenville'. Act of December 12, 1811.[23]

8 Another road project ran 'from the line established by the treaty of Grenville, to the North Bend in the state of Ohio'. Act of January 8, 1812.[24]

9, 10 These were two road repair projects. One extended from 'Columbia, in the state of Tennessee' to 'Madisonville, in the state of Louisiana'[25]. The second ran 'between Fort Hawkins, in the state of Georgia to Fort Stoddard' in the Mississippi Territory. Act of April 27, 1816.[26]

11 This road ran from Shawnee Town IL (on the Ohio river) to Kaskaskia 'in the Illinois territory'. Act of April 27, 1816.[27]

12 This road ran from Reynoldsburgh TN 'through the Chickasaw nation' to Chickasaw Old Town MS. Act of March 3, 1817.[28]

13 Congress designed this project as the southerly extension of the Cumberland Road. Congress planned this route to angle off from Wheeling VA and proceed west – along a route south of the existing Cumberland Road – with a terminus at St. Louis MO. Act of May 15, 1820.[29]

Monroe noted that Congress planned a five-project national road network (1806, 1820). Three national roads were to run through northern, central and southern Ohio toward the Mississippi River. A fourth road would connect Athens GA and New Orleans in the Orleans Territory. A fifth road would run from Nashville TN to Natchez in the Mississippi Territory. Only in the case of the Cumberland Road (running from western Maryland and into central Ohio) did Congress require state consents. All five roads involved considerable lengths of *intra*state roadway to be constructed. All five roads were funded, at least in part, by direct federal appropriations. Monroe is citing the reader to these five projects (along with the other eight) for the proposition that Congress acted as if it had the power to build national roads.

> Appropriations have never been limited by congress to cases falling with the specific powers enumerated in the constitution, whether those powers be construed in their broad, or their narrow sense.[30]

Justice Story's remarks appear immediately after his praise for Monroe's 'Views', noted above.[31] Taken as public sector benefits that maximize private choice, did transportation projects enjoy a special status? In other words, was transportation legislation presumed to deliver productivity gains? 'Good roads, canals, and navigable rivers, by diminishing the expense of carriage', Adam Smith declared in the *Wealth of Nations* (1776), 'put the remote parts of the country more nearly upon a level with those in the neighbourhood of the town. They are upon that account the greatest of all improvements'.[32] Following Smith's thinking, Story noted that the predicates 'narrow' and 'broad' did not cure the fundamental flaw that inhered in textual reasoning that drew its strength from notions of 'higher law'. Reasoning via such adjectives could not to grips with the concrete details that an assembly would be obliged to address when it set about launching transportation projects and – more generally – spending tons of money.[33]

'There has never been an instance before of so unanimous an opinion of the people'

My comments on Monroe's survey of Congressional precedents follow:

1 Arranging his precedents in chronological order served to remind Monroe's readers that Thomas Jefferson had referred to lawmakers of the 14th Congress, 1st Session as the '1500.D. a year' Congress because members voted themselves a pay rise in the Act of March 19, 1816.[34] Referring to the Act of February 6, 1817,[35] Congressmen serving in the 14th Congress, 1st Session who survived the 1816 biennial elections promised voters to repeal the pay hike. The 14th

Congress, 2nd Session had no difficulty interpreting the message that the voters sent to Congress.[36] Referring 'to the law giving themselves 1500.D. a year', Jefferson lettered Gallatin, 'there has never been an instance before of so unanimous an opinion of the people [disapproving of an Act of Congress]'.[37]

Take Congress's plan to run a new national road on the southerly route from Wheeling VA to St. Louis MO. If the plan had seriously offended voters, then the *congressional* elections of 1820 gave voters an opportunity to express themselves. Voters could also have expressed their displeasure in the *presidential* election taking place in that year. Monroe thereby offered a very unsubtle hint that presidential elections – and their margins of victory – matter. Monroe won reelection by a near-unanimous margin.[38]

2 Monroe's list included a road project that James Madison signed into law on the same day he vetoed the Bonus Bill. Monroe referenced the Act of March 3, 1817.[39] This was a rare instance of Monroe casting serious shade at his predecessor. Astute politicians would take the full measure of that citation. The Act that Madison did *not* veto funded an *intra*state stretch of national road from Nashville to Tennessee's border with the Mississippi Territory.

3 Monroe named projects launched during the administrations of Jefferson and Madison. Monroe omitted mention of bills passed during the presidencies of Washington and Adams. The first two presidents approved bills in the 2nd, 3rd, 4th and 6th Congresses that batch-processed 101 intrastate postal routes.[40] The early republic also undertook other types of projects, such as a federally funded state harbor project in Savannah GA which the 6th Congress launched in the final year of the Adams administration. This was a first in American political history.[41] Monroe also excluded projects that Jefferson approved before the Cumberland Road bill. Worth special mention: To launch a construction project in the Delaware River at Philadelphia, Congress tasked a state body to fulfill a federal program (1806).[42]

4 Monroe's list drew attention to Congress's role as the national brokerage for improvement projects. When Congress considered multiple projects in a single bill, wheeling and dealing accommodated competing interests. The Act of April 21, 1806 distributed benefits (three national road projects) among at least three states (Georgia, Tennessee and Ohio) and two territories (Mississippi and Orleans). Weeks earlier the Act of March 29, 1806 distributed benefits (the Cumberland Road) among four states: Maryland, Pennsylvania, Virginia and Ohio.

Taken together these two statutes offer a fair sampling of the parochial and territorial entities receiving transportation benefits. I refer to four types of beneficiaries. (a) A ratifying state (Georgia), (b) an admitted state (Ohio), (c) a bulk territory (Mississippi Territory) and (d) the Orleans Territory, then being configured as a nascent state.

5 Monroe opened and closed his data-set with statutes that launched and curated the Cumberland Road. Monroe's emphasis on that project is justified. On 10 occasions in the 14-year interval 1806–1820 Congress composed statutes devoting attention to various aspects of the Cumberland Road. See Appendix D: The Cumberland Road.

6 Take Maryland's consent to the Cumberland Road. This appeared in Maryland Session Law c. 70 (1806/1807).[43] The issue of title to the land – on the surface of which the future highway (and adjoining facilities) would be laid out – was carefully avoided. 'The full and entire consent [of Maryland] is hereby given [and] the president of the United States is hereby authorized to cause the said road to be laid out, opened and improved, in such way and manner as by the before recited act of congress is required and directed'.[44] Lawmakers in both Washington and Annapolis acted (in apparent concert) by *not* detailing how a footprint for the road was to be acquired, managed and, eventually, disposed of.

7 Another perspective may be gained by referring to Senator Eli Ashmun's speech during the debate on the Bonus Bill (26 February 1817). He pointed out that Congress held all the high cards when it offered to build infrastructure within a state's borders. Congress could resort to bribery or coercion in dealing with state legislatures. 'Congress may and will say, to a State, that the money shall be applied in constructing a road or canal in a particular place; otherwise it cannot be applied at all within the State. ... A consent obtained under such circumstances', the Senator declared, 'is no consent'.[45]

8 Monroe's data-set is not as complete as my survey listing 388 projects launched or curated before 4 May 1822 (a subset of the 1,147 projects launched or curated on or before 3 March 1837). However, any member of Congress who gave the 'Views' even a casual reading could see that for every project that Monroe mentioned, there might be 10 or 20 others equally worthy of attention. And for every *type* of project he mentioned, there could be a half-dozen other *types* of projects. And for every funding vehicle referenced in the statutes Monroe reviewed, there would be four other *types* of funding vehicles.

Did H.R. 50, the Cumberland Road repair bill, deserve to be treated as an outlier? Tollgates and tollhouses were the sticking point. One might surmise that these structures required a footprint. But so did the road surface itself. Monroe's failure to close out his data-set with a reasoned judgment on H.R. 50 may be charitably overlooked. In 1823 Congress hosed $25,000 at the problem and funded a superintendent to oversee the necessary repairs.[46] In the

1824 elections, voters did not revolt at this spending. J.Q. Adams – who became the nation's sixth president – was even more committed to launching infrastructure projects than Monroe.[47]

'The creed of our political faith, the text of civic instruction'

I gather key words and phrases that Monroe employed in his 'Views'. In his 1819 essay, I count 'focus' words and phrases. These are:

Field for legislation and internal government ¶78
Power of indefinite and unlimited extent ¶96
Power of such vast extent and so indefinite ¶98
National purposes ¶99
Immediate and local interests ¶154

What did these phrases have in common? First, they assured readers that Monroe adhered to the 'two governments' formula. Second, the list demonstrated that Monroe considered divided allegiance to be a virtue. If two governments were calling upon inhabitants to divide their loyalty, voters had a choice in the matter. They might view themselves as rejecting Congressional programs (they find distasteful) *or* they might support future state action in lieu of federal programs of which they disapproved. Third, no matter how divided voters might be on issues of the day, inhabitants expected that programmatic action would deliver benefits to their doorstep. One might suppose that satisfying inhabitants' needs should compel the two governments of a nation to cooperate. Accordingly, Monroe signaled – in his 1822 essay – that 'great harmony' would prevail when two governments got down to the business of doing the people's business.

> I do not think that in offices of this kind there is much danger of the two Governments mistaking their interests or their duties. I rather expect that they would soon have a clear and distinct understanding of them and move on in great harmony. ¶106.

During the Monroe presidency, superminoritarians were compelled to concede that their Article V weaponry had failed them. And for this reason: 'The national sentiment is in favor of internal improvements', Sen. Hardin assured the US Senate, on the same day that Sen. Ashmun's remarks (quoted above) entered the record.[48] In Monroe's 1822 essay, I counted 14 'focus' words and phrases; these resonate to the same effect as the five I gathered from Monroe's 1819 essay.

Definite, safe and useful meaning ¶105
Original grant, with unlimited power ¶105

Clear understanding ¶106
Distinct understanding ¶106
Strictly local ¶106
Purposes strictly local ¶106
Very important national purposes ¶107
Measures as operate internally ¶121
Distinct and specific power ¶128
Special objects ¶134
Operations of a general nature ¶147
Internal and local purposes ¶147
Beyond the faculties of the General Government ¶147
Particular and local interests. ¶149

In employing these phrases Monroe assured Americans that they need not worry about 'consolidation'.

> It is only when the expansion shall be carried beyond the faculties of the General Government so as to enfeeble its operations to the injury of the whole that any of the parts can be injured. The tendency in that stage will be to dismemberment and not to consolidation. ¶147

The foregoing approach enabled Monroe to incorporate votarian discipline into his 'Views'. There were no constitutional or statutory norms to guide and govern the conduct of voters at the polls. Jefferson gave this point a light brush in his first Inaugural Address (1801). What 'should be the creed of our political faith', Jefferson asked? His response directed the attention of his listeners to 'the text of civic instruction, the touchstone by which to try the services of those we trust'? Jefferson also declared that 'creed', 'text' and 'touchstone' were to be found in 'principles' that might be useful to voters when they went to the polls to 'try the services' of lawmakers. Jefferson did not explain where these 'principles' were to be found.[49] I suggest that Monroe crafted his bright line phrases – local against general, internal versus national – for the purpose of aiding voters when they went to the polls. Monroe charged voters with the duty to disapprove national programs (a) that were composed to meet 'internal and local purposes' ¶147, *or* (b) that were 'beyond the faculties of the General Government, ¶147 *or* (c) that devoted inordinate attention to 'particular and local interests'. ¶149 On this account, if voters assessed programmatic action not to deserve their disapproval, then – after the election – lawmakers might gauge that voters were speaking for the nation's inhabitants and were therefore united 'in common efforts for the common good'.[50] In Chapter 5, this volume, I will arrange the relevant concepts into a pattern marked by the mottos 'needs', 'gets' and 'wants'.[51] Voters have an important role to play in dissuading lawmakers from launching projects of which they disapprove.

Could voters or politicians claim to be ignorant that voting has a double purpose? I fast forward to an argument that Andrew Jackson made. Voters enjoyed the opportunity to signal their disapproval of a president's policies – implemented in his first term – by denying the president a second term in office. Voters could accomplish this purpose, even if their message must be filtered through the convoluted votarian machinery known colloquially as the 'electoral college'.

> If I have mistaken the interests and wishes of the people the Constitution affords the means of soon redressing the error by selecting for the place their favor has bestowed upon me a citizen whose opinions may accord with their own.[52]

'Equal rotation is equal vicissitude in government through the free election of the people'

What transpired when agents of legislative candidates invited voters to shop their preferences was not a mysterious business in the eighteenth and nineteenth centuries. In Charles Dickens's *Pickwick Papers* Slumkey's election agent played his walk-on role to perfection. In Chapter XIII Slumkey's agent 'solicited the honor of a private interview with these intelligent, these noble, these patriotic men'.[53] 'Eatanswill' was the village in which Mr. Pickwick recorded these events. At a higher level of abstraction, Marshall and Monroe attempted to explain how representative government worked in the nineteenth century. Voters stabilized legislative delivery of goods and services by administering the death blow to programs which they (properly) regarded as outliers. They must, however, make their anger clear to politicians by voting at least some politicians out of office. The debacle of the 'Fifteen Hundred Dollar' Congress – events centering on the 1816 Congressional elections – showcased anger that voters aimed at incumbent Congressmen of the 14th Congress. You don't have to vote a lot of Congressmen out to make your point but you must boot some lawmakers out of the office to get your objections to rise above the noise of biennial contests taking place across the length and breadth of the nation.

Taken in this light, Madison, Marshall and Monroe may be put down as followers of James Harrington's political science. I refer to the expression 'equal rotation is equal vicissitude in government'; this phrase appeared in Harrington's essay 'Preliminaries', a short composition that opens Harrington's magnum opus, his *Oceana*.[54] 'Equal rotation' would oblige incumbent lawmakers to delay their return to the assembly for an interval equal to their service in that body. This is Harrington's 'equal vicissitude'. After the fact, behavior that voters exhibited at the polls will populate data-sets – that is, election results – from which lawmakers can draw their post-election conclusions. May one claim that elections (doing double duty as I have argued) are a species of the labor-saving device? The evidence supports Monroe's reasoning on this point, with both the affirmative and negative prongs of his method directing attention to lawmakers' assessment of the results of the 1822 election. Monroe and Marshall would argue that the results of the 1822 election encouraged Congress to pass the bill that became the Act of February 28, 1823, 17th Congress, 2nd Session [$25,000 to fund road repair east of Wheeling; no tollgates]. In this case, direct appropriations were an instance of an acceptable pattern of Congressional lawmaking. The 18th Congress, 1st Session failed to enact H.R. 9 [installing tollgates]; the bill may be regarded as an outlier, given the act just mentioned.[55]

Events surrounding the launch of *Constitution II* – and the instrument itself – effectively put a biennial election into the *middle* of the work of any given Congress. Here 'Congress' is taken as two sessions of legislative activity bracketing a biennial election. This was the case until the Twentieth Amendment reconfigured this arrangement (1933).[56] Put another way, voter assessment of a given program – should voters care to venture their disapproval – was nested between lawmakers' initial assessment and lawmakers' post-election reassessment. This is the single most important piece of parliamentary science that the Philadelphia convention and the Confederation Congress, working together, got right. I point to the interplay of Article I, Section 4, Clause 2 ['The Congress shall assemble ... on the first Monday in December'] *and* Article I, Section 2, Clause 1 ['The House of Representatives shall be composed of Members chosen every second Year by the People of the several States']. Take 1816, an even-numbered year and therefore a 'second Year'.[57] The 15th Congress – elected during 1816 – did not begin work until 1 December 1817 when its first session opened for business. The 15th Congress, 1st Session adjourned on 20 April 1818. State legislatures were free, however, to select dates for their biennial elections as tradition, fashion and convenience dictated. When the 15th Congress, 2nd Session opened for business (Congress advanced the date to 16 November 1818 from the 'first Monday in December' of that year[58]) that second session would either (a) follow most of the electioneering in 1818 or (b) – at the choice of individual states – biennial electioneering could take place while Congress was in session. It was not until 1872 that Congress fixed the first Tuesday after the first Monday in November (in even-numbered years) as the date on which states were required to conduct elections for seats in the House of Representatives.[59]

There is a related lesson to be teased out of the historical record. On 17 September 1787, the Philadelphia convention instructed the Confederation Congress to set two dates as soon as the ninth state ratified *Constitution II*. I note that this is one of two transmittals for which the Philadelphia convention is responsible.[60]

> That ... as soon as the Conventions of nine States shall have ratified this Constitution, the United States in Congress assembled should [set in motion the electoral machinery to elect the president] and the Time and place for commencing Proceedings under this Constitution. Senators and Representatives [shall then be] elected.[61]

Three points bear on the Philadelphia convention's direction to the Confederation Congress. (a) The ninth state ratified in June, 1788 and (b) 1788 was an even-numbered year and (c) the next even-numbered year would be 1790. Article I, Section 2, Clause 1 ['The House of Representatives shall be composed of Members chosen every second Year by the People of the several States'] dictated the 'second year' cycle. I have already noted that a broad measure of initiative was transferred to state legislatures and election officials with regard to the votarian mechanics involved in electing members of the House of Representatives.[62]

There is another cycle at work. This is the annual parliamentary cycle, which was governed by Article I, Section 4, Clause 2 ['The Congress shall assemble ... on the first Monday in December']. The faster that nine states ratified, the more time would remain on the various state electoral clocks before the 1st Congress convened. The operative interval here was bracketed by the ninth state's ratification (New Hampshire, 21 June 1788) *and* the calendar day, month and year that the Confederation Congress fixed as the 'Time ... for commencing Proceedings under this Constitution'. Assume that *Constitution II* called for Congress to convene on the 1st Monday in April. Under this hypothetical, the 1st Congress, 1st Regular Session would begin work in April, 1789. The 1st Congress, 2nd Regular Session would begin its work in April, 1790. Congress could wrap up that session's business in the summer of 1790. This schedule would allow time for biennial elections (in 1790) to *follow*, and not *precede*, the 2nd Session of the 1st Congress.

In line with the foregoing, each state decided how much, if any, *federal* legislating would take place after (at least some) *state* electioneering. For example, the first regular session of the 1st Congress convened on 4 January 1790; Congress postponed the date for the 1st Congress to reconvene from the 'first Monday in December' 1789 to 4 January 1790.[63] New York Congressional elections, for example, were set for 27–29 April 1790.[64] By conducting its first regular biennial elections under the Second Republic in April, New York guaranteed that its voters would have a chance to react to developments in the 1st Congress as one of its three sessions was in progress. I note that organic arrangements in the GB/UK did not call for the outgoing House of Commons to reconvene after a general election. In this case, Americans achieved a significant advance over British-style governance.

It is worth noting that making sense of two very unBritish arrangements in the organic affairs of the new republic required significant cooperation among many different lawmakers and officials.

'After he had now read it through, a general silence ensued'

According to J.Q. Adams, Monroe's Secretary of State, the President began work on his 1819 essay in the 'last winter' of that year. It is possible that Monroe was composing his 1819 essay at the same time that Marshall and his colleagues were hearing oral arguments in the *McCulloch* case (21 February-3 March 1819).[65] Moving forward to December, 1819: Adams' diary entry relates what transpired at the cabinet meeting of 3 December 1819. Monroe 'produced a manuscript long enough itself for two moderate Messages, recommending the proposal by Congress of an Amendment to the Constitution, authorizing them to make internal improvements by Roads and Canals; with an elaborate argument to prove that the authority has not been given by the Constitution'.[66] Adams's diary supplies additional details of the relevant events.

> It is a paper which he drew up last winter, and was then anxious to communicate in some way to Congress – He then read it at a Cabinet Meeting – but finally postponed producing it to the public at that time. After he had now read it through, a general silence ensued.[67]

As of 1819 Monroe believed the persuasive effect of his essay would stimulate Congress to propose a suitable constitutional amendment. However, Monroe decided against publishing this essay in 1819. As it happened, 29 months transpired before his two essays reached Congress and the public. As noted above, the 1822 essay contradicted many of the positions Monroe reached in his 1819 essay.[68] However, Monroe never abandoned the formula 'two governments' and its corollary 'divided allegiance'. How would Monroe make divided allegiance, at one pole, and stability-inducing programmatic action, at the other, link up one with one another? Programmatic action, Monroe argued in 1822, could be an allegiance-building enterprise, if it healed the nation. The Second Republic discovered opportunities to bring disparate regions of the nation together early in the nineteenth century. 'It was foreseen at the early period at which [the Ohio Enabling Act] passed that the expansion of our Union to the Lakes and to the Mississippi and all its waters would not only make us a greater power, but cement the Union itself'. ¶117.[69] Federal funding of Monroe's 'good roads and canals', ¶107, would reconcile geographically disparate communities and regions.

I suggest that the foregoing quotations bring the reader into the heart of Monroe's way of thinking. There was never going to be another hero, wounded in the First War for American Independence, who could credibly advocate majoritarian accomplishments to superminoritarians, especially those residing south of the Mason-Dixon line. In his 1822 essay Monroe declared:

> Good roads and canals will promote many very important national purposes. They will facilitate the operations of war, the movements of troops, the transportation of cannon, of provisions, and every warlike store, much to our advantage and to the disadvantage of the enemy in time of war. ¶107

In his 1822 essay, Monroe expressed himself as follows:

> Our union is not held together by standing armies or by any ties other than the positive interests and powerful attractions grow up among us who may promise to themselves advancement from a change, and by practicing upon the sectional interests, feelings, and prejudices endeavour under various pretexts to promote it. ¶146.

Monroe placed into public discourse the notion that 'positive interests' – inhabitants acknowledging the needs of fellow inhabitants – would stimulate 'powerful attractions'. The task of the unitary government was to nurture these feelings, thereby enabling inhabitants to embrace the common good.

Conclusion

At this point in his 1819 essay Monroe touched a chord both poetic and Eurocentric. 'They had every motive to bind [themselves] together' in refounding the national government, 'which could operate on the interests and affections of a generous, enlightened, and virtuous people'. The passage carves out European American political culture as the touchstone of organic development in the United States.

> Established in the new hemisphere, descended from the same ancestors, speaking the same language, having the same religion and universal toleration, born equal and educated in the same principles of free government, made independent by a common struggle and menaced by the same dangers, ties existed between them which never applied before to separate communities. They had every motive to bind them together which could operate on the interests and affections of a generous, enlightened, and virtuous people, and it affords

inexpressible consolation to find that these motives had their merited influence. ¶27.

Monroe confidently declared that European Americans were a 'generous, enlightened, and virtuous people' and, given those characteristics, 'ties existed between them which never applied before to separate communities'. Therefore, 'separate communities' of settlers could be relied upon to build new 'ties', one community to the next. These ties would be stronger than the links that previously 'existed between them'.[70] True, European Americans faced geographical hurdles in settling the American half-continent. However, given that they had 'every motive to bind [themselves] together' it should not be surprising that 'these motives had their merited influence'. On this account, Monroe declared that some settlers are better qualified to settle the southern, western and northwestern territories than others. Monroe's statement was fact-testable. How do you go about finding settlers qualified to 'go west' – as Bishop Berkeley rhapsodized[71] – without employing such biographically-based criteria as 'born equal' and 'educated in the ... principles of free government'? Or, more precisely, is Monroe on the right track, emphasizing biography, although his criteria requires fine-tuning?

I turn from the text that Monroe composed in 1819 to text that Congress composed in 1818. I refer to the Illinois Enabling Act.[72] Congress outlined the qualifications required of prospective inhabitants (of the nascent state of Illinois). Congress employed these qualifications to mark factors to contour the process of organizing a state constitutional convention. Congress authorized the territorial legislature to 'form a constitution and state government'. Section 4. Four qualifications follow: (a) There must be 'not less than forty thousand inhabitants' in the Illinois Territory. (b) To vote for 'representatives to form [the] convention' a voter must be a 'white male citizen'. (c) He must also be '21 years' old and (d) have been a resident 'in the said territory [for] six months'.[73]

I now compare Monroe's 1819 and Congress's 1818 qualifications. Congress does not care about pioneers' 'virtue'; Monroe does. Monroe requires that his preferred settlers should be 'educated in the ... principles of free government'. Congress is silent on this point. In essence, Monroe is dealing with variables assignable to an individual's biography. Congress traffics in demographic variables.

I compare and contrast these two approaches. Had Congress omitted the demographic requirement that voters must be 'white male citizens' – in (b) above – I doubt that the other three requirements, then or now, would raise an eyebrow. But if I tidy up Congress's social science – some tranches of the Illinois population are better qualified to cast ballots for delegates to the Illinois constitutional convention – I should also refine Monroe's. Monroe's biographical approach, suitably updated to post-modern standards, was preferable to Congress's reliance on demography. This requires recalibration of the variable calling for a settler to exhibit a pedigree traceable to a 'generous, enlightened, and virtuous people'[74] Suitably sorted, Monroe argued that prior life experience mattered to the well-modulated development of political organizations on the frontier. In other words, Monroe attempted to connect the potential contribution of settlers to political life on the frontier with their past life experiences. As I have argued in this study, developments in the interval 1817–1825 opened the way for methodologies to mature open-ended performance thresholds for those seeking to participate in the political life of the Second Republic. Slapdash predicate-attaching (here Congress's over-reliance on demographic variables) gave way to (a) creation of templates to guide and govern fulfillment of tasks assigned to institution agents, (b) application of Smithian productivity analytics and (c) employment of the method of Congressional precedents. Identify the qualities that would best enable an individual voter to participate in electing delegates to a state constitutional convention. If these are qualities that can be acquired – biography overpowering demography – then offer training to all comers and let them compete on equal terms. The US frontier would seem to offer suitable opportunities for inhabitants who were not 'born equal and educated in the same principles of free government' to acquire the skills required to navigate the pathways of representative government and contribute to the political life of a new state on the US frontier. If Congress can make a new state, why can't it enable new citizens to remake themselves? Every newcomer, over time, should have an equal chance to make a valuable contribution to the interconnected life that human beings were interweaving into a common social experience in the nascent states that Congress was legislating into existence.

Notes

1. See memory.loc.gov/ammem/amlaw/lwaclink.html; *Annals*, 17th Congress, 1st Session, 1872-1874.
2. *Ibid.*, Sec. 4.
3. Appendix D: The Cumberland Road.
4. 2 Stat 173; c. 40, Act of April 30, 1802, Sec. 7, *Third* [Ohio Enabling Act]; 3 Stat 289, c. 57, Act of April 19, 1816, Sec. 6, *Third* [Indiana Enabling Act]; 3 Stat 428, c. 67, Act of April 18, 1818, Sec. 6, Third [Illinois Enabling Act].
5. 2 Stat 357, c. 19; 9th Congress, 1st Session; Act of March 29, 1806; 3 Stat 206, c. 43; 13th Congress, 3rd Session; Act of February 14, 1815.
6. 3 Stat 426, c. 60, Act of April 14, 1818.
7. *Ibid.*, Sec. 2.
8. See Macadam [last retrieved 22 June 2021].
9. See memory.loc.gov/ammem/amlaw/lwsllink.html; 2 Stat 517, c. 17, Act of February 16, 1809.

10. 2 Stat 570, c. 26, Act of April 20, 1810.
11. See presidency.ucsb.edu/documents/veto-message
12. *Ibid.*
13. See presidency.ucsb.edu/documents/special-message-the-house-representatives-containing-the-views-the-president-the-united
14. See presidency.ucsb.edu/documents/veto-message
15. *Ibid.*
16. 'It is the peculiar felicity of the proposed amendment that while it will enable the United States to accomplish every national object, the improvements made with that view will eminently promote the welfare of the individual States, who may also add such others as their own particular interests may require'. ¶149.
17. See text at 113.
18. *Statistical Abstract*; Series P 40-49, Government Elections and Politics – Bills ... and Resolutions: 1789-1945.
19. In accordance with modern practice my endnotes cite to *The Public Statutes at Large* edited by Richard Peters (Little, Brown; 1st vol. published 1845). Monroe referred his readers to the Bioren & Duane edition of the *Laws of the United States of America*, in 5 volumes (Philadelphia PA and Washington City, 1816). For the latter edition, see catalog.hathitrust.org/Record/010473393. Congress authorized publication of this edition 'in four volumes, royal octavo'. 3 Stat 129, c. 69, Act of April 18, 1814; Sec. 1.
20. 2 Stat 357, c. 19. See text at 27.
21. 2 Stat 396, c. 41, Sec. 7.
22. 2 Stat 444, c. 43. The statute omits the following cross-reference. 'A road on the same route' (in Sec. 2) directs the reader to 2 Stat 396, c. 41, Sec. 7.
23. 2 Stat 668, c. 8.
24. 2 Stat 670, c. 12. For discussion of the Treaty of Grenville, see text at 35n56.
25. This may be 'Jackson's military road'. See Jackson's_Military_Road [last retrieved 26 January 2021].
26. 3 Stat 315, c. 112.
27. 3 Stat 318, c. 131.
28. 3 Stat 377, c. 67.
29. 3 Stat 604, c. 123.
30. Story, *Commentaries*, 456-457; Sec. 988.
31. See text at 43-44.
32. Smith, *Wealth*, 163.
33. I build on Smith's remarks as follows. A well-constructed and well-maintained road connects Town A to Village B. A horse-drawn wagon can cover the distance in a day. The route from Town A to Village C follows a track that is barely passable. After the road is rebuilt, a horse-drawn wagon can cover the distance in three days. Smith's case study permits this computation: both Village B and Village C are on the same 'level', that is, goods can be conveyed over equal distances in equal intervals of travel time, thanks to the 'improvements' constructed on the A to C route. Now to productivity gains. Smith considers this factor by noting that 'improvements' will bring about productivity gains thanks to 'diminishing the expense of carriage'. Strictly speaking, however, there is a still a financial penalty attached to remote living. Goods shipped back and forth between Town A and Village C will cost more than goods shipped between Town A and Village B. Improvements can ameliorate opportunities for economic advancement, but improvements can't equalize all geophysical hurdles to

business activity. I turn to proportionality, which Smith regards as the most important productivity analytic. Village B's producers will have to compete with Village C's products; this will require that Village C's producers accept a reduced profit margin thanks to the two additional days required to get their produce to the market in Town A. Smith correctly assumed that private choice would settle these (and related) issues. As far as Smith was concerned (a) government should intervene in the geophysical reality of the nation. Thanks to well-honed projects of 'improvements' remote villages will get their 'level' opportunity to cover equal distances in equal times when producers ship their products to market. (b) Thereafter, Smith 's caution against 'encroachment' or 'violation' of 'natural distribution' comes into play. Smith, *Wealth*, 673. Thus, governments should not intervene in private choice once productivity gains via improvements in physical infrastructure have been distributed. There's much more to be said on this subject. Is it perfectly clear that producers named in this case study would continue to enjoy the title 'private' after the geophysical reality of the planet has been rearranged to bring about the productivity gains Smith has projected?

34. 3 Stat 257, c. 30.
35. 3 Stat 345, c. 9.
36. *Ibid.*
37. See founders.archives.gov/documents/Jefferson/03-10-02-0263; 'Thomas Jefferson to Albert Gallatin, 8 September 1816'. See also Dubin, *Congressional Elections* ['Statistical Overview' pp. xx-xxi]. Take the first entry in that table appearing. Of 56 Congressmen seeking reelection from the 1st to the 2nd Congress, 15 were defeated; the fraction yields a 73% reelection rate. Of 100 Congressmen running for reelection (from the 14th Congress to the 15th Congress) only 56% were successful. This data quantifies Jefferson's assessment that the '1500.D'. Congress would be going down to defeat.
38. See 1820_United_States_presidential_election [last retrieved 3 March 2021].
39. 2 Stat 377, c. 67, Act of March 3, 1817 ['road through the Chickasaw nation'].
40. The first in this series was 1 Stat 232, c. 7, Act of February 20, 1792 [16 projects] and the last was 2 Stat 125, c. 35 Act of March 3, 1801 [20 projects].
41. 2 Stat 18, c. 15, Act of March 17, 1800.
42. 2 Stat 353, c. 12, Act of February 28, 1806.
43. C. 70, Act of 4 January 1807, 608:41.
44. *Ibid.*, Sec. II.
45. *Annals*, 14th Congress, 2nd Session, 180, 26 February 1817. Eli Ashmun served in the US Senate from 1816 to 1818; an old school Federalist, he is buried in Northampton MA. See bioguideretro.congress.gov
46. 3 Stat 728, c. 17, Act of February 28, 1823.
47. See text at 166.
48. *Annals*, 14th Congress, 2nd Session, 176, 26 February 1817. Sen. Hardin served from 1816 to the end of the 14th Congress, 3 March 1817. He is now buried in the State Cemetery at Frankfort.
49. See millercenter.org/the-presidency/presidential-speeches/march-4-1801-first-inaugural-address.
50. *Ibid.*
51. See text at 117-118.

52. Jackson's remarks appear in his Second Annual Message to Congress (6 December 1830). See millercenter.org/the-presidency/presidential-speeches/december-6-1830-second-annual-message-congress In that essay, Jackson referred back to the Maysville Road and the Rockville Road projects; both disapprovals were dated in May, 1830. Jackson's references to 'Maysville' and 'Rockville' (in his Second Annual Message) do not perfectly align with the titles of the bills he vetoed. I begin with his reference to the Maysville project. The veto message appears at millercenter.org/the-presidency/presidential-speeches/may-27-1830-veto-message-regarding-funding-infrastructure The bill, as introduced, authorized 'a subscription of stock in the Maysville, Washington, Paris, and Lexington Turnpike Road Company'. The text of H.R. 285 appears at memory.loc.gov/cgi-bin/ampage?collId=llhb&fileName=012/llhb012.db&recNum=114 The 'Rockville Road' inspired Jackson's veto message four days later (31 May 1830). That brief message incorporated Jackson's previous message regarding the Maysville project. See presidency.ucsb.edu/documents/veto-message-472 As introduced S. 27 authorized 'a subscription of Stock in Washington Turnpike Road Company'. The text of what Jackson referenced as the 'Rockville Road' bill appears at memory.loc.gov/cgi-bin/ampage?collId=llsb&fileName=011/llsb011.db&recNum=75
53. Dickens, *Pickwick Papers*, c. 13 (1837).
54. Harrington, *Oceana* ['Preliminaries'], 51.
55. See memory.loc.gov/cgi-bin/ampage?collId=llhb&fileName=005/llhb005.db&recNum=34
56. See text at 49-50.
57. See https://memory.loc.gov/ammem/amlaw/lwjc.html *Continental Congress Journals*, 34:522-523, 9 September 1788 ['that the first Wednesday in March next (4 March 1789) be the time and the present seat of [the Confederation] Congress (New York City) be the place for commencing proceedings under the said constitution'.].
58. 3 Stat 433, c. 71, Act of April 18, 1818.
59. 17 Stat 28, c. 11, Sec. 3, Act of February 2, 1872.
60. Farrand, *Records*, 665-666.
61. *Ibid.*
62. See text at 49.
63. 1 Stat 96, c. 27, Act of September 29, 1789.
64. See 1790_United_States_House_of_Representatives_elections_in_New_York [last retrieved 14 May 2021].
65. See Introduction, this volume.
66. See masshist.org/jqadiaries/php/doc?id=jqad31_1 John Quincy Adams, Diary 31, 221-222; entry for 3 December 1819.
67. *Ibid.*
68. See text at 38-40.
69. 2 Stat 173, c. 40, Act of April 30, 1802.
70. The organization that maintains Highland, Monroe's plantation near Charlottesville, records that Monroe owned as many as 250 enslaved persons during his lifetime; Monroe manumitted only one. See highland.org/highland-and-slavery [last retrieved 2 July 2021].
71. Given that documentation for Horace Greeley's (frequently attributed) quotable is not undisputed, see Go_West,_young_man, it seems preferable to credit the Bishop as the ultimate source for the idea. See text at 24.
72. 3 Stat 428, c. 67, Act of April 18, 1818.
73. See text at 53-54.
74. See text at 52-53.

References

Primary Sources

Burke, Edmund, *Reflections on the Revolution in France* (1790), *in* oll.libertyfund.org/title/canavan-select-works-of-edmund-burke-vol-2; HTML version used; original pagination in [] single brackets.

Dickens, Charles, *The Pickwick Papers* (London, 1837).

Records of the Federal Convention of 1787 (New Haven, CT, 1911, 3 vols; Max Farrand, ed.; rev. ed. 1937, 4 vols.).

Harrington, James, *The Oceana and Other Works* (London, 1771); see https://oll-resources.s3.us-east-2.amazonaws.com/oll3/store/titles/916/0050_Bk.pdf

Jefferson, Thomas, *A Manual of Parliamentary Practice. For the Use of the Senate of the United States* (Washington City, DC; printed by Samuel Harrison, 1801; rev. end 1812, published at Georgetown by Joseph Milligan and William Cooper).

Story, Joseph, *Commentaries on the Constitution* (Boston, MA, 1833; 1st ed.).

Secondary Sources

Aschenbrenner, Peter, *British and American Foundings of Parliamentary Science, 1774-1801* (Abingdon-on-Thames, Oxfordshire, UK, 2017).

Dubin, Michael J., *United States Congressional Elections, 1788-1997: The Official Results of the Elections of the 1st through 105th Congresses* (Jefferson, NC, 1998).

[United States] *Historical Statistics of the United States 1789-1945, A Supplement to the Statistical Abstract of the United States* (Washington, DC, 1945), available at census.gov/library/publications/time-series/statistical_abstracts.html.

3 'Powers to Create and to Preserve'

'The sum of twenty-eight millions of dollars shall be subscribed'

Chief Justice John Marshall's opinion for the Supreme Court in *McCulloch v. Maryland*, 17 US (4 Wheat.) 400 (1819) offers scholars a summit of constitutional reasoning. The justices of the Supreme Court were unanimously of the opinion that the state of Maryland could not tax the business operations of the Second Bank of the United States in that state.

After a bill to recharter the First Bank went down to defeat (1811),[1] in 1815 and 1816 Congress passed two bills chartering the Second Bank of the United States. President James Madison, however, vetoed the first bill (30 January 1815). In his message the President invited Congress to draft a revised bill. Madison approved the revised bill on 10 April 1816.[2] The Act of Congress establishing the Second Bank fixed the capital stock of that institution at $35 million. The 'sum of twenty-eight millions of dollars, shall be subscribed and paid for by individuals, companies, or corporations'. The Treasury's investment – $7 million – was to be 'be subscribed and paid for by the United States'.[3] On 6 March 1819 the Supreme Court upheld the charter that Congress granted. These are *McCulloch*'s two holdings:

- Congress had the power to charter a national banking institution.
- Maryland lacked the power to tax that institution's business operations in Maryland.

In short order, I will return to the oddity that the reader will certainly have noticed. The Supreme Court declared the charter of the Second Bank to be a valid exercise of Congress's power (to establish a national financial institution). This declaration took place in a case in which the Second Bank was not a party.

The Second Bank claimed a pedigree that went back to Hamilton's First Bank (1791)[4] and that institution owed significant inspiration to

DOI: 10.4324/9781003019381-4

the Bank of North America (1781).[5] The Confederation Congress chartered that institution under its 'Plan for establishing a national bank in the United States of North America'. The Bank of North America could trace many of its features to the charter that Parliament granted the Bank of England (1694).[6] All four of these banks were hybrids. That is, to varying degrees, they functioned both as public and proprietary institutions. As to the former function, a fiscal intermediary facilitated Treasury access to private cash. Given the unpredictable arrival of gold and silver into the Treasury, short-term loans from the Second Bank to the Treasury covered calls made on the Treasury's resources of specie. The preamble to the First Bank's charter declared that the bank would 'tend to give facility to obtaining of loans, for the use of the government, in sudden emergencies'.[7]

When John Marshall declared that Congress possessed the power to establish a public-private bank, his arguments anticipated those that James Monroe offered when he promoted the construction of 'good roads and canals'.[8] Technocratically-inclined politicians and scholars frequently recycle and expand on each other's ideas. But there is more here than brilliant minds reasoning in chorus. Marshall and Monroe framed arguments to point up the postwar generation's opportunity to refashion the Second Republic's reason to exist. They set out to define what the Second Republic was and where it was going.

My background to *McCulloch* begins with Maryland Session Law c. 156 (1817/1818). [9] Maryland charged the Second Bank a fee of $15,000 per year to do business in Maryland. It also offered the Second Bank an alternative. The Bank could purchase stamped paper to issue its bank notes. The Bank's cashier would then issue these stamped notes to its customers in return for their gold and silver. Maryland also made the cashier of the Second Bank personally liable for penalties (that the Maryland act scheduled) if the cashier issued banknotes to customers without using the state's paper for that purpose.

There is an interesting sidebar in the run-up to the *McCulloch* decision. James W. McCulloch bought US government bonds (in his name) with cash he stole from the Second Bank's vaults. See Appendix H: James W. McCulloch, John Marshall and the US Sinking Fund. I draw attention to the connection between Marshall's service as a Commissioner of the US Sinking Fund (by virtue of his office as Chief Justice) *and* details of McCulloch's embezzlement of funds. The clerk of the Supreme Court docketed *McCulloch*'s case in September 1818.[10] On 6 March 1819 Marshall's opinion for the Court disposed of Maryland's challenge. I conclude that John Marshall was aware, from at least 5 February 1819, that James W. McCulloch was an embezzler.[11] This is a month before the *McCulloch* decision was announced.

Two centuries of scholars have offered divergent opinions on Marshall's textual and structural arguments. I sampled thirty-six studies published from 1826 to 2012. To some the word 'necessary' was critical in parsing *McCulloch*. This term brings in a reference to Article I, Section 8, Clause 18, the Necessary and Proper Clause. 'The Congress shall have Power ... To make all Laws which shall be necessary and proper for carrying into Execution the foregoing Powers, and all other Powers vested by this Constitution in the Government of the United States, or in any Department or Officer thereof'. On this account *McCulloch* is a case about constitutional text. James Kent's *Commentaries on American Law* (1826) grounded the 'whole opinion [on] the idea that ... the bank was necessary and proper', as does James Bryce's *American Commonwealth* (1888) which also relies on the Necessary and Proper Clause.[12] To Kent and Bryce the constitutional text authorizing Congress to make laws 'necessary and proper' served as the foundation for Marshall's reasoning.

Another school of thought – nearly half of the scholars surveyed – ignored the Necessary and Proper Clause altogether. These scholars referred to arrangements set in place when the Philadelphia convention composed *Constitution II,* after which it was ratified by the 13 original states (1787–1790). On their account *McCulloch* was a case about constitutional structure. For example, Charles Warren's *Supreme Court in United States History* discarded the court's reasoning.[13] The 'degree of [the bank's] necessity was solely for ... Congress' to decide, a position that Jean Edward Smith embraced in his *John Marshall, Definer of a Nation.*[14] Alexander Bickel concurred with Warren: his study *The Least Dangerous Branch* found the 'nature' of the constitution offering 'hospitality to large purposes', relieving Bickel of the chore of citing to the constitution. Bickel relied heavily on James Bradley Thayer's article 'Origin and Scope of the American Doctrine of Constitutional Law'.[15] G. Edward White's *The Marshall Court and Cultural Change* likewise followed the minority view.[16] His contribution to *The Oliver Wendell Holmes Devise History of the Supreme Court of the United States* made *McCulloch* turn on 'implied sovereign powers', powers both vast and unenumerated.[17]

This survey suggests that scholars have not arrived at a common understanding of what Marshall accomplished in the opinion. Did Marshall himself entertain second thoughts? From April to June/July, 1819 Marshall composed 11 essays to supplement the opinion he composed in the *McCulloch* case. A fellow Virginian attacked the *McCulloch* opinion in articles that the Richmond *Enquirer* published in April, 1819. Marshall composed two essays in response and arranged for publication in the Philadelphia *Union* under the pseudonym 'A Friend to the Union'. When those essays drew fire from another Virginian, Marshall responded with nine more essays. In publishing these essays in the Alexandria (Virginia) *Gazette* Marshall employed the pseudonym 'A Friend of the Constitution'. Marshall's 'Friend' essays did not receive their due of scholarly attention until 1965 when Gerald Gunther – also credited on the title page of G. Edward White's study[18] – published these essays, sorting them into the right order and introducing them to scholars as 'materials that have come to the surface after a century and a half'.[19]According to Gunther it was 'probably Judge William Brockenbrough, as Marshall himself believed', who launched the initial attack on *McCulloch*'s reasoning.[20] Brockenbrough penned two essays under the pseudonym 'Amphictyon', to which Marshall responded with two essays of his own. Gunther unmasked Spencer Roane as 'Hampden', the author of the four essays to which Marshall responded with nine essays.[21]

Why didn't Marshall include this material – or at least some of his second thoughts – in the *McCulloch* opinion? Marshall's first task was to secure his colleagues' support for his draft opinion. Adding another 30,000 words – the length of the essays he composed to supplement his *McCulloch* opinion, itself comprising 10,000 words – would bloat his opinion into an impossible read, conveying the impression that the Supreme Court had no real idea what to make of the case. Second, Marshall may have been confident that a detractor would publish an attack on the Court's decision. A battle in newsprint – if the Chief Justice concealed his identity – would afford Marshall the opportunity to supplement his opinion. All things considered, there may have been a number of factors – the parties' collusion, McCulloch's embezzlement – that encouraged Marshall to place his further and better thoughts into the public record.

'Throughout this vast republic from the Atlantic to the Pacific, revenue is to be collected and expended'

On three occasions Marshall connected the phrase 'the power to tax' with phrase 'the power to destroy' in *McCulloch*. The relevant passages follow:

- 'That a power to destroy, if wielded by a different hand, is hostile to, and incompatible with these powers to create and to preserve'. 17 US 400, 426.
- 'That the power to tax involves the power to destroy; that the power to destroy may defeat and render useless the power to create'. 17 US 400, 431.

Marshall played fast and loose with the political science involved in assessing tax policy. Governments must access private activities and resources. Without a tax base, a civil government would go out of business. Marshall lacked evidence for the sweeping proposition that such a 'power ... *may* defeat and render useless the power to create'. If one tidies up Marshall's argument against the validity of the Maryland tax on the bank, it is possible to construct a better argument. Here it is.

First, there is no coherent Smithian argument that permits a taxing authority to drive an enterprise out of business and thereby *decrease* that authority's gross tax revenues. Smith's tax maxim on this point follows: Every 'tax ought to be so contrived [so as not to] diminish, or perhaps destroy, some of the funds which might enable [taxpayers] more easily to [satisfy the tax burden]'.[22] Because Maryland sought to tax the Second Bank out of business in Maryland, the state violated this maxim. In other words Maryland could not fashion tax policy as a weapon for the purpose of enabling Maryland lawmakers to pick winners and losers among enterprises engaged in a legitimate line of business. In a rather bone-headed piece of lawyering, Maryland's Attorney-General stipulated that the validity of the Second Bank's charter was an issue for the Supreme Court to decide.[23] This gave away Maryland's game. The purpose of the Maryland statute was not to raise revenue but to cobble a litigation strategy out of hyperminoritarian shoe-leather.

Second, in arranging the posture of its tax collection suit against McCulloch, the Second Bank's cashier, the state of Maryland never put the validity of the Bank's charter into play.[24] Assume the following. James McCulloch fails to pay state income tax. Could Maryland levy a tax on the proceeds of McCulloch's illegal activity? Yes. Can the state get double-mileage from a criminal prosecution or a civil tax collection effort by arguing that the legality or validity of the Second Bank was relevant to Maryland's efforts to raise revenue by taxing McCulloch's income? No. Can James McCulloch defend Maryland's tax collection case by arguing that his employer is likely to sue him to recover the funds he stole? No. I note US Supreme Court authority on these points.[25] The foregoing points shed light on the collusive arrangement that the Second Bank and Maryland's Attorney General entered into. I detail this point in Appendix I.

In the *McCulloch* opinion, Marshall drew the reader's attention to the benefits that government distributed to its inhabitants.

> Throughout this vast republic, from the St. Croix to the Gulf of Mexico, from the Atlantic to the Pacific, revenue is to be collected and expended, armies are to be marched and supported. The exigencies of the Nation may require that the treasure raised in the north should be transported to the south, that raised in the east, conveyed to the west, or that this order should be reversed. Is that construction of the Constitution to be preferred which would render these operations difficult, hazardous and expensive? 17 US 400, 408.

It was the job of Congress to assess the demands of the material world – Marshall calls them as 'exigencies of the Nation' – and legislate accordingly. In other words, externalities justify taxation (as with any other programmatic action). The features of a proposed tax scheme must be evaluated in light of a methodology that has proved itself a reliable means of sifting and weighing the variables that the tax invokes. For purposes of this chapter I employ the productivity analytics that Adam Smith brought forward in his essay 'Of Taxes' in *Wealth of Nations*.[26] In my ordering, these variables are feasibility, longevity, proportionality and diminishing returns. From this point forward, I use my term for Smith's tax 'maxims', referring to them as 'productivity analytics'.

'Resting confidently on the interest of the legislator and on the influence of the constituent'

It is possible to tease out from the *McCulloch* opinion an argument – based on the Smithian factor 'proportionality' – that supports the US Supreme Court's decision to invalidate the Maryland tax. The Maryland legislature offered an alternative method of compliance to the Second Bank of the United States. That institution might 'relieve itself from the operation of the provisions aforesaid, by paying annually to the treasurer of the western shore, the sum of fifteen thousand dollars'.[27] Assume that the Second Bank paid the $15,000 annual fee that Maryland required and obtain a license to do business in Maryland. The Second Bank could recoup this cost at its discount window (by offering less favorable discounts on bills of exchange in Baltimore) and by boosting interest charges levied on Maryland business owners. Marshall introduced his discussion of tax policy as follows. 'We first must be permitted to bestow a few considerations on the nature and extent of this original right of taxation'. 17 US 400, 427–428. Marshall then shifted his emphasis to the following variation on proportionality.

> It is admitted that the power of taxing the people and their property is essential to the very existence of Government ... The only security against the abuse of this power is found in the structure of the Government itself. In imposing a tax, the legislature acts upon its constituents. This is, in general, a sufficient security against erroneous and oppressive taxation. 17 US 400, 428.

Marshall framed his analysis of proportionality by reference to the terms 'erroneous and oppressive'. Did the Maryland statute deserve these features? This proposition is fact-testable. Data extracted from the 1820 census shows that the population of the United States would exceed 9 million inhabitants in the year following the *McCulloch* decision. The population of Maryland would number 407,000.[28] 'The people of a State', Marshall explained, 'give to their Government a right of taxing themselves and their property'. 17 US 400, 428. This was exactly what Maryland was *not* doing. The state legislature was not 'taxing [the inhabitants of that state] themselves ... or [acting] upon its constituents'.

Any claim to this effect sinks out of sight under the weight of the proportion (rounded down) 9,000,000 to 400,000. As 'the exigencies of Government cannot be limited', Marshall declares, 'they prescribe no limits to the exercise of this right, resting confidently on the interest of the legislator and on the influence of the constituent over their representative to guard them against its abuse'. 17 US 400, 428. Marshall properly equates 'abuse' with 'erroneous and oppressive taxation'. Maryland plundered benefits that Congress intended the nation to enjoy in common.

The Smithian proportionality analytic backstops Marshall's observation that 'the influence of the constituent over their [representatives] guard them against its abuse'.[29] Marshall grounded 'abuse' in the fact that out-of-state voters had no 'influence' in Maryland state elections; that is, voters in federal elections had no means of protecting their access to benefits Congress intended that they enjoy. On this account, the 'only security against the abuse of this power', Marshall declared, was to be 'found in the structure of the government itself'. 17 US 400, 428. Employing a counterfactual, I shift the emphasis. Instead of the inhabitants of the United States residing outside Maryland being injured, local prejudice might target a 'discrete and insular' minority of Maryland inhabitants. To enable an ethnic or religious minority of Marylanders to redress abuses directed at their members, the state of Maryland (and its various affiliated actors and bodies) must offer viable political avenues – to be 'found in the structure of the government itself' – suitably contoured to achieve this purpose. In *United States v. Carolene Products Company*, 304 U.S. 144, 152 n. 4 (1938), Stone J speaking for the Court, referenced the passages in *McCulloch* that I have quoted above. 'Prejudice against discrete and insular minorities may be a special condition, which tends seriously to curtail the operation of those political processes ordinarily to be relied upon to protect minorities, and which may call for a correspondingly more searching judicial inquiry. Compare *McCulloch v. Maryland*, 4 Wheat. 316, 428 ...'.[30] As these examples show – I draw on *McCulloch* and *McCulloch* through *Carolene Products* – the Supreme Court put itself squarely in the business of policing trust violations (a) that generated 'abuse' of votarian mechanics or (b) that threatened to inflict such abuse.

The foregoing discussion bears more scrutiny. John Marshall drew attention to the hostility of Maryland lawmakers to the economic interests of the 8.6 million *Americans* who had no adequate means, through Maryland's votarian mechanics, of protecting their interest in the benefits that Congress expected the Second Bank to deliver to them. Justice Stone inverted Marshall's perspective by turning the lens to deficiencies (in opportunities for political redress) that might burden only *Marylanders*. Chief Justice John Marshall's attention was not devoted to a 'discrete and insular minority' inhabiting Maryland; Justice Stone's was. Marshall's attention was directed to a majority; Stone's to a minority. But the cornerstone of each justice's analysis was the failure of votarian mechanics to enable challenges to lawmakers who might be tempted to pursue a legislative agenda hostile to those who lacked the means to defend themselves. Put another way, both Marshall and Stone agreed on the following. It was the job of voters to discipline lawmakers (among other actors and bodies in political society). This is 'votarian discipline'.[31] Absent pre-fabricated avenues 'in the structure of the government' that *facilitated* such challenges, inefficiencies in the delivery of benefits were certain to occur and these were chargeable against state actors and bodies. In other words, inefficiencies counted as trust violations.[32] Put crudely, governments ran on trust, among other fuels. Wasting energy, measured in trust, counted as an unacceptable inefficiency.

Monroe touched on this point as well. 'The several States enjoy all the rights reserved to them of separate and independent governments, and each is secured by the nature of the Federal Government, which acts directly on the people, against the failure of the others to bear their equal share of the public burdens'. 'Views' ¶27. Aligning Monroe's remarks with those of Marshall and Stone, Monroe would argue that Maryland must deny itself the pleasure of driving the Second Bank's Baltimore branch out of business. It is, therefore, the job of the federal government to take action against Maryland lawmakers. The duty to police trust violations devolved from the national government's relationship with 'the people' – on whom the 'Federal Government' acted directly – which relationship was 'completely distinct from and independent of' the relationship state governments enjoyed with 'the people'. 'Views' ¶27.

'This system in its twofold character and in its great principles of two governments'

In this section I draw on Monroe's 'Views' and Marshall's *McCulloch* opinion along with his 'Friend' essays. I focus attention on their employment of the 'two governments' formula. That expression makes 11 appearances in these 15 compositions. The reader will find the relevant passages in Appendix E: The 'Two Governments' Formula.

Marshall touches on the 'two governments' formula in his recitation of events leading up to the ratification of *Constitution II*. 'The government proceeds directly from the people; is ordained and established, in the name of the people; and is declared to be ordained, in order to form a more perfect union, establish justice, insure domestic tranquility, and secure the blessings of liberty to themselves and to their posterity'. 17 US 400, 404. Marshall elaborates this point as follows:

> The powers delegated to the state sovereignties were to be exercised by themselves, not by a distinct and independent sovereignty, created by themselves. 17 US 400, 404

Of Marshall's references to the 'two governments' formula, the sentence that follows is the most consequential.

> Much more might the legitimacy of the general government be doubted, had it been created by the states.

I note that Marshall does not exclude the possibility that – post-Ghent – the tables might be turned. State governments might find *their* legitimacy under assault. After all, Congress was competing with state governments to win the loyalty of the nation's inhabitants. As the following passages demonstrates, when two governments exercise the power to tax 'concurrently', they compete with each other for access to private wealth and income.

> That the power of taxation is one of vital importance; that it is retained by the states; that it is not abridged by the grant of a similar power to the government of the union; that it is to be concurrently exercised by the two governments – are truths which have never been denied. 17 US 400, 425.

Marshall was fond of this passage and recycled these remarks twice in his 'Friend' essays.[33] 'The government "while moving within its proper sphere", is supreme. What authority is above it?'[34]

For his part Monroe repeated the 'two governments' formula eight times in his 'Views'. Five references appear in his 1819 essay and three in his 1822 essay.[35] 'There were two separate and independent governments established over our Union', Monroe argued. 'One for local purposes over each State by the people of the State, the other for national purposes over all the States by the people of the United States. The whole power of the people, on the representative principle, is divided between them'. ¶26. Monroe argued that

> The National Government begins where the State governments terminate, except in some instances where there is a concurrent jurisdiction between them. ¶26

The loyalty of inhabitants to the national government was a matter that inhabitants would settle, given that each individual's personal autonomy was at stake. The national government's 'powers are granted by [the people], and are to be exercised directly on them, and for their benefit'. 17 US 400, 405. The passage that follows is Monroe's most aggressive invocation of the 'two governments' formula.

> It is impossible to speak too highly of this system taken in its twofold character and in its great principles of two governments, completely

> distinct from and independent of each other, each constitutional, founded by and acting directly on the people, each competent to all its purposes, administering all the blessings for which it was instituted, without even the most remote danger of exercising any of its powers in a way to oppress the people. ¶27.

I draw the following conclusions from the points that Marshall and Monroe made in the passages (they composed) that reference the 'two governments' formula.

1 Allegiance is the freely conceded loyalty of individuals. It is charged against the personal autonomy of each individual. National and state governments (the latter fractured across a half-continent) are free to make their respective and competing claims on the allegiance of inhabitants. State governments are likewise free to disparage claims to legitimacy that the national government makes.
2 Governments are committed to self-preservation. 'The manner in which Congress was appointed would warrant, and the public good required', Hamilton reasoned, 'that they should have considered themselves as vested with full power to preserve the republic from harm' (1780).[36] To survive, a national government – as any other – must design and execute programs that harmonize, one with another, and – more importantly – are purposed to preserve its stability.
3 Assume that a nation's political society is occupied by two governments. 'It is owing to the simplicity of the elements of which our system is composed', James Monroe declared in his 'Views', 'that the attraction of all the parts has been to a common center, that every change has tended to cement the union, and, in short, that we have been blessed with such glorious and happy success'.[37] A government can make stability-promoting programmatic action serve two purposes. (a) It can develop a strategy that coerces or bribes parochial governments to serve as its institution agents. Institution agents will, on this account, carry out the national government's programs. (b) Assuming a broad spectrum of federal, state, local and private agents are harnessed, this strategy would also reduce, gently or forcefully, parochial governments to a subordinate role in addressing the 'exigencies of the Nation', a phrase of John Marshall.[38] In other words, the unitary government could treat the power of parochial governments as a national resource, one that was available to serve the center's purposes.
4 The tipping point in the political history of a 'two governments' arrangement occurs when the national government achieves ascendency over state governments. The national government obtains the submission of state governments (a) on a service mission by service

mission basis or (b) on a program-by-program basis. The national government can then assume that the worst days of the struggle for ascendency are over.

5 Congress weaponized transportation and communication infrastructure by planning a national network to launch projects. Planning national distribution of these benefits compelled all other public and private actors and bodies to take into account the logical choices remaining to them. (a) A state could coordinate its local build out with the national government. (b) A state could also build the proverbial 'bridge to nowhere' and waste money as foolishly as parochial dignity demanded. (c) Finally, a state could build feeder routes and small-scale facilities that imposed inefficiencies on the movement of people and products through the state.

6 States could, on the other hand, become the authors of their own fates. State governments could encourage their Congressmen and Senators to participate in the national brokerage for bills launching national transport and communication projects. They would then live with a plan's pinches and ouches. But so would other states. I refer to George Washington's call for ratification of *Constitution II* (17 September 1789). When rational actors in a state took into account 'her interest', according to Washington's analysis of the situation, they would avoid inflicting 'consequences ... particularly disagreeable or injurious to [other states]'.[39] For example, State A can refuse to build feeder roads, thereby injuring business owners in States B and C. This effort is easily countered. State A's leaders will rapidly grasp that failure to build local infrastructure (feeder roads leading to national roads) is a strategy of marginal utility, if it is a strategy at all. States B and C will have equal or better means of inflicting 'consequences [that might be] particularly disagreeable or injurious' to State A.

7 In line with the foregoing, a state government could refuse to coordinate state spending with the federal government. This refusal would come to an end when that state's business owners threw in the towel. I refer to events recited in the 'letter from sundry Persons of the State of Rhode Island addressed to the honorable the Chairman of the General Convention' (11 May 1787). Business owners in Rhode Island groveled before the Philadelphia convention. 'As the Object of this Letter is chiefly to prevent any impressions unfavorable to the Commercial Interest of this State, from taking place in our Sister States'.[40] The eagerness of private actors (to obtain federal benefits) offered national leadership a grand strategic opportunity.

Having adopted *Constitution II*, the Philadelphia convention pointedly declined to transmit a copy of that instrument to Rhode Island (17 September 1787).[41] Less than three years later Rhode Island ratified *Constitution II*, a text in which it played no part in crafting. Congress effectively shoved *Constitution II* down Rhode Island's throat, a result that Rhode Island richly deserved. To bring about this result, the 1st Congress declared that Rhode Island-flagged ships were to be treated as foreign after January 15, 1790. I refer to the Act of September 16, 1789. In that act Congress also imposed duties on rum, loaf sugar and chocolate imported through Rhode Island and into the United States.[42] This lesson was not lost on the superminoritarians. In any serious showdown between a state government and the national government, majoritarians would find allies in local business owners. Truculent state politicians might raise the flag of resistance to the power of the center but local business owners knew that resistance was a ticket to impoverishment.

8 The Philadelphia convention adopted organic arrangements that set national and state governments at each other's throats. Divided allegiance could have made instability a permanent feature of US political society. Post-Ghent, however, the contest was never really in doubt. At least by its own lights the Second Republic lived up to its obligations as the winner. Long ago, a poet gave expression to duties incumbent on national leadership. 'Govern power by power, while not forgetting your arts: impose peace, shower the fallen with your mercy and crush the proud'.[43]

9 The talent pool was insufficient to staff all governments with those offering the most aggressive grasp of skills and logics that statecraft in civil government required. Better talent rose to the national level. State governments came to be regarded as stepping-stones in an official's cursus honorum. There was a single most desirable destination for ambitious men and women. The City of Washington in the District of Columbia offered opportunities for technical accomplishment that attracted ambitious talent to the center. Simply put, there was a superior cachet involved in planning on a grand scale, opening up new lands to settlement and spending tons of other people's money.

10 On the other hand, when state politicians blocked transportation projects, their dog-in-the-manger approach reduced to the claim that impassable roads and rock-strewn shoals deserved to be viewed as objects of state pride. Even if state leaders were proud of primitive infrastructure, why would a state's inhabitants regard themselves as suffering nobly in the cause of destabilizing the national government? Did it really degrade the legitimacy of the national government to sweat your product to market when neighboring regions thrilled to the sound of 'steamboat comin' round the bend'?

11 Water and steam. The following confluence was not overlooked. (a) The surface of the North American continent was crisscrossed by big rivers (effectively rendering state management of geophysical resources inefficient) and (b) Monroe and Marshall helmed two pyramids' worth of national institutions at a time when (i)

commercially feasible steam-powered transportation *on water* had reached its longed-for maturity (1807) and (ii) steam-powered transport *on land* would shortly become feasible in the United States (1831).[44] The center commanded the *power to improve* access to remote communities and regions. In so doing Congress (in the nineteenth century) made sense of geophysical realities whose configurations British ministers (among others) had seriously botched and bobbled in the seventeenth century. State governments – all of them ratifying states – began the process of rationalizing their boundaries via state cessions (1781), the last of which was completed in 1802.[45] Credit must be given to the state governments that participated in this process. From that point forward, it was left to the federal government to settle the boundaries of the 37 admitted states, which it accomplished in the interval 1791–1960.[46]

12 In 1807 those booking passage on Fulton's steamboat could travel from New York City to Albany on the surface of the Hudson River. 'Rain, steam and speed' drove the superminoritarians to an early grave, long before J.W.M. Turner exhibited the canvas of that title at the Royal Academy, London (1844).[47]

'Powers are to be put at rest by the practice of the Government'

I turn to Marshall's exposition of the method of Congressional precedents. Marshall puts the affirmative face of this method on full display. The following declaration appears at the opening of Marshall's opinion in *McCulloch*.

> It has been truly said that this can scarcely be considered as an open question entirely unprejudiced by the former proceedings of the Nation respecting it. The principle now contested was introduced at a very early period of our history, has been recognized by many successive legislatures, and has been acted upon by the Judicial Department, in cases of peculiar delicacy, as a law of undoubted obligation. 17 US 400, 401.

1 The constitutionality of national banking legislation is not 'an open question' because it's been decided. Who resolved the question? The Supreme Court ducked one opportunity to resolve the issue (1809).[48]

2 Marshall directed his readers to search through 'proceedings of the Nation' and locate answers in the proceedings of 'many successive legislatures'. This was a bit problematic. The 11th Congress bobbled its chances to settle the issue when the Senate split on the recharter bill leaving the bill to be disapproved by the Vice-President (1811).[49]

On the other hand, one might survey returns for the biennial elections following the First Bank's charter (1791), the attempted recharter of that institution (1811), the new charter that proposed to establish the Second Bank (vetoed, 1815) and the successful new charter (1816). Voters did not sack members of the House of Representatives in such numbers that knowledgeable observers would judge that they rejected national banking institutions as programs unsuitable for national action.[50]

3 The following paragraph is Marshall's most complete statement of the method of Congressional precedents (1819). (Monroe will publish his exposition of the method in 1822 and Marshall will revisit his exposition of the method in 1824.) 'It will not be denied that a bold and daring usurpation might be resisted after an acquiescence still longer and more complete than this. But it is conceived that a doubtful question, one on which human reason may pause and the human judgment be suspended, in the decision of which the great principles of liberty are not concerned, but the respective powers of those who are equally the representatives of the people, are to be adjusted, if not put at rest by the practice of the Government, ought to receive a considerable impression from that practice. An exposition of the Constitution, deliberately established by legislative acts, on the faith of which an immense property has been advanced, ought not to be lightly disregarded'. 17 US 400, 401.

4 Every statute that Congress enacted, Marshall declared, was presumptively an 'exposition of the Constitution'. Marshall argued that if there were a number of statutes on a given topic, constitutional 'exposition [was] deliberately established by legislative acts'. 17 US 400, 401. If the proposed program, as its features were visualized, lay outside the 'practice of the Government' – as revealed by its position in a scatter graph populated with dots representing past 'legislative acts' – then the bill deserved to be considered an outlier. If the proposed program was consistent with an existing pattern, the program was eligible and could be merged into the pattern. Inclusion of the new instance within an existing pattern recontoured the pattern. Consequently, the patterns under examination always presented a moving target. This was evident as soon as a new candidate for inclusion in an existing pattern entered the picture. The method of Congressional precedents demonstrated that the Second Republic was always in a state of becoming.

5 I have reserved this oddity for the last point. Marshall declared that the validity of a national banking institution 'has been acted upon by the Judicial Department, in cases of peculiar delicacy, as a law of undoubted obligation'. I have pointed out that the Supreme Court declined to rule on the constitutionality of the First Bank in 1809.[51] What was Marshall driving at? I suggest that Marshall was

fast-forwarding to a future time when reference to Supreme Court holdings would become a reliable resource for actors and bodies searching for acceptable patterns of decision-making.

Can holdings in Supreme Court decisions be regarded as supplementing acts of Congress? In 2014 I gathered official action taken by legislators, executive and judicial officers in the subject matter area national banking legislation (1781–1846). At the time I termed used the term 'child-entities' to refer to 'institution agents'.[52] My tabled data appears at slide no. 4 in the presentation. I sliced official action involved in the build out of national finance arrangements into 10 discrete event states extending over that 65-year interval. If Program XYZ were challenged and the Supreme Court approved that program, then it would be an expanded pattern that embraced a recognition of Program XYZ's validity. This would be the case even if the pattern contained many other types of official action but only one judicial decision. This is sort of, but not precisely, like arguing that once the Supreme Court has settled an issue – as a matter of its own jurisprudence – one can stop counting Acts of Congress.[53]

'Machinery tends to produce the desired effect'

In the second of Marshall's 'A Friend to the Union' essays (I refer to the first tranche published in April, 1819) Marshall unleashed a direct assault on the textual reasoning of Amphictyon. The latter proposed to limit Congress's power to launch programmatic action. His method would invoke free-wheeling predicate-attaching.[54] Only 'means which directly and necessarily tend to produce the desired effect' were constitutionally permissible.[55]

Like Adam Smith, John Marshall was fond of constructing and employing case studies. These brief passages compressed fact-like events and thereby offered fabricated data to substitute for a survey of real-world events. 'Let us apply these different definitions of ... words to any of the most common affairs of human life'.[56] I repeat that Marshall aims his analysis at textual reasoning.

> A leases to B a mill for a number of years on a contract that A shall receive half the profits, and shall pay half the expenses of all the machinery which B may erect therein, and which shall be *"necessary and proper"* for the manufacture of flower. Pending this lease, the elevator and hopper boy are invented, and applied, with great advantage, to the manufacture of flower. B erects them in his mill. A is very well satisfied with receiving the increased profits, but is unwilling to pay half the expense of the machinery, because, as he alleges, it was not *"necessary"* to the manufacture of flower.[57]

A 'flower mill' operates a horizontally-positioned millstone that rotates above a stationary counterpart. As grain falls into the center of the moving millstone, chaff is thrown off. On the floor below workers bag or barrel the flower. Because the trajectory of the grain and flower is gravity driven, the miller must load the grain up to a floor where it can drop freely into the rotating millstone. The 'hopper boy' and 'elevator' were devices for raising grain from a horse-drawn wagon or oxcart to the mill floor located above the millstones. These two devices were designed as labor-saving equipment. I employ Adam Smiths' productivity analytics to parse Marshall's case study.[58]

1 Was the new equipment feasible? When the case study opens, the mill operator has put the equipment to work. Presumably he is not the first to hire or buy the equipment.[59]
2 What is the useful life of this equipment? It can't extend for any significant interval beyond the termination of the lease. If it did the mill operator would be burdened with an investment that (on the happening of that event) enjoyed marginal economic value. To manage this risk (a) the operator should obtain an extension of the current lease with the mill owner or (b) the operator will be obliged to move his operations, renting another mill owner's plant. What's required is an assessment of future efficiencies that employment of the hopper boy and elevator promised to the operator. 'Cocktail napkin' arithmetic may be required. For example, the mill operator may conclude that the labor thereby saved will permit him to assign one-half of an existing worker's effort to the task of loading the customer's wagons with sacks or barrels of flour processed. This estimate then permits/requires the mill operator to price enhancements in customer service into his business model.
3 Are the benefits of the investment proportional to burdens undertaken? Because the mill operator did not know whether the mill owner would object to the investment, the operator must have priced the investment to account for the following three contingencies. (a) The mill owner may not object. (b) The mill owner may agree to renegotiate their profit-sharing arrangement. (c) The mill owner may declare that he will not share in the additional cost of the new equipment. As a prudent business owner, the mill operator will have priced each of these possibilities and determined that, no matter what action the mill owner takes, the mill operator can still make a decent profit from his investment.[60]
4 What events will reliably signal that the use of the equipment has become marginally rewarding? If the equipment requires frequent repair, even if the repairs may be done quickly and cheaply, mill downtime signals that replacement of the equipment should be seriously considered. You don't need to know when this further employment

> of equipment will become marginally efficient. However, at the time you invest in new equipment you need to ask yourself, 'do I have any idea of how I will be able to recognize the signal "this equipment has become marginally useful"?'.[61]

As in Adam Smith's essay 'Of Taxes', Marshall's employment of the four productivity analytics offers two pairs of variables that work in tandem.

- Longevity may be considered a special case of feasibility. If a piece of new equipment has very short useful life, then a search for a prior successful application of the equipment will be disappointing. The feasibility hurdle cannot be cleared.
- Diminishing returns may be considered a special case of proportionality. If a piece of new equipment is very expensive and the repair downtime is lengthy, then the operator may well conclude that he should investigate the acquisition of a more reliable version of this equipment.

'I was afraid I had said some foolish things but it was not half so bad as I expected'

It's a charming anecdote, narrating as it does an episode in the public life of John Marshall. If it is to be credited, it also includes a private exchange between the Chief Justice Marshall and Associate Justice Joseph Story. In 1833 Story will become the Supreme Court's leading published scholar. I refer to his *Commentaries on the Constitution* (1833).[62] Story served as Marshall's wingman on the court. He offered the Marshall court diligent judicial scholarship. Story was, as one might expect, a reliable supporter of Marshallian methods.

The anecdote's first appeared in a biography of Alexander H. Stephens, who served as the Vice-President of the Confederate States of America. His biographers published editions in 1878 and 1883. G. Edward White relates a slightly different version of this anecdote in *The Marshall Court and Cultural Change, 1815–1835*.[63] White substitutes Luther Martin (1748–1826), Maryland's Attorney General, for Martin's co-counsel Chapman Johnson (1777–1849).

Stephens (through his biographers) preambles his readers as follows. He is relating 'an anecdote of Marshall, which Story told as having occurred in a case involving the constitutionality of the United States Bank'.[64] Stephens' biographers relate Justice Story's anecdote as follows:

> Chapman Johnson, who was arguing upon the side to which the Chief Justice's views were supposed to be adverse, after a three days' argument, wound up by saying that he had one last authority which

> he thought the court would admit to be conclusive. He then read from the reports of the debates in the Virginia Convention what Marshall himself had said upon the subject, when the adoption of the Constitution was discussed. Story relates that at this point, 'Marshall drew a long breath with a sort of sigh. After the court adjourned he rallied the Chief Justice on his uneasiness, and asked him why he sighed', to which Marshall replied, 'Why, to tell you the truth, I was afraid I had said some foolish things in the debate [at Richmond]; but it was not half so bad as I expected'. Story indulges in a great many such anecdotes.[65]

The facts, insofar as they can be ascertained, don't smoothly line up with Stephens' relation of events. I start with (what should be) a reliable bit of evidence. The United States Reports (in Henry Wheaton's syllabus) summarizes Luther Martin's argument to this effect: 'We are now called upon to apply that theory of interpretation, which was then rejected by the friends of the new constitution, and we are asked to engraft upon it powers of vast extent, which were disclaimed by them, and which if they had been fairly avowed at the time, would have prevented its adoption'. 17 US 372-374 [syllabus].

What transpired at the Virginia ratifying convention (1788) that might have troubled Marshall in 1819? I suggest the following remarks might have given Marshall an opportunity for sober second-thoughts.

> Have we no navigation in, or do we derive no benefit from, the Mississippi? How shall we retain it? By retaining that weak government which has hitherto kept it from us? .... We cannot expect that a government which hitherto has not been able to protect it, will have the power to do it hereafter.[66]

Marshall concluded these remarks as follows: 'I trust we can prove that no danger to the navigation of that river can arise from the adoption of this Constitution'.[67] *Constitution II* did not, however, grant Congress control over inland navigable waters. Nor was it obvious that a government with a superior claim to the bed of a navigable river was powerless to control traffic on the river's surface. Nor was it clear how a contractor could go about removing obstructions protruding from a riverbed (rocks, snags and sandbars) or deepening the channel or constructing by-pass canals without reconfiguring the riverbed itself.

On the other hand, Marshall may have been crazy like a fox. Maryland controlled the riverbed underlying the Potomac River, thanks to the wording of its royal charter. Challenges, ripostes and details noted.[68] Marshall may have calculated that Congress should control traffic on that river rather than Marylanders.[69] The Supreme Court decided that point in *Gibbons v. Ogden*, 22 US (9 Wheat.) 186 (1824).

What the record at the Richmond convention does reveal is Marshall's well-contoured grasp of the challenges posed by the material world. 'Who can penetrate into futurity? How can any man pretend to say that our future exigencies will be less than our present? The exigencies of nations have been generally commensurate to their resources'.[70] Marshall thereby turned economies of scale head-on-end. He argued that if a nation were rich in resources, then that munificence (plenty, abundance) should serve as the metric by which the nation was entitled to measure its ambitions. This is another formulation of the equivalency 'can = should'. More than any other two political scientists of their day, Monroe and Marshall explored the potential of that equivalency. To their way of thinking, voters flashing a red-light to projects would mark the outer limit of permissible legislation.

Conclusion

In the maturity of his judicial career, Marshall looked beyond heroic one-off judicial opinions featuring bold generalizations that supported Congress's leadership role in the evolution of the Second Republic. No future Chief Justice, he calculated, would have the opportunity to reshape the Second Republic as he had done. In the passage following Marshall visioned the Supreme Court as a body tasked to create patterns of judicial decision-making. I draw on *Gibbons v. Ogden*, 22 US (9 Wheat.) 186 (1824) for this purpose.

> The Court is aware that, in stating the train of reasoning by which we have been conducted to this result, much time has been consumed in the attempt to demonstrate propositions which may have been thought axioms. It is felt that the tediousness inseparable from the endeavour to prove that which is already clear is imputable to a considerable part of this opinion. But it was unavoidable. The conclusion to which we have come depends on a chain of principles which it was necessary to preserve unbroken, and although some of them were thought nearly self-evident, the magnitude of the question, the weight of character belonging to those from whose judgment we dissent, and the argument at the bar demanded that we should assume nothing. 22 US 186, 221-222.

By assembling 'a chain of principles which it was necessary to preserve unbroken', justices – through their internal decision-making – licensed themselves to create and exploit data sets consisting of propositions that might be drawn from the case under consideration. This effort would enable the Supreme Court to deliver a more nuanced and complete exposition of the 'conclusion to which we have come'. 22 US 186, 221-222. By breaking down judicial reasoning (in a given case) into discrete 'propositions' – of their making – judges could construct a 'train of reasoning' or 'chain of principles'. This effort would be rewarded if the reader were to accept that these 'trains' and 'chains' were constructed from near-axiomatic propositions. Marshall denied that his approach was 'refined and metaphysical'. 22 US 186, 222. At a more general level of abstraction, the passage (quoted above) offers insight into Marshall's fascination with decision-making options available to the Supreme Court. Marshall was serious about exploring methodologies that judges could employ in assessing the validity of acts of Congress. Or, as in *Gibbons*, the *presumed* will of Congress.

Notes

1. The 11th Congress, 3rd Session took up final passage of the First Bank recharter bill in January-February, 1811. On 20 February 1811 the recharter bill went down to defeat in the US Senate. Vice President George Clinton cast the tie-breaking negative. *Senate Journal*, 4:577-578. On 4 March 1811, the charter of the First Bank of the United States expired; this was the date fixed in the Act of February 25, 1791. 1 Stat 191, c. 10, Act of February 25, 1791.
2. See memory.loc.gov/ammem/amlaw/lwsl.html; 3 Stat 266, c. 44.
3. *Ibid.*, Sec. 1.
4. 1 Stat 191, c. 10, Act of February 25, 1791.
5. See memory.loc.gov/ammem/amlaw/lwjc.html; *Continental Congress Journal*, 20:545-48; 26 May 1781. Madison's negative on the bank proposal is recorded at 547. See also Hammond, *Banks and Politics,* 48-53. See also siue.edu/~rblain/debtproblem.html [last retrieved 21 June 2021] for details of Robert Morris's activities as Superintendent of Finance. 'I mean to render this [the Bank of North America] a principal pillar of American credit, so as to obtain the money of individuals for the benefit of the Union, and thereby bind those individuals more strongly to the general cause by the ties of private interest'.
6. 5 & 6 Will & Mary, c. 20; The Bank of England Act *also known as* The Tonnage Act (1694).
7. 1 Stat 191, c. 10, Act of February 25, 1791, Preamble.
8. 'Views', ¶107.
9. 'Provided always, that any institution of the above description may relieve itself from the operation of the provisions aforesaid, by paying annually, in advance, to the treasurer of the western shore, for the use of the state, the sum of fifteen thousand dollars'. Sec. 1.
10. White, *Marshall,* 3:543.
11. See text at 185-186.
12. Kent, *Commentaries*, 1:239; Bryce, *American Commonwealth*, 1:369.
13. Warren, *The Supreme Court*, 1:510.
14. Smith, *Marshall*, 440-445.
15. Bickel, *Least Dangerous Branch, 36*; Thayer, 'American Doctrine', 150-151.
16. White, *Marshall,* 3:544.
17. *Ibid.*
18. See text at 81.
19. Marshall, 'Friend', 17.
20. *Ibid.*, 13.

21. *Ibid.*, 15-16.
22. Smith, *Wealth*, 826.
23. See text at 185-186.
24. See Appendix H: James W. McCulloch, John Marshall and the US Sinking Fund.
25. *James v. United States*, 366 U.S. 213 (1961)[embezzler's ill-gotten gains taxable income, despite his liable for restitution to his employer].
26. *Ibid.*, 825-827.
27. See text at 60n9.
28. See census.gov/history/www/through_the_decades/overview [last retrieved 19 November 2020].
29. See text at 17 US 400, 428.
30. 304 U.S. 144, 152 n. 4.
31. See text at 108, 113, 119, 156.
32. See text at 14, 65, 66.
33. Marshall, 'Friend', 101, 193.
34. *Ibid.*, 188.
35. 'Views' at ¶¶26, 27, 58, 64, 97, 106, 114, 123.
36. See founders.archives.gov/documents/Hamilton/01-02-02-0838; 'Alexander Hamilton to James Duane, 3 September 1780'. See also Aschenbrenner, *Foundings*, 53-57.
37. 'Views'. ¶30.
38. See text at 63.
39. Farrand, *Records*, 2:666-667
40. *Ibid.*, 3:18-20. Gouverneur Morris brought this letter to the attention of the convention on 28 May 1787. *Ibid.*, 1:9.
41. *Ibid.*, 2:665-666.
42. 1 Stat. 69-70, c. 15, Secs. 2,3. Congress meted out the same treatment to North Carolina but nobody hated North Carolina with the passion that everybody hated Rhode Island. North Carolina promptly rose to the occasion, reconvened its ratification convention and ratified *Constitution II* (23 November 1789). See Fayetteville_Convention [last retrieved 22 December 2020].
43. Vergil, *Aeneid*, 6:847-853.
44. See Albany_and_Schenectady_Railroad [last retrieved 22 May 2021].
45. The last such cession was concluded 24 April 1802 and is known in the scholarly literature as the Compact of 1802. Congressional confirmation of the Compact does not appear in the Public Statutes at Large nor is any action referenced in the Senate (Legislative) Journal or Senate Executive Journal. See State_cessions [last retrieved 22 August 2021].
46. See text at 92-94.
47. See www.nationalgallery.org.uk/paintings/joseph-mallord-william-turner-rain-steam-and-speed-the-great-western-railway.
48. *Bank of the United States v. Deveaux*, 9 US (5 Cranch) 61 (1809). Hammond, *Banks and Politics*, 222-223 has further details.
49. See text at 92-94.
50. Marshall, 'Friend', 173.
51. See text at 71n48.
52. 'Managing the Endowment of Child Entities in Complex Systems: The Case of National Banking Legislation, 1781-1846'. See www.rhsmith.umd.edu/files/Documents/Centers/CCB/peter_aschenbrenner_presentation.pdf In my survey I distributed 29 official events, including the *McCulloch* decision, among these 10 discrete event states. Bayesian

decision-makers could, at the opening of a new event state, evaluate the conditional probability of a given course of action in light of the cumulative pattern that was (at that time) discernible.

53. See text at 159-160.
54. Aschenbrenner, *Foundings*, 132-133.
55. Marshall, 'Friend', 102.
56. *Ibid.*
57. *Ibid.*
58. Smith, *Wealth*, 825-827.
59. Smith addresses feasibility in the fourth of his tax maxims. Smith, *Wealth*, 826-827. However, considered functionally, parliamentary assemblies should take up feasibility – as the first order of business – when new programmatic action is proposed.
60. Smith addressed proportionality as the first of his four tax maxims. Smith, *Wealth*, 825.
61. Smith addressed diminishing returns/marginal utility in the second of his tax maxims. *Ibid.*, 826.
62. Story, *Commentaries.*
63. White, *Marshall Court,* 3:239.
64. Johnston and Browne, *Stephens.*
65. *Ibid.,* 183.
66. See memory.loc.gov/ammem/amlaw/lwed.html; Elliot, *Debates*, 223.
67. *Ibid.*, 231
68. See nsglc.olemiss.edu/SandBar/SandBar2/2.4supreme.htm
69. See virginiaplaces.org/boundaries/mdboundary.html; last retrieved 20 November 2020.
70. Elliot, *Debates*, 235.

References

Primary Sources

Records of the Federal Convention of 1787 (New Haven, CT, ed. Max Farrand; rev. ed. 1937; 4 vols.).

Gunther, Gerald, *John Marshall's Defense of McCulloch v. Maryland* (Stanford, CA, 1969).

Smith, Adam, *An Inquiry into the Nature and Causes of the Wealth of Nations* (Oxford, 1976; R.H. Campbell, A. S. Skinner and W.B. Todd, eds.; the 'Glasgow' edn). See text at 37 for details on pagination.

Johnston, R.M. and Browne, W.H., *Life of Alexander H. Stephens* (Philadelphia, PA, 1883; 2nd edn).

Story, Joseph, *Commentaries on the Constitution* (Boston, MA, 1833; 1st edn).

Secondary Sources

Aschenbrenner, Peter, *British and American Foundings of Parliamentary Science, 1774-1801* (Abingdon-on-Thames, Oxfordshire, UK, 2017).

Bryce, James, *The American Commonwealth* (New York, NY, 1888).

David Currie, *The Constitution in Congress: The Jeffersonians* (Chicago, IL, 2001).

Hammond, Bray, *Banks and Politics in America, From the Revolution to the Civil War* (Princeton, NJ, 1957).
Kent, James, *Commentaries on American Law* (New York, NY, 1826).
Marshall, John, 'A Friend to the Union' [and] 'A Friend of the Constitution' *in John Marshall's Defense of McCulloch v. Maryland* (Stanford, CA, 1969; Gerald Gunther, ed.).
McDonald, Forrest, *E Pluribus Unum, The Formation of the American Republic 1776-1790* (Indianapolis, IN, 1965).
Warren, Charles, *The Supreme Court in United States History* (Boston, MA, 1923).
Bickel, Alexander, *The Least Dangerous Branch: The Supreme Court at the Bar of Politics* (New Haven, CT, 1986).
Thayer, James Bradley, 'The Origin and Scope of the American Doctrine of Constitutional Law', *Harvard Law Review* 7:129 (1893).
White, G. Edward, *The Marshall Court and Cultural Change, 1815-1835* (New York, NY, 1988).
Smith, Jean Edward, *John Marshall, Definer of a Nation* (New York, NY, 1996).

4 'Captivating Improvements to Seduce Their Constituents'

'Surveys of national importance in a commercial or military point of view'

On the 'first Monday in December' (1 December 1823) the 1st Session of the 18th Congress convened.[1] The following events took place during this session.

- On 2 March 1824 Chief Justice John Marshall announced the Supreme Court's decision in *Gibbons v. Ogden*, 22 US (9 Wheat.) 186 (1824) [federal control over the surface of inland navigable waters upheld].
- On 30 April 1824 President Monroe approved the General Survey Act, 4 Stat 22, c. 46. The act empowered the president to assess the feasibility of national road and canal projects that he selected for evaluation.
- On 24 May 1824 Monroe approved a project-specific bill to 'improve the navigation of the Ohio and Mississippi rivers'. 4 Stat 32, c. 139.

Taken together, these three texts supply an epilogue to the 15 essays that Monroe and Marshall published between March 1819 and May 1822. Via the General Survey Act, the president was 'authorized to cause the necessary surveys, plans, and estimates, to be made of the routes of such roads and canals as he may deem of national importance, in a military or commercial point of view, or necessary for the transportation of the public mail'.[2] If the president ordered a survey, the engineers' report would include cost estimates. The General Survey Act boosted the chances that advocates of a specific road or canal project could successfully lobby Congress on behalf of a region's transportation needs. Congress did not include navigation projects in the General Survey Act (1824). Congress dealt with navigation projects in 1824 Ohio-Mississippi navigation act, which it passed 24 days after the General Survey Act. In this Act, Congress named five sandbars that impeded steam-powered navigation on the Ohio River. These obstructions were located (generally) between

DOI: 10.4324/9781003019381-5

the extreme northern neck of (what is now) West Virginia – at the West Virginia-Pennsylvania state line – and (what is now) Cairo IL. Congress instructed the president's engineers to pick two of the five sandbars. 'Experiments shall first be made upon two of the said bars, and if in his judgment they shall be successful, then, and not otherwise, he is hereby authorized to cause improvements to be made upon the remaining bars'.[3] The combinatorial formula yields ten different choices of two sandbars for the president's engineers to dredge or blast away. The act did not require the President to obtain the consent of any state to launch construction activity in the bed of the Ohio River.

Over 20 years later the Supreme Court held that 'the shores of navigable waters, and the soils under them, were not granted by the Constitution to the United States, but were reserved to the States respectively'. *Pollard's Lessee v. Hagan*, 44 US (3 How.) 219, 230 (1845). This doctrine (apparently) secured to state governments the title to submerged lands (within their borders) (a) at the Declaration of Independence (in the case of ratifying states) or (b) at admission to statehood (in the case of admitted states). I turn to the Act of May 20, 1826. This launched 23 projects, 11 of which required a permanent or temporary federal footprint in the riverbed of a navigable waterway.[4] In the Act of May 23, 1828, Congress launched 21 projects. In 19 of these projects, Congress permanently recontoured state submerged lands or directed that federal engineers and contractors access riverbeds for construction purposes. In one case Congress ordered that $20,000 be spent on 'dredging machines, to be worked by steam and employing the same for the removal of the shoals forming obstructions'.[5] Congress eventually gave the 'submerged lands' doctrine the force of statutory law. The Submerged Lands Act of 1953 followed an interval of 133 years in which Congress funded projects reconfiguring state-owned riverbeds to its purposes without obtaining consents from those states.[6]

In 1820 Congress ordered surveys of the Mississippi and Ohio river systems. In 1824, 1826 and 1828 Congress funded obstruction-removing projects on these and other rivers.[7] All of these projects were designed to promote *increased* steam-powered river traffic. National transportation policy (a) was unhindered by crazy-quilt geography, (b) featured a 'boots on the ground' mentality – hire contractors and get workers to the jobsite – and (c) was supported by a national court system which vigorously promoted an *increase* in the supply of transportation services. In other words, national policy assumed that supply and demand would sort out winners and losers. Energy wasted in the private sector, in other words, was to be accounted an acceptable cost of national policy. Thanks to this trade-off, Capt. Tootalot might be driven out of business because he chose the wrong waterway on which to whistle up custom. Most importantly, US transportation policy was successful because it offered a well-modulated geophysical expression of the

Second Republic's ambition to give something to everybody. Martin Van Buren might tut-tut (in Edmund Burke's company) that distribution of benefits on a national scale would be a Bad Thing. But as James Monroe demonstrated in his 'Views', it was also a Necessary Thing.

There is a second assumption, both significant and troubling, that is not readily teased from the day-to-day work of Congress in the postwar era. Laws promoting the productivity of households and businesses, in all their Smithian glory, assumed the following. Enhancing the productivity of this or that household or business (by type) did not necessarily take something from anyone. There were no victims when Congress funded physical infrastructure.[8] 'Good roads, canals, and navigable rivers' Adam Smith declared, are 'the greatest of all improvements'.[9] Put another way, distribution machinery – promoting productivity gains – did not commit Congress to programs of *re*distribution. Programs of *re*distribution committed Congress to promote one person's economic gain by inflicting economic loss on another. This was not only a Bad Thing, it was also a French Thing and was, therefore, a *Very* Bad Thing.

'Persons navigating with vessels moved by steam or fire shall forfeit such boat'

I background the Supreme Court's decision in *Gibbons v. Ogden,* 22 US 186 (1824). In 1808 New York granted Livingston and Fulton the 'exclusive navigation of all the waters within the jurisdiction of that State, with boats moved by fire or steam'.[10] The New York legislature granted Livingston and Fulton the opportunity to cartelize steam-powered transport in that state. New York also authorized Livingston and Fulton to sublicense their rights to operators of other 'steam-boats or vessels'. For every operator (like Ogden) who associated his vessels with the Livingston and Fulton cartel, the cartel's life would be extended for another five years. Lawmakers capped the life of the cartel at 30 years. Section I.

New York's statutory arrangement was a bit wobbly on remedies. Section III authorized the cartel to sue violators in state court for 'penalties ... incurred'. Section II. 'The said person or persons, so navigating with boats or vessels moved by steam or fire, in contravention of the exclusive right of [Livingston and Fulton] shall forfeit such boat ... together with the engine, tackle and apparel thereof, to [Livingston and Fulton] and their associates'. Chancellor James Kent granted injunctive relief to Ogden, an associate (licensee) of the Livingston and Fulton cartel. This relief barred Gibbons' 'two steamboats ... the *Stoudinger* and the *Bellona* [from] running between New York and Elizabethtown [NJ], in violation of the exclusive privilege conferred'. 22 US 1, 2 [Syllabus]. The 'boats employed by him were duly enrolled and licensed', Gibbons pleaded in his defense, 'under the act of Congress, passed the 18th of February, 1793, c. 3 entitled, "An act for enrolling and licensing ships and vessels to be employed in the coasting trade and fisheries, and for regulating the same"'.[11] Section 1 of that Act provided that a vessel (so enrolled and licensed) was 'entitled to the privileges of ships or vessels employed in the coasting trade or fisheries'. Marshall may have assumed that he could leverage the Act of February 18, 1793 to the same effect that he employed the Act of April 10, 1816. That act chartered the Second Bank of the United States. If Congress could occupy the field of national finance, then Congress should also be well-positioned to claim an ascendent role in managing traffic on the surface of coastal navigable waters.

The Act of February 18, 1793 targeted waterborne customs evaders. Alexander Hamilton designed the licensing scheme as a 'get out of jail free' card, so to speak. If boarded (more likely hailed) by a US revenue cutter, the master could demonstrate his 'right to sail' in US coastal waters. The purpose of the act was to protect US Treasury revenues from smugglers. The Act of February 18, 1793 did not, however, support the result that Marshall wanted *Gibbons* to deliver into the US Reports. For example, the state of Maryland had not granted the Second Bank's competitors – private or state banks – the right to seek a decree forfeiting the assets of the Second Bank's Baltimore Branch. Had Ogden sought relief in the form of a decree of *forfeiture*, Marshall might have been able to revisit *McCulloch*'s reasoning. 'The power to forfeit', Marshall could have argued, 'is the power to destroy'. Ogden, however, sought *injunctive* relief in the New York court system. Another approach did – if only momentarily – occur to Marshall. Perhaps the New York legislature (through Livingston and Fulton) could persuasively argue that it possessed the power to license a cartel to promote new technology. At the opening of *Gibbons*, Marshall promised to address the constitutional grant of power 'to promote the progress of science and useful arts'. 22 US 186. At the conclusion of *McCulloch*, however, Marshall yawned that this argument has lost its appeal. 'I have not touched upon the right of the States to grant patents for inventions or improvements, generally, because it does not necessarily arise in this cause'. 22 US 186, 239.

Was Marshall left with this thin reed? A competitor to the New York cartel steamed his vessel from the Hudson River to a waterside structure in New Jersey. Would a reduction in the number of steamboats crossing the Hudson River and entering Newark Bay, 'restrain a free intercourse among the States'? Such an approach would align with the framing that Article I, Section 8, Clause 3 supplied. 'The Congress shall have Power ... To regulate Commerce ... among the several States'. States cannot exercise any power they possess 'so as to restrain a free intercourse among the States'. 22 US 186, 239.

The reasoning that Marshall employed in *Gibbons* was, however, almost completely untethered from the historical record of Congress's regulation of interstate commerce. I begin with 'can = should' and restrict the lens to Congress's regulation of inland navigable waters. That equivalency declares that if the federal government can successfully launch a mission specific project, then a decent prospect of success for programmatic action (measured via Smithian productivity analytics, for example) furnishes a sufficient justification for doing so. I turn to the converse. If states can't fulfill the responsibilities that should be shouldered by an efficient manager of surface waters, the equation 'can't = should' justifies the federal government's role in declaring and managing national transportation policy. Put another way, if it was geophysically impossible for states to regulate waterborne traffic, then it was inevitable that the federal government would do so.

I expand on this point by turning to the topological challenges facing provincial/state governments. Thanks to ministers and mapmakers in London, US rivers fell into three categories. (a) The main channel of some waterways served as state borders. This was the situation in *Gibbons v. Ogden*. The states of New Jersey and New York shared the waterway that connected the Hudson River to Newark Bay and Elizabethtown NJ (now Elizabeth NJ). (b) Some waterways were (more or less) wholly assigned to one province or another. Maryland's grant embraced the Potomac River. In these cases, the bank of the river – not the middle (or 'thread') of the main channel – served as the boundary between two states.[12] (c) Finally, a number of major waterways on the North American continent, such as the Susquehanna and Arkansas, played no role as state borders.[13]

'Steamboats lost on western rivers fell victims to snags or obstructions'

Geophysical patterns (including those surveyed above) made a topological mess of provincial and (later) state governments' chances to govern traffic on the surface of inland waters.[14] Agreed-upon state cessions rearranged some boundaries and were an important step towards geophysical rationalization. The possibility of future cessions added credibility to the promise that the Continental Congress made to its ranks and officers in the Continental Army. I refer Congress's commitment to distribute land in territories won on the battlefield and at the negotiating table (16 September 1776).[15] These events underline that state governments were unequal to the task of getting people and products across the country via the natural rivers and lakes within their borders.[16] I sort out three cases.

a Take the Ohio-Mississippi river system. From Pittsburgh to New Orleans, the following states possessed governance or resource claims to the halfway mark of those rivers. Virginia, Ohio, Kentucky, Indiana, Illinois, Missouri, Tennessee, Arkansas, Mississippi and Louisiana. This list of ten matured in 1836 when Congress admitted

Arkansas to the Union. Keep in mind that Article I, Section 10, Clause 3 provides: 'No State shall, without the Consent of Congress … enter into any Agreement or Compact with another State'. In 1803 Virginia would be obliged to negotiate with Kentucky and Ohio for a compact to govern river traffic on the stretch of the Ohio River that these three shared. These states would then be compelled to obtain the consent of Congress to such an agreement, thanks to Article I, Section 10, Clause 3 just quoted. In 1816, Indiana statehood would require the renegotiation of that compact. This would continue until nine states negotiated with Arkansas on its admission in 1836. This 10-state compact would enable that (newly-admitted) state's management of its half-slice of the Mississippi River.

b I turn to the case of Maryland and Virginia. Maryland might build a bypass canal to enable vessels to reach the Potomac River above the Falls of Maryland. Virginians, however, might float down the Potomac without paying user-fees to Maryland. That state would be compelled to launch a fleet of gun boats to patrol the river.

c Pennsylvania might draw up plans to render the Susquehanna River navigable for the entire length of that river within the state's borders, from the Maryland border (south of Peach Bottom PA) to the New York border (north of Sayre PA). It does not obtain the agreement of Maryland to this scheme. Maryland stations gunboats at the mouth of the Susquehanna River and charges exorbitant fees for the right to steam 15 miles of that watercourse from the open waters of Chesapeake Bay to the Maryland-Pennsylvania border.

The foregoing explains, in part, why states were reluctant to take on the responsibility for building out a national system of waterborne transport. According to the Army Corps of Engineers 'between 1811 and 1851, more than 40 percent of the steamboats lost on western rivers fell victims to snags or similar obstructions'.[17] There was no certainty that if state X made a river safe for steamboats, that states Y and Z would reciprocate and invest in projects that extended the efficiencies that state X planned along its segment of that river. When Congress clears snags and sandbars from a river, it thereby designates that waterway as a commercially feasible avenue and that designation also grounds the declaration that such a river – in which national dollars have been invested – is a river suitable for federally-regulated transport because only Congress can make the river safe for waterborne transport. By design the previous sentence loops around on itself to expose the ontological fragility that inheres in this reasoning. Congress gets to declare what its powers are *and* one of those powers includes the power to declare that it has the power to make such declarations. 'It's elephants (or turtles, your choice) all the way down'.[18] Be that as it may, surveys assessing the 'most practicable mode of improving navigation' permitted Congress to leverage a modest expenditure into the power to designate navigable waterways as *national* waterways.

- In 1820 Congress ordered up 'a survey, maps, and charts, of the Ohio and Mississippi rivers, from the rapids of the Ohio at Louisville, to Balize [LA]'.[19]
- In 1823 Monroe duly transmitted the 'Survey of the Ohio and Mississippi Rivers' to Congress (23 January). The Survey listed 21 sandbars and like obstructions between Shippingport Island KY (visible from the Muhammed Ali Center in Louisville) and the confluence of the Ohio and Mississippi Rivers. Monroe's engineers then reported on 'the means which art and experience may present for removing these obstacles, (a result greatly to be desired)'.[20]
- In 1827 Congress ordered that 'all snags, swayers, stumps, logs, and obstructions of every description, which tend to endanger the steamboat navigation of the Ohio river, at any navigable stages of the water ... shall be removed so that navigation of said river, shall be rendered at all times safe'.[21] Section 1.

I have already noted details of the Act of May 24, 1824.[22] The act directed that 'experiments shall first be made upon two of the said bars'.[23] I recast the features of this statute at a slightly elevated level of abstraction. (a) Congress assigns a task to agents that it names, (b) these agents (such as the president's engineers) fulfill their orders and (c) report results to Congress. I move to an even higher level of abstraction. (a) The principal engages an agent and assigns a task to the agent, elaborating its reasonable expectations as to results it seeks, (b) the agent fulfills these tasks and (c) the agent's report relates how the agent's fulfillment of its duty satisfies the principal's reasonable expectations. This reduction assumes that it is the agent who will make the vast majority of decisions involving expenditure of energy. That much is inevitable. The performance standard – for which the principal is wholly responsible – offers to the agent the principal's understanding of how well it expects the agent to do its job. On this account, the performance standard frames – for the agent – the accomplishment that the principal would find satisfactory. 'That two experiments shall first be made upon two of the said bars', the performance standard of the Ohio-Mississippi navigation act declared, 'and if in [the President's] judgment they shall be successful, then, and not otherwise, he is hereby otherwise to cause improvements to be made upon the remaining bars'. Put crudely, if Capt. Han Solo can sail a steamboat down the stretch of the Ohio River on which engineers have conducted their 'two experiments' and emerge with his hull intact, federal engineers should go ahead and rip the remaining sand bars out of the river.

The principal's formulation of performance standards expresses the principal's confidence that it has a role to play in adding value (a) to its order-giving and (b) to the agent's task-fulfilling. Collective wisdom (that a parliamentary assembly may bring to bear on assigning tasks) supplies a fertile opportunity for constructing performance standards. The reader may ponder by what other effort the principal may add value to the principal-agent relationship. In the case of parliamentary assemblies, the reflective, contemplative and introspective faculty might be brought to bear on this challenge.[24]

'The sense of mankind, the practice of the world have clearly established the right of Congress'

The foregoing the Chief Justice declared that the prosperity of Americans was 'inseparable' does not, however, supply a complete picture of the North American waterscape. *Gibbons* did not take into account the following geophysical reality. North America is well-stocked with *intra*-state lakes and rivers. For example, Lake Cayuga, the largest lake wholly within the borders of New York state, is an *intra*state navigable lake. Nevertheless, its surface is regulated by the federal government. Readers may travel any number of *state*-branded highways to Ithaca NY where they will discover, proximate to the shores of Lake Cayuga, a *federally*-branded US Coast Guard Auxiliary Station at 508 Old Taughannock Blvd. Had Ogden's and Gibbons's dueling steamboats paddle-wheeled Lake Cayuga's waters – waters both *intra*state and navigable – Chief Justice John Marshall would have been hard pressed to argue that he was relying on the Commerce Clause in composing his opinion for the Supreme Court. How could Gibbons' steamers – offering scenic tours of Cayuga's waters, that is, sailing 'its waves of blue' from the boathouse at Cornell University[25] – affect 'commerce ... among the several states'? Marshall could not rest his entire case on the Commerce Clause. And John Marshall was not a 'let's do things by halves' kind of guy. The Chief Justice was not tempted to surrender to state governments the power to regulate traffic on *intra*state navigable lakes and rivers.

As in *McCulloch v. Maryland*, Marshall employed the method of Congressional precedents. The following timeline might be useful. Marshall's opening exposition of the method appeared in *McCulloch* (1819), five years before Marshall appealed to that method in *Gibbons* (1824). Monroe elaborated and expanded the method of Congressional precedents in his 'Views' (1822). Monroe's survey gathered data from nine statutes and 13 projects. We know that Marshall was aware of Monroe's data-gathering – taken as a social science technique in support of his political science – because Marshall acknowledged to Monroe, in a letter referenced in Appendix J (13 June 1822), that Marshall had carefully studied Monroe's 'Views'.[26]

Marshall's appeal to the Marshall-Monroe method of Congressional precedents runs as follows. 'The contemporaneous assumption and continued exercise of the power, and universal acquiescence, have so clearly established the right of Congress over navigation'. 22 US 186, 230–231. I gather the data to support this fact-testable proposition by locating 12 navigation projects in eight statutes. My survey appears in the margin. I began with the Act of March 17, 1800 (6th Congress) and completed my data-gathering with the Act of April 20, 1822 (17th Congress).[27] Each project (that Marshall could have mentioned) offered an instance of Congress's 'assumption and continued exercise ... of the right of Congress over navigation'. 22 US 186, 230–231. For example, in the 1802 Act of Congress granted its permission for the state of Virginia to improve the 'Appomatox river'[28] while the 1804 Act of Congress gave Virginia permission to improve the James River.[29] Nothing concedes the power of the unitary government to engage in ABC-related activity like a parochial government asking the unitary government for permission to launch programmatic action for the same purpose. My survey supports Marshall's declaration that states conceded the 'right of Congress over navigation' including power over *intra*state navigable waters as far back as 1800. For example, the Appomattox River was (and still is) an intrastate waterway. The James River was an *intra*state waterway up to 1863 when Congress transformed the James River into an *inter*state waterway by detaching counties in western Virginia and admitting them to the Union as the newly-minted state of West Virginia. This transformation of an *intra*state waterway into one of *inter*state dimensions – the James River flowing majestically eastwards through two states – called on magic that only the national government commanded.[30] And, I hasten to add, Congress did not require the assistance of elephants or turtles to deploy this power, provided that voters and lawmakers approved its work *after the fact*. John Marshall's 'acquiescence' to federal power is a convenient posture for a constitutional historian to note when federal gunboats steam local rivers and federal troops are camped outside state capitols. I have quoted phrases from John Marshall's invocation – in his *Gibbons* opinion – of the method of Congressional precedents. Here is Marshall's passage in full.

> But, it is almost labouring to prove a self-evident proposition, since the sense of mankind, the practice of the world, the contemporaneous assumption, and continued exercise of the power, and universal acquiescence, have so clearly established the right of Congress over navigation, and the transportation of both men and their goods, as not only incidental to, but actually of the essence of, the power to regulate commerce. 22 US 186, 231.

'Assumption, exercise, acquiescence'

I suggest that the geophysical point of view was, effectively, the only perspective that mattered to John Marshall. Now subtract navigation from *Gibbons*. In this recasting, 'transportation of both men and their goods' would serve as 'the essence of the power to regulate commerce'.

The following difficulty sinks this analysis and in some very shallow water. Congress did not have a significant track record when it came to composing statutes devoted to *inter*state regulation of commerce. Building roads, obviously, is not the same thing as establishing weight- and length-limits for big rigs and hiring cops-on-hogs to enforce these regulations. To make a commerce-based analysis successful, Marshall needed a data set that would support the following 'if x, then y, else z' statement: '[federal] assumption, [federal] exercise ... and [state] acquiescence' to establish 'the right of Congress over ... transportation of both men and their goods'. Absent such data, Marshall would be thrown back to a very unMarshallian grounding for his decision. He would be forced to settle for a garden-variety gloss on Article I, Section 8, Clause 3. 'The Congress shall have Power ... To regulate Commerce ... among the several States'. As the saying goes, 'no hundred of millions of acres of watery patrimony for you'.

Marshall's declaration – that the federal government enjoyed supreme power over North American inland navigable waters – aligned (and quite nicely) with federal ownership of the above-the-water-line national domain. I refer to the 400,000,000 acres of land that shrewd negotiation won for the First Republic (Paris, 1783) and good fortune brought the US in the Louisiana territory (Paris, 1803).[31] Thanks to John Marshall, the federal government successfully claimed ownership of all US navigable waterways, intrastate and interstate. Was the grand total 600,000,00 or 700,000,000 acres? In 1824 Marshall confirmed that the federal government was the nation's largest owner of land and water rights in every proprietary sense of the word. But that wasn't all. Congress's power to legislate its will into the 'law of the land' – to launch and curate programs managing and disposing of its patrimonial rights and powers – put the federal government in charge of the nation's destiny.

In 1899 Congress converted *Gibbons*'s declaration of federal supremacy over navigable waters into federal codelaw. The Rivers and Harbors Act (1899) provided that: 'The creation of any obstruction not affirmatively authorized by Congress, to the navigable capacity of any of the waters of the United States is prohibited'.[32] This effectively blocked any actor or body from accessing a state-owned riverbed – and thereby obstructing navigation (or more broadly the 'capacity' for navigation) – without the prior authorization of Congress. The Rivers and Harbors Act overturned the practical effect of Taney's holding in *Pollard's Lessee v. Hagan*. This was not the first or last time that the jurisprudence of the Taney court found a welcoming home in the dustbin of history. On the other hand, John Adams has yet to receive acknowledgment for approving the Act of March 17, 1800 [Congress funds state harbor project in Savannah GA by permitting Georgia to tap federal tax resource].[33] That act launched a century's worth of power creep. In that enactment Congress offered Georgia (in effect) a juicy federal tax subsidy; this eased the state of

Georgia along a path whose terminus was, according to John Marshall in *Gibbons*, the surrender of state power over all navigable waters.[34]

'A range of States puts us essentially at ease'

The foregoing discussion backgrounds the reader on the evolution of new state-making in the Second Republic. From 1607 (Virginia) to 1732 (Georgia) British ministers and mapmakers had their opportunity to make topological sense of British North America when they granted provincial charters. In hindsight, rendering provincial boundaries a crazy-quilt was the British empire's best chance to hobble the ambitions of American provinces to unite and seek independence from the homeland. It was left to the Second Republic to launch the process of building out new states in a geophysically reasonable (if not always pretty) pattern.[35] New state-making went into high gear when Congress settled on the following two-stage process. This process teamed an enabling act of Congress with an admitting act or resolution. From 1802/1803 through 1849/1850, Congress admitted 15 states into the Union by employing these twinned processes. Exceptions will be noted. The Confederation Congress did not admit a single new state to the Union. The Confederation Congress did, however, craft nation's first enabling act; this was designed to tempt the Republic of Vermont into the Union.[36]

The following survey lists pathways (by type) that mark off the journeys by which 37 states joined the Union. *Constitution II* invited the first 13 states to join by ratification. These 37 remaining states are the states that Congress admitted to the Union. (I omit reference to *re*admitted states.) In this survey I refer to 'a nascent state' as the entity that was the subject of a Congressional enabling act. This phrase makes clear that – most of the time but not invariably – a nascent state's pedigree may be traced back to a larger geophysical reality. I do not supply all the instances of every class that my survey names. States may be assigned to more than one class.

- New state-making may detach a tract of land from one state and assign it to new state. Vermont, Kentucky, Tennessee, Mississippi, Alabama and Maine were instances of this type.
- Detachment may take place during rebellion against the national government. West Virginia is an instance of new state-making that Congress employed to punish Virginia (1863).
- States may be created from (former) stand-alone foreign colonies: Florida and Alaska fall into this pattern.
- States may be admitted/annexed/absorbed from stand-alone republics (Texas and California) or a kingdom (Hawaii) or a prone-to-wander republic (Vermont).

- States may be admitted (with tracts assigned to it) that the United States acquired in settlements that concluded international armed conflict. The Northwest Territory was acquired in the Treaty of Paris (1783). The Indiana Territory was carved out from this bulk territory in 1800. Further tracts were detached from the originally-configured Indiana Territory. I refer to tracts assigned (more or less entire) to the states of Illinois and Wisconsin along with smaller tracts, later assigned to the future states of Michigan and Minnesota. After slicing and dicing the geophysical reality at its disposal, Congress admitted Indiana to the Union (1816).
- The evolution of Nevada (almost) parallels that of Indiana. The Treaty of Guadalupe Hidalgo combined a forced cession of land with US payment of compensation to the United Mexican States (1848). Having admitted California (1850), Congress organized the remaining tracts (acquired in the Mexican War) into a northern slice (the Utah territory) and a southern slice (the New Mexico territory). Congress then prepared Nevada for statehood by creating the Territory of Nevada (1861). The Nevada territory twice (successfully) urged Congress to slice off tranches of the (remaining) Utah territory. I note the short-lived existence of the 'State of Deseret' and the California 'Bear Flag' Republic.[37]
- States may be admitted with lands assigned to the state that represent a small portion of a continental-sized tract that United States acquired from a foreign nation by purchase of its claims. Louisiana is an example here.
- The United States may acquire a relatively small tract from a foreign nation by purchase of its claims and reserve this tract for incorporation into states scheduled for later admission. Congress assigned Arizona and New Mexico portions of the Gadsden Purchase in their respective statehood acts.
- A state may be admitted and, shortly after admission, a relatively small tract is assigned to that state *in addition to* its original configuration. Louisiana is an example. I term this 'resizing'.
- States may be admitted with tracts assigned to it, which tracts the United States acquired in a border settlement with a foreign nation that *almost* resulted in outright conflict. Oregon, Washington and Idaho are examples of this pattern.
- A state may be admitted with tracts assigned to it but the border is so muddled that international arbitration is required to settle the issues. Alaska is an example.
- A state may be admitted with tracts assigned to it *and* the border is disputed *but* international arbitration fails to resolve the issues. Instead, the state's border gets defined in treaty negotiations. Maine is an example.

- A state may be admitted retroactively. In the case of Ohio 150 years transpired before Congress remembered that it forgot to pass an act admitting Ohio to the Union.[38]
- A state may be admitted to the Union after a predecessor national government passed the enabling act that circumstances called for. Vermont is an example.
- A state may be admitted with tracts that included reservations guaranteed to Indian tribes. Oklahoma is an example.
- A state may be admitted with most (but not all) of the indigenous people's claims outstanding and unsettled. Alaska is an example.

These points highlight the enabling/admitting process. Congress admitted new states for the purpose of – among other goals – stabilizing frontier regions and pushing potential frontier instability west, south and northwest. There was no 'one size fits all' approach to new state-making. No single instrument could possibly supply all the prescriptions needed to reliably guide and govern enabling and admitting legislation whose objects were splashed across a continent's worth of geophysical reality. Moreover, no single generation was responsible for getting it entirely right; no generation got it entirely wrong.

Take a frontier republic on the North American continent that was not formally aligned with the US. Such an entity might be tempted to link its political fortunes with those of a foreign power. Capital cities that might warm to such a prospect included London, Paris, Madrid, Moscow and Mexico City. Monroe was well aware of the threat that breakaway republics posed to frontier stability. In his 'Views' Monroe observed that:

> A range of States on the western side of the Mississippi, which already is provided for, puts us essentially at ease. Whether it will be wise to go further will turn on other considerations than those which have dictated the course heretofore pursued. At whatever point we may stop, whether it be at a single range of States beyond the Mississippi or by taking a greater scope, the advantage of such improvements is deemed of the highest importance. It is so on the present scale. The further we go the greater will be the necessity for them. 'Views', ¶148.

Monroe's sentiments were in sync with the temper of the times. In a report to Congress on developments in Georgia, Monroe transmitted an assessment of the negotiations with the Cherokee Nation. The federal government had launched extinguishment of its claims within the state of Georgia. The report declared that the federal government's purpose in extinguishing such claims was to organize 'new states and having them settled, and populated, for the better defence of the country in case of war' (1824).[39] In his 'Views', Monroe hinted – in the passage quoted above – that the future build out of the US might be governed by 'other considerations than those which have dictated the course heretofore pursued'.[40] Monroe's reference to 'other considerations' was a genteel way of saluting power for the sake of power. If European Americans could dominate the continent, 'can' supplies the justification for Americans to do so.

The threat of breakaway republics offered a convenient opportunity for the federal government to flex its considerable and growing muscles. This was not an imaginary concern. A band of disgruntled Vermonters succumbed to the temptation of recolonization.[41] After preliminaries for Vermont's union with the remaining colonies of British North America gained traction, the Confederation Congress made a counteroffer to Vermonters (21 August 1781). This offer laid out the conditions for Vermont's eventual admission to the Union.[42] New York surrendered its claims to Vermont lands in 1790.[43] These events eased the admission of the Vermont Republic into the Union (1791).[44] I note Aaron Burr's attempt to make himself head honcho of someplace in the west.[45] Although scholars may tut-tut at the Jefferson administration's failed prosecution of Burr, the federal government gained valuable support, functionally speaking, for its argument that pacifying North America required US control over the geophysical reality located within the borders of existing states and territories. Breakaway threats need not be fact-based to be useful to the center's ambitions.

'The advantage of such improvements is deemed of the highest importance'

I note Monroe's confidence that the 'advantage of such improvements is deemed of the highest importance. It is so on the present scale. The further we go the greater will be the necessity for them'. 'Views', ¶148. A sprawling landmass required a national transportation network. Accordingly, all existing and contemplated modes of transport should be designed to mutually support one another. Managing a continent's worth of land and water called on the specialized know how required to design, construct and maintain transportation projects. To illustrate this point, I reviewed statutes offering guidance enacted in Great Britain (1773) and the state of Indiana (1817). The former statute was designed to facilitate a future legislature's crafting of statutory text to launch a given public highway project. In other words, the British statute sought to enhance legislative competence. In the latter statute, the Indiana General Assembly drilled down to the level of administrative competence.[46] In this case the legislature tasked agents to fulfill the principal and ancillary processes that lawmakers spelled out in this statute. Agent initiative was yoked to the purposes of the principal by the energy-tracking devices that these processes outlined.

In 1773 Parliament enacted the Public Highways Act, 13 Geo. 3, c. 78. This statute provided a template for future lawmaking. Section XIV (first half) of the Public Highways Act follows:

> And be it further enacted, where the Ditches, Gutters or Watercourses which have been usually made, or which are hereinbefore directed to be made, cleansed and kept open, shall not be sufficient to carry off the Water which shall lie upon and annoy the Highways, that then and in every such case, it shall and may be lawful for the said Surveyors, by the Order of any one or more of the said Justices, to make new Ditches and Drains in and through the said Land and Grounds adjoining or lying near to such Highways, or in and through any other Lands or Grounds, if it shall be necessary, for the more easy and effectually carrying off such Water from the said Highways, and also to keep such Ditches, Gutters or Watercourses scoured, cleansed and opened.

Parsing out titles and officeholders:

- Surveyors laid out a route for a public highway; after it had been constructed, these officials were charged with the duty of maintaining the road surface.
- Justices of the Peace were available to supervise (and later on, justify) the performance of the Surveyors.
- Landowners or their tenants (on either side of the road, whose holdings are 'not Waste or Common') also played a role in the two processes referred to.

When the House of Commons took up a future highway project, the Public Highways Act guided proceedings on such a bill. An MP might come up with a good reason to depart from the pre-fabricated features that the template contained. But that only proves the point under consideration. Taken in this light, the Public Highways Act (1773) should be considered a labor-saving device. Another type of labor savings – directed to administrators not legislators – made its appearance shortly after Congress admitted Indiana to statehood on 11 December 1816. The Indiana General Assembly promptly opened its doors for business. By 3 January 1817 that body had enacted seven laws. Here I draw on 'an Act for repairing and opening public Roads and Highways'.[47] Section 12 of that Act reads:

> And in order to enable the supervisors the more effectually to discharge their duty, it shall and may be lawful for the supervisors aforesaid, or any other person or persons by his or their order and directions to enter upon any lands adjoining or lying near the public

> roads and highways within their respective townships and to cut or open such drains or ditches through the same as he or they shall judge necessary completely to carry off and drain the water from such roads.

The British Parliament and the Indiana General Assembly composed semi-regimented sentences to solve the same problem. A deluge of rain inundates roads in Great Britain and in the United States, floods a roadway and renders it impassable. In Britain 'it shall be ... lawful for the said Surveyors, by the Order of any one or more of the said Justices, to make new Ditches and Drains in and through the said Land and Grounds adjoining or lying near to such Highways ... the more easy and effectually carrying off such Water from the said Highways ...'.[48] In Indiana 'it shall be ... lawful for the supervisors ... to enter upon any lands adjoining or lying near the public roads and highways ... and to cut or open such drains or ditches through the same as he or they shall judge necessary completely to carry off and drain the water from such road'.[49]

- A British Surveyor (with the approval of a Justice of the Peace) possessed the authority 'to cut or open such drains or ditches through the same as he or they shall judge necessary completely to carry off and drain the water from such roads'.
- His American cousin – elected to the county board of supervisors – could 'cut or open such drains or ditches through the same as he or they shall judge necessary completely to carry off and drain the water from such roads'.

Template statutes address one of the fundamental difficulties that confronts the work of parliamentary assemblies. Statutes are crafted in semi-regimented sentences; all energy that lawmakers expend must be passed forward to aid future lawmakers or future agents via these sentences. As noted above, in the case of the Public Highways Act, the House of Commons directed its labor-saving efforts to a future session of that body. In the case of the Indiana General Assembly, that body anticipated tools that local officials might find handy when they resist the inevitable and random-like push-back that the material world will reliably throw at any program that the Generally Assembly has crafted.

'If the Ditches shall not be sufficient to carry off the Water then it shall be lawful'

Based on the foregoing, I can identify three different phases of templating effort that lawmakers undertake. (a) Framing initiative transfers. These transfers are inevitable because the principal can never compose a volume of instructions sufficient to automate the agent's fulfillment of the mission, given the material world's inevitable resistance to the success of the mission. Declaring performance standards and offering labor-saving tools to its agents are frequently the best the principal can do when it comes to adding value to its mission-specific instructions.

(b) Heuristics or thumbnail tests. (i) Take economies of scale. The principal's goal is to discover how little energy he can invest in problem-solving while, at the same time, the principal transmits to its the agent a suitable volume of instructions, with the hope that these will save energy on the agent's part. (ii) Take Aristotle's heuristic complete, consistent and proximate.[50] Instructions passed to the agent should include everything he needs to know, but exclude extraneous instructions that are likely to be overcome by events. Once these instructions are tentatively available for the principal's further consideration, the principal should scale its instructions. That is, instructions to the agent should align with the features of the situations that the agent is likely to face. (iii) I turn to the heuristic 'what is' which I contrast with 'how is'. This heuristic operates by disciplining easy-to-say definitions with robust algorithms. Definitions license investigators to attach predicates (features, properties) to persons, places, things and situations. There is a trap, however. When the principal slaps predicates on situations, it is prone to convince itself that it is making significant progress towards constructing a suitable body of instructions (to be passed forward to its agent). Early branching error occurs when the principal postpones crafting 'if x, then y, else z' instructions. Employing that formula retards the principal's temptation to slap predicates on features of the initiative to be transferred and announce that its 'work is done'. This deceleration comes about because the principal must give thought to the three empty slots in the 'if x, then y, else z' formula that the principal must fill.

(c) Chaining and nesting processes. The investigator constructs primary process P_1 in the form 'if then else', explained above. The principal must then decide, 'do I chain P_2 to P_1? Or do I chain ancillary process A_1 to P_1?' Another choice: 'do I nest ancillary process A_2 within P_1? Or do I chain ancillary process A_2 to A_1?'

I return to Section XIV of the Public Highways Act.[51] I start with the text, quoted above, commencing: 'where ... Ditches, Gutters or Watercourses which have been usually made, or which are hereinbefore directed to be made, cleansed and kept open, shall not be sufficient to carry off the Water which shall lie upon and annoy the Highways, that then and in every such case, it shall and may be lawful ...'. Preliminarily I restate this text:

> [If] the Ditches shall not be sufficient to carry off the Water ... then ... it shall and may be lawful for the said Surveyors ... to make new Ditches in and through the said Land adjoining to such Highways [else].

I rephrase the foregoing, dispensing with text irrelevant to my purpose. 'If Ditches made, cleansed and kept open shall not be sufficient to carry off the Water, *then Surveyors [shall] make new Ditches and Drains in and through the said Land and Grounds adjoining or lying near to such Highways ...*'. The text serving as the chained process appears in italics.

What happens when British Surveyors notice that the 'Ditches' are silting up? Lawmakers could invoke an ancillary process, one that is nested (not chained) to the primary process.

> In every such case where the Ditches shall not be sufficient to carry off the Water which shall lie upon and annoy the Highways, then it shall and may be lawful for the said Surveyors, *by the Order of any one or more of the said Justices,* to make new Ditches and Drains in and through the said Land and Grounds.

The text that captures the ancillary process appears in italics. It explains what happens in the time slice occurring immediately *before* 'said Surveyors ... make new Ditches and Drains'. Justices of the Peace will issue orders authorizing the Surveyors 'to make new Ditches and Drains'. I sum up the energy-tracking that these two pathways trace. When you nest an ancillary process, you map out your return to the primary process. But when you chain a process to another process – as in 'if x, then y' – this pathway marks out an opportunity for the assembly to move forward and, consequently, to declare other variables that might render the program Smith-compliant.

As the parliamentary assembly tests various configurations of text – employing the template formula (and its variations noted above) – opportunities to secure energy-savings to future legislators or administrators will stimulate the ambition of lawmakers. Within 50 years after the Public Highways Act had been written into the statute books, John Loudon McAdam published his study *Remarks on the Present System of Road Making; with Observations, Deduced from Practice and Experience, with a View to a Revision of the Existing Laws, and the Introduction of Improvement in the Method of Making, Repairing, and Preserving Roads, and Defending the Road Funds from Misapplication.*[52] As of 1823 this work had gone through seven editions. As the title indicates McAdam directed his attention to achieving (a) efficiency in lawmaking – 'A View to a Revision of the Existing Laws' – along with (b) efficiencies in road construction. As to the latter, I note that McAdam's title refers to 'the Method of Making, Repairing, and Preserving Roads'. On both subjects McAdam made himself the internationally acknowledged expert.[53] McAdam's research and experiments on the subject of road-making supported his conclusion 'that under a better system of management a better road would be produced'.[54] I have drawn on his 1823 testimony before a House of Commons Select Committee.

McAdam explained how this was accomplished and in so doing justified his *Remarks on the Present System of Road Making* as a species of 'how-to' literature (1823). If a 'better road' is desired, then competent administrators must be engaged. They will apply their administrative competence to achieve that end by employing 'a better system of management' to the purpose of road-building. But they can't do it by themselves. Competent lawmakers must template variables that will supply a 'system of management' to guide and govern the agents' fulfillment of their respective duties.

'The Model Form of Government most readily and easily adopted upon a Sudden Emergency'

A single figure dominated the political science of the First Republic when it came to template creation. On three occasions John Adams made himself the undisputed master of that contribution to political science (1775–1776). If the reader harbored doubts that templates were a well-recognized species of bourgeois artwork, Adams's virtuoso performances should resolve the question. (a) Adams penned a template to guide future constitution writers. I refer to this template by drawing on Adams's phrases (stitched together to read) 'the Model ... Form of Government ... most readily and easily adopted upon a Sudden Emergency' (15 November 1775).[55] In the margin I note James Harrington's precursor *The Rota: Or, A Model of a free State, or equal Commonwealth* (1659).[56] Adams's 'Model ... Form' enjoyed a spectacular success. A total of 523 constitutional instruments were adopted or proposed in the interval January 1776-November 1815.[57] (b) Adams immediately revisited the subject of new state-founding with a resolution he proposed to the Continental Congress (10 May 1776). 'Where no Government sufficient to the Exigencies of their Affairs, hath been hitherto established, to adopt such Government as shall in the Opinion of the Representatives of the People best conduce to the Happiness and Safety of their Constituents in particular, and America in general'.[58] That body incorporated Adams's text into the resolution that it adopted a few days later (15 May 1776).[59] (c) Adams then followed up these accomplishments with his Model Treaty (24 September 1776). 'There shall be a firm, inviolable, and universal Peace, and a true and sincere Friendship between A. and B. and the Subjects of A. and of B'.[60]

I draw on the first sentence of Adams' 'Model ... Form' to illustrate the power of Adams' formula. Adams' text reads: 'a Legislative, an Executive and a judicial Power, comprehend the whole of what is meant and understood by Government. It is by ballancing each of these Powers against the other two, that the Effort in humane Nature towards Tyranny, can alone be checked and restrained and any degree of Freedom preserved in the Constitution'.[61] I recast the foregoing according to the formula 'if x, then y, else z', omitting italics or other signals. 'If text composers wish to check and restrain the Effort in humane Nature towards Tyranny, then they will balance texts establishing each of these Powers – Legislative, Executive and a judicial Power – against the other two, else any degree of Freedom will not be preserved in the Constitution'. The suppleness of Adams' template-creating discipline arises in a remarkable self-regarding sense. When the draft constitution is completed, a reader will notice that the force of the text vesting 'Legislative ... Power' in a parliamentary body is checked by text creating 'Executive ... Power', for example. But in a second and broader sense, Adams is saying that when text composers go to work, they must solve this problem, writing *this* text, before they tackle the next problem, which they do by composing *that* text. This second sense calls on text-writers to step back and, in real time, assess how well they are going about their text-crafting. Step-by-step crafting effort will be facilitated if lawmakers refer back to Adams's template while text-crafting is in progress.

Two accomplishments may be regarded as the technical offspring of Adams' facility with templates and especially his exploitation of the formula 'if x, then y, else z'. The Confederation Congress crafted the first enabling act in US history (21 August 1781).[62] In this act Congress provided for a contractual-like address to the people of the Republic of Vermont. This aligns with John Adams's urging that inhabitants of the respective provinces provide for 'Government sufficient to the Exigencies of their Affairs' (10 May 1776).[63] In my recasting of the Confederation Congress's enabling act, Congress declared that if the people of Vermont 'explicitly relinquish all demands of lands or jurisdiction on the east side of the west bank of the Connecticut River [along with other tracts]', then Vermont will qualify for statehood, that is, it will enjoy Congress's 'recognition of the independence of the people inhabiting the territory of Vermont'.

Less than five years later Congress took another step forward. The declaration embodying this accomplishment appeared in the Northwest Ordinance (13 July 1787). Congress devised a series of chained and nested processes suitable to bring new states into the Union from the (bulk) Northwest Territory.[64] I recast the first sentence of Section 9 of the Ordinance. '[If] there shall be five thousand free male inhabitants of full age in the district, [then] they shall receive authority, with time and place, to elect a representative from their counties or townships to represent them in the general assembly'.[65] The Northwest Ordinance sets forth various primary and ancillary processes in Sections 9 through 13. In the latter section Congress declares the final payoff, which it addresses to all potential beneficiaries of the Ordinance. This payoff is expressed in the now-familiar formula, reduced to two variables. I recast as follows. '[If you do all of the foregoing things, then Congress will] provide for the establishment of States, and permanent government therein, and for their admission to a share in the federal councils on an equal footing with the original States, at as early periods as may be consistent with the general interest'.[66]

Conclusion

When S. Augustus Mitchell teamed up with a Philadelphia businessman to launch a publishing firm specializing in reference works, a niche market was theirs for the asking. Appealing to business owners and general readers alike, Mitchell & Hinman brought forth *Mitchell's Compendium of the Internal Improvement of the United States Comprising General Notices of all the Most Important Canals and Rail-Roads, throughout the Several States and Territories of the Union* (1835). Mitchell noted that transportation 'projects which a few years ago would have seemed visionary and chimerical, have been carried into execution, with results outstripping the most sanguine calculations'.[67] Accordingly, Mitchell heaped extravagant praise on the Second Republic. 'Nothing but physical impossibilities are beyond the sober hopes of a great and growing people, whose national wealth is accumulating, and whose physical resources are constantly developing'.[68] Mitchell then declared that 'immense expenditures of capital have been made, and investments still more enormous are contemplated throughout every part of the Union for the construction of these important works, which are destined to revolutionize the inland commercial intercourse of the civilized world'.[69]

Mitchell also appealed to the attractive force of the expression 'political economy' when he proclaimed that advocates of transportation and communication projects had been engaged in a 'demonstration of [the] power in political economy'. Did Mitchell assume that this 'power' was an American discovery?

> It has been discovered, as a new demonstration of power in political economy, that works of internal improvement, if wisely executed, enrich, instead of impoverishing a country.[70]

Mitchell drew the connection between transportation – promoting augmentation of the net worth of households and business – and incorporation of remote communities and regions. In the outline following, I emphasize the geophysical dimension, as did John Marshall in his phrase 'this vast republic'.[71]

It's a big continent. If we don't dominate it, we'll have to share it. That's unacceptable, so we'll dominate it. To dominate it, we'll have to populate it. For this purpose, we prefer to settle European Americans in the back country because their life experience includes participation in political cultures whose norms we find acceptable. Populating means eventual political incorporation because we can't settle remote tracts with inhabitants who expect to live in a condition of perpetual subordination on the margins of our evolving civilization. They wouldn't go out there *and* we wouldn't want them out there. It's remote out there and remoteness is an enemy of incorporation. Remoteness can be overcome by moving people and products better, faster, cheaper. Overcoming remoteness is our preferred means of binding outlying communities and regions to the center of gravity. Two mottoes grace the temple. 'Expand *or* die'. 'Paralysis is death'.

Based on the foregoing, the unitary government possessed the right and duty to resort to self-help for the purpose of evolving systems, structures and institutions in political society to meet the challenges and exploit the opportunities that the material world reliably delivered. As of 1824, on the eve of Monroe's departure from office, it was clear that the two governments/divided allegiance formula yielded ascendency to the majoritarians. Political society on the North American continent pitted representative governments, one against many. The will to survive and the cash to flourish resolved the contest.

'The unity of Government which constitutes you one people, is also now dear to you', President George Washington declared in his 'Farewell Address' (1796).[72] Washington anticipated the Monrovian connection between brand loyalty, on the one hand, and, on the other hand, programmatic action that reliably promoted *national* prosperity and thereby stabilized political society. Allegiance to the 'national Union' had 'immense value', Washington declared. Be on guard, he warned, against attempts to 'alienate any portion of our country from the rest, or to enfeeble the sacred ties which now link together the various parts'.[73] Monroe commenced his first term as president with the confidence that official behavior in his administration would be both 'efficient' – delivering stability – and, since public officials fulfilling these service missions could 'never become oppresive', the center would reap the benefits of the brand loyalty it had worked so hard to gain.[74]

Notes

1. 'The Congress shall assemble at least once in every Year, and such Meeting shall be on the first Monday in December, unless they shall by Law appoint a different Day'. Article I, Section 4, Clause 2. See also text at 49.
2. See memory.loc.gov/ammem/amlaw/lwsllink.html; 4 Stat 22, c. 46, Act of April 30, 1824; Sec. 1.
3. 4 Stat 32, c. 139, Act of May 24, 1824; Sec. 1.
4. 4 Stat 175, c. 78.
5. 4 Stat 288, c. 73.
6. 67 Stat 29, P.L. 83-31, Act of May 22, 1953, since codified at 43 USC Sec. 1301 et seq. ['title to and ownership of the lands beneath navigable waters within the boundaries of the respective States [is] vested in and assigned to the respective States'. Sec. 1311(a)].
7. See text at 82-83.

8. See text at 121.
9. See text at 43.
10. Laws of the State of New York; 21st Session, c. 225, Act of April 11, 1808, 407-408. Sec. I; see also 22 US 1, 2 [Syllabus].
11. 1 Stat 305, c. 8.
12. See List_of_river_borders_of_U.S._states [last retrieved 20 June 2021].
13. See List_of_longest_rivers_of_the_United_States_(by_main_stem) [last retrieved 22 March 2021].
14. See State_cessions [last retrieved 21 April 2021].
15. Aschenbrenner, *Foundings*, 57.
16. See vault.georgiaarchives.org/digital/collection/adhoc/id/420
17. See usace.contentdm.oclc.org/digital/collection/p16021coll4/id/156 ['Working in the Dry: Cofferdams, In-River Construction and the United States Army Corps of Engineers'], 20 [last retrieved 9 January 2021].
18. Locke, *Essay*, Book II, Chapter XXIII, Section 2. In the text I have paraphrased the following passage which I have drawn from Locke's *Essay*. 'The world was supported by a great elephant [which] rested on a great tortoise'.
19. 3 Stat 562, c. 45, Act of April 14, 1820.
20. See memory.loc.gov/ammem/amlaw/lwsp.html American State Papers/ Commerce and *Navigation*, 740-748, Document No. 260.
21. 4 Stat 241, c. 92, Act of March 3, 1827, Sec. 1.
22. See text at 82.
23. 3 Stat 562, c. 45, Act of April 14, 1820.
24. See text at 113.
25. See www.youtube.com/watch?v=_SiInyGmA9M ['Far above Cayuga's waters'].
26. 'Each author assumes that social science can be mobilized to support the political science he advocates'. Aschenbrenner, 'Can Nation-states Self-stabilize?'
27. 2 Stat 18, c. 15, Act of March 17, 1800 [Baltimore and Savannah harbors; as to Savannah, a tax subsidy reserved to Georgia]; 2 Stat 152, c. 23, Act of April 14, 1802 ['Appomatox river']; 2 Stat 269, c. 22, Act of March 16, 1804 [James River]; 2 Stat 353, c. 12 Act of February 28, 1806 [Philadelphia Port Wardens and tax subsidy]; 2 Stat 484, c. 47, Act of April 16, 1808 [renewal of Baltimore and Savannah assents, provided that Georgia refrain from taxing steam-powered transport]; 3 Stat 125, c.60, Act of April 16, 1814 [renewal of Baltimore and Savannah assents]; 3 Stat 301, c. 77, Act of April 26, 1816 [James River]; 3 Stat 665, c. 29, Act of April 20, 1822 [renewal of Baltimore and Savannah assents].
28. See text at 26.
29. See text at 26.
30. See en.wikipedia.org/wiki/The_Sorcerer%27s_Apprentice
31. See text at 132.
32. 30 Stat 1151, c. 425, Sec. 10, Act of March 3, 1899.
33. 2 Stat 18, c. 15 [Baltimore and Savannah harbors; Georgia granted tax subsidy].
34. *Ibid*., Sec. 1.
35. See text at 92.
36. See text at 101.
37. See State_of_Deseret; see also California_Republic [both sites last retrieved 28 June 2021].
38. 67 Stat 407, P.L. 83-204, Act of August 7, 1953.

39. See babel.hathitrust.org/cgi/pt?id=uc1.31158000787118&view=1up&seq=271&skin=2021 The quotation in the text is sourced to the *Public Documents printed by Order of the Senate during the First Session of the Eighteenth Congress*. I refer to Doc. No. 63 ['Message from the President of the United States, transmitting certain papers relating to the compact between the U. States and the State of Georgia of 1802, &c. April 2, 1824'] and, drilling down further, to the 'Communication ... made to the council of the Cherokee nation' (16 October 1823), 24.
40. See text at 40.
41. See Haldimand_Affair [last retrieved 26 December 2020].
42. *Continental Congress Journals*, 21:892-893; 21 August 1781. The Supreme Court reviewed the relevant historical details in *Vermont v. New Hampshire*, 293 US 593 (1933).
43. See text at 92.
44. 1 Stat 191, c. 7, Act of February 25, 1791.
45. Isenberg, *Founder*; Chapters 8 and 9 detail Burr's western adventures and the follow-on trial.
46. See text at 95.
47. 1st General Assembly, Session Law 7.
48. See text at 96.
49. See text at 96.
50. Aristotle, *Posterior Analytics*, 73a21-73b6 [de omni per se quatenus ipsum].
51. See text at 96-97.
52. London, 1823; 7th edn.
53. See Macadam [last retrieved 22 May 2021].
54. *Ibid.*, 223.
55. See founders.archives.gov/documents/Adams/06-03-02-0163; 'From John Adams to Richard Henry Lee, 15 November 1775'.
56. See oll.libertyfund.org/title/toland-the-oceana-and-other-works#lf0050_head_179, 587-598. At 6,400 words Harrington's *Rota* is about 12 times longer than Adams's 'Model ... Form of Government'.
57. Aschenbrenner, 'Tracing the Sources'. In that essay I cite to Dippel's surveys which appear in *Constitutions of the World*.
58. *Continental Congress Journals*, 4:341 (10 May 1776).
59. Adams's text was approved and wrapped into a lengthier resolution whose text was devoted to the subject of new state-founding during international conflict. *Ibid.*, 4:357-358.
60. *Continental Congress Journals*, 5:813-817; see also Aschenbrenner, *Foundings*, 18-20.
61. See text at 100n55.
62. *Continental Congress Journals*, 21:892-893.
63. See text at 100.
64. See avalon.law.yale.edu/18th_century/nworder.asp.
65. *Ibid.*
66. *Ibid.*
67. Mitchell, *Compendium*, v-vi.
68. *Ibid.*
69. *Ibid.*
70. Mitchell, *Compendium*, v.
71. *McCulloch*, 17 US 400, 408.
72. See avalon.law.yale.edu/18th_century/washing.asp
73. *Ibid.*
74. 'Views', ¶5.

References

Primary Sources

Locke, John, *Essay Concerning Human Understanding* (London, 1689).

[Mitchell, S. Augustus] *Compendium of the Internal Improvement of the United States Comprising General Notices of all the Most Important Canals and Rail-Roads, throughout the Several States and Territories of the Union* (Philadelphia, PA, 1835).

Smith, Adam, *An Inquiry into the Nature and Causes of the Wealth of Nations* (Oxford, 1976; R.H. Campbell, A. S. Skinner and W.B. Todd, eds.; the 'Glasgow' edn). For details on pagination see text at 37.

Mill, James, 'Essay on Government' (1820) *in The Political Writings of James Mill*. See oll.libertyfund.org/titles/2520

Secondary Sources

Aschenbrenner, Peter, *British and American Foundings of Parliamentary Science, 1774-1801* (Abingdon-on-Thames, Oxfordshire, UK, 2017).

Aschenbrenner, Peter, 'Can Nation-states Self-stabilize? From Aristotle through Adam Smith to Hans Kelsen', *Journal of Parliaments, Estates & Representation*, vol. 41, no. 3 (December 2021), 259–279. doi.org/10.1080/02606755.2021.1949567.

Aschenbrenner, Peter, 'Tracing the Sources of Parliamentary Procedure in the French Constitution of 3-4 September 1791', *Journal of Parliaments, Estates & Representation*, vol. 39, no. 2 (July 2019), 184–201. doi.org/10.1080/02606755.2019.1595380.

David Currie, *The Constitution in Congress: The Jeffersonians* (Chicago, IL, 2001).

Dippel, Horst, ed., *Constitutions of the World from the Late 18th Century to the Middle of the 19th Century* (Munich and Berlin, 2004–2014; 47 vols; with numerous other editors).

Isenberg, Nancy, *Fallen Founder, The Life of Aaron Burr* (New York, NY, 2007).

5 'There Is More Than One Mode of Accomplishing the End'

'An act of the State of Georgia authorizes a duty of three pence per ton for clearing the river Savannah'

At mid-century, the United States ranked its states and territories from sea to sea with the admission of California (1850) and Oregon (1859) to the Union. New modes of transportation and communication were put to work uniting the Second Republic into a single market. The steamboat and railroad entered commercial use in the US (1807, 1831).[1] Samuel F.B. Morse demonstrated the telegraph to be a feasible means of instantaneous communication (1844).[2] In the interval 1805–1865, Congress enacted a total 4,834 public bills and resolutions into law.[3] The 9th Congress (1806–1808) and the 38th Congress (1863–1865) serve as end points for this survey. The 26th Congress (1839–1841) passed the fewest bills. These totaled 55 public bills and resolutions. Knowledgeable readers will not be surprised that the 37th Congress (1861–1863) passed the most bills and resolutions; the total is 428. It probably wasn't a good idea for Southern Congressmen to stage their walkout in 1861, if raw totals of legislative product matter. From 1805 to 1864 no Congress proposed a constitutional amendment to state legislatures (for their ratification) that states then ratified.

During the Monroe administration (1817–1825), the build out of the Second Republic gathered speed. Congress successfully obtained the cooperation of state, local and private actors and bodies. I term these 'institution agents'. They assisted Congress in fulfilling (a) service missions (transportation, communication) or (b) mission specific tasks (harbor improvements at Savannah and Philadelphia[4]). These state and private institution agents joined the ranks of federal employees that Congress commanded (engineers, commissioners) along with federal contractors that executive branch departments hired (Department of War, Post Office Department) or lesser federal entities (General Land Office, Army Corps of Engineers). Institution agents shared a common appetite for cash, land and other benefits that Congress commanded. What was the principal source of federal revenue? In the interval 1817–1825 customs

DOI: 10.4324/9781003019381-6

duties on British industrial and luxury goods funded the expansion of the federal government.[5] In other words, when Americans satisfied their need for imported goods, they also bought themselves a national government committed to giving them more *of what it thought* they needed.[6] Put another way, when US households bought Chippendale furniture and US printers purchased Koenig & Bauer steam-powered presses from UK manufacturers, they effectively supported the economic ambitions of the federal government, whose ambitions – as this study shows – readily crossed over the divide between the public and private sectors.[7]

I introduce the concept of 'autonomy rental'. At times, actors and bodies in political society might take offense at official action that they regarded as negatively impacting their interests (tastes, wants). In these cases, actors or bodies conducted themselves as if they had an investment in political society worth defending. Put another way, government officials rightly assumed that those impacted by their official conduct (misconduct or non-feasance) would respond to these acts or omissions as insults to their autonomy. Only by renting the autonomy of individuals (households, businesses) could officials assure themselves that they would receive signals of displeasure at their behavior. Negative signals gave officials their cues to adjust policies or double-down and plow ahead.

How did this play out in the immediate post-Ghent interval? What were the instances in which actors or bodies conducted themselves as if it was worthwhile for them to challenge official conduct that (they believed) negatively impacted their autonomy? I break this out as follows: (a) Congress passed a bill. (b) Another actor or body in political society challenged the Act of Congress. (c) Congress revisited the issues that this challenge raised. (i) Congress then retreated and conceded the merits of the challenge, *or* (ii) Congress engaged in temporizing action (such as amending the enactment challenged) *or* (iii) Congress doubled down and moved forward, even if it also accommodated (in some respects) the merits of the challenge. The following schema outlines the key points that votarian discipline exposed:

- initial enactment by Congress,
- challenge by another actor or body to the Act of Congress and
- reassessment and further action by Congress.

I surveyed seven challenges that took place during the interval 1815 to 1824.

- The (first iteration of the) Second Bank Bill (1815),
- The Congressional Pay Rise bill (1816),
- The Bonus Bill (1817),
- The *McCulloch* case involving the Second Bank (1819),
- The Missouri Compromise (1820),

- The Cumberland Road Repair bill (1822) and
- The *Gibbons* case involving Hamilton's anti-smuggling scheme (1824).

'Indications, in different modes, of the general will of the nation'

On 30 January 1815, President Madison challenged Congress after that body enacted its first version of the Second Bank's charter. Madison referred to 'repeated recognitions under varied circumstances of the validity of such an institution in acts of the legislative, executive, and judicial branches of the Government, accompanied by indications, in different modes, of a concurrence of the general will of the nation'.[8] Madison did not gather data to support this fact-testable proposition. In 1816 Congress acknowledged the validity of Madison's challenge, revised the bill, passed it and Madison signed it.[9]

In 1816, voters challenged Congress after that body enacted the bill granting members of Congress a pay rise. Madison approved it. In 1817 Congress acknowledged the validity of the challenge and repealed the offending law, which Madison also approved.[10]

On 3 March 1817, President Madison challenged Congress after that body passed the Bonus Bill. In the course of his veto message Madison referred to 'insufficient precedents' to justify enactment.[11] On 14 March 1818 the House of Representatives adopted a resolution that outlined a narrower version of Congress's power to launch improvement projects, implicitly accepting a measure of Madison's criticism.[12] I supply further details in Appendix K: Notes on the Bonus Bill (Act of March 3, 1817) and the 1818 House Resolution (14 March 1818).

In 1818, the state of Maryland challenged Congress's enactment of a bill establishing the Second Bank. In 1819 the United States Supreme Court referred to 'the practice of the Government', stating that 'an exposition of the Constitution, deliberately established by legislative acts ought not to be lightly disregarded'. The state of Maryland was forced to accept the Supreme Court's approval of Congress's 1816 enactment: Congress could charter the Second Bank.[13]

In 1820, Congress authorized the Territory of Missouri to call a constitutional convention and adopt a constitution for Congress's review. I refer to the Missouri Enabling Act.[14] The Missouri convention inserted a clause challenging Congress's authority over interstate travel.[15] In 1821 Congress stripped the clause of offensive meaning by inserting text to that effect in the resolution admitting Missouri to the Union.[16]

On 4 May 1822, Congress converted a national road into a pay-to-travel highway; revenue from tolls would be exclusively directed to road repairs. President Monroe challenged the bill by surveying similar legislation. The acts of Congress he surveyed did not install tollgates and tollhouses. Congress acknowledged its mistake by passing a revised version of the Cumberland Road repair bill in 1823. The revised bill did not include such structures.[17]

On 18 February 1793, Congress enacted a bill requiring registration of vessels sailing the coasts of the United States. New York challenged the law by establishing a state-licensed cartel that claimed exclusive control over *inter*state and *intra*state navigable waters.[18] In *Gibbons v. Ogden*, 22 US (9 Wheat.) 186 (1824), the Supreme Court declared that New York lacked the power to regulate traffic on the surface of navigable waters, whether *inter*state or *intra*state (2 March 1824).[19]

I summarize the foregoing points. Voters in the 1816 biennial elections were willing – and eager, on Thomas Jefferson's account[20] – to go to the polls to disapprove an Act of Congress. Other actors and bodies took advantage of circumstances and objected to federal action. These objections were stimulated, at least in part, by the number and cost of programs launched and the resulting pace of change in organic arrangements. In the seventeenth and eighteenth centuries, two investigators considered the optimal rate of change in political society. These investigators laid the intellectual groundwork for the Second Republic's aggressive approach to self-directed evolution. I note, however, that these two investigators would be surprised to learn that their studies supplied the methodological foundation for an ambitious republic to proclaim its ambitions and structure the pathways it designed to fulfill these self-declared destinies.

'A chronological view of our laws and their successive mutations'

Wm. Blackstone surveyed instances of organic change in his *Commentaries on the Laws of England* (1765–1769). He gathered his data sets within the final chapter of his *Commentaries*, Book IV, Chapter 33. Blackstone titled this essay 'Of the Rise, Progress and Gradual Improvements, of the Laws of England'.[21] Blackstone gathered surveys of 'gradual improvements'. He arranged time-slices beginning in pre-Norman times and concluding in 1765, the year that he began to send volumes of his *Commentaries* to press. The last of Blackstone's intervals (from 1688 to 1765) gathered data from 16 Acts of Parliament, four instances of executive acquisition of power and 15 instances of judicial reform. Blackstone computed 'successive mutations at different periods of time'.[22] In total Blackstone's survey gathered 35 changes in the most recent 77-year interval. This worked out to one instance of 'organic change' (my term) or 'mutation' (Blackstone's) every 2.2 years. The Vinerian furnished the reader 'an historical review of the most remarkable changes and alterations, that have happened in the laws of England'.[23] As surveyed and arranged, Blackstone's approach would enable him to mark out 'outlines of an English juridical history, by taking a chronological view of the state of our laws, and their successive mutations at different periods of time'.[24] Blackstone's ultimate purpose was to examine the quality of lawmaking, that is, 'to demonstrate the elegant proportion' of the whole body of laws. The scope of his pattern-discovering swept in both statutes and holdings in cases that appellate courts had decided. This project enabled Blackstone to evaluate the 'harmonious concurrence of those several parts'. He took care to underscore that his *Commentaries* did not 'conceal' the 'faults' that he assigned to British political society. He passed off these 'defects' as 'chiefly arising from the decays of time, or the rage of unskillful improvements in later ages'.[25]

Blackstone's survey omitted significant events in his survey of 'Gradual Improvements' (1688 to 1765). He noticed few programmatic achievements other than the creation of a 'standing army' which he noted – with sincere disdain – as a 'vast acquisition of force'.[26] Blackstone omitted events in any foreign theatre, despite the regular outbreak of foreign wars from 1688/1689 forward. Rebellions (1716, 1745) also went unnoticed. I suggest that a smaller number of 'mutations' was more consistent with his purposes. A greater number of elements in any data set, as a matter of methodology, would render it more difficult to demonstrate the harmony and elegance that Blackstone hoped to expose in the evolution of 'English laws'.

I draw on Blackstone's survey of organic changes to measure the Second Republic's rate of change. The US ratified 12 constitutional amendments in 13 years (1791–1804). Taken as changes in organic arrangements, the US rate of change computed to .92 changes per year. From 1804 to 1864, however, the US ratified no constitutional amendments. We might generously concede the boost Jerome Bonaparte and his Baltimore bride (almost) gave to this dismal total. I refer to the not-quite-ratified Titles of Nobility Amendment.[27] The US rate of change – accordingly – computes to .178 changes per year over the interval 1791–1864. This paltry rate would leave Wm. Blackstone thoroughly unimpressed. On his side of the pond, the Vinerian computed that .45 'mutations' transpired each calendar year. The cumulative British score is 35 changes in organic arrangements in 77 years (1688–1765).[28] 'You're probably not counting statutes and court decisions', Blackstone would sniff at the US's feeble count. 'The Industrial Revolution – now running at full tilt in your nineteenth century – surely obliges the US to bring in more, not fewer, of my "Gradual Improvements".' Madison, Monroe and Marshall would agree. Blackstone anticipated their searches for precedents. Pattern-discovering, they would agree, grounded their conclusions regarding the 'practice of government'.[29]

'Time discovers day after day new inconveniencies and doth successively apply new remedies'

Blackstone was not the first investigator to study the rate of change in political society. I refer to an essay attributed to Sir Matthew Hale (1609–1676) who enjoyed a long and distinguished career, capped by his service as Chief Justice of King's Bench. In 1787 the antiquarian Francis Hargrave published 'A Collection of Tracts relative to the Law of England ...'. Hargrave attributed to Hale an essay (appearing in that collection) titled 'Considerations Touching The Amendment Or Alteration of Lawes' (1690).[30] There may be more of Hale's essays to be recovered.[31] Garden-variety lawmaking drew Hale's attention. Hale divided his examination of lawmaking within three headings.

1 Concerning the several extreams relating to the amendment and alteration of lawes; and therein touching the extreame in the excesse of over hastiness and forwardness to alteration in lawes.
2 Touching the reasons and grounds, that ordinarily move men to this excess and itching after changes in laws.
3 Touching the other extreame, the over-tenacious holding of lawes, not withstanding apparent necessity for and safety in the change; the danger and occasions thereof.[32]

Given that Hale lived through the Civil War, the Protectorate and into the Restoration, one would suppose that Hale would have plenty to say about large-scale changes in British political society. These events did not interest Hale. Instead, Hale directed his attention to garden variety legislation and the holdings of appellate courts. I total Hale's references to 'common law' (1) and 'common laws/common lawes' (18 + 95 = 113) at 114 mentions. I tease three functions from Hale's essay 'Considerations Touching The Amendment Or Alteration of Lawes'. (a) A parliamentary assembly considers a bill that, if enacted, will add a new law to a body of existing laws within a given subject matter area. A parliamentary assembly's consideration of such a bill employs a 'successive' function. (b) In composing a new statute or amending or altering a law already in the statute books, lawmakers must also harmonize the bill's text with the contents of an existing body of laws. That is, they must employ a 'cumulative' function; Hale defines this as a 'kind of aggregation of the discoveries results and applications of ages and events'.[33] (c) Finally – and this is Hale's most explicit recommendation – lawmakers should ask themselves if the new law would be a suitable addition to the existing body of laws. I call this a 'quality assurance' function.

> So that in truth ancient lawes, especially, that have a common concern, are not the issues of the prudence of this or that council or senate, but they are the production of the various experiences and applications of the wisest thing in the inferior world; to wit, time, which as it discovers day after day new inconveniencies, so it doth successively apply new remedies: and indeed it is a kind of aggregation of the discoveries results and applications of ages and events; so that it is a great adventure to go about to alter it, without very

great necessity, and under the greatest demonstration of safety and convenience imaginable.[34]

Hale's 'Considerations' offered the following guidance to lawmakers. It was a parliamentary assembly's job to see that the provisions of a bill would change the existing body of laws 'for the better'.[35] The assembly, Hale also declared, should set its sights on the 'greatest demonstration of safety and convenience imaginable'.[36] By weighing choices, the legislative assembly will commit itself to improve statutory text. Hale envisioned this as an intramural effort. Hale assumed that the lawmakers (in a parliamentary assembly, such as the House of Commons) could sort issues – and thereby launch or curate programmatic action – without interacting with anyone else in political society. Hale's key recommendation? MPs should engage in 'a kind of aggregation of the discoveries results and applications of ages and events'.[37] I have previously termed this an introspective or contemplative function. 'The contemplative moment must be isolated from the noise of day-to-day life'.[38]

In assigning no role to another actor or body, Hale did not take into account review of bills or enactments by executive leaders, review by another legislative body or review by a national court system for corrective purposes. Likewise, Hale's functions did not take into account voter approval, disapproval or acquiescence/non-disapproval of an assembly's text-writing efforts. Blackstone, following Hale's lead, offered lawmakers only vague guidance, warning them against 'unskillful improvements'. Other than pattern-discovering, Blackstone offered no technical analysis to guide lawmakers when they took up bills that may – or may not – produce acceptable 'gradual improvements' to a nation's organic arrangements.[39] Like Hale, votarian discipline did not play a role in Blackstone's understanding of the constraints that operated when lawmakers went to work.

To sum up this point: parliamentary assemblies were obliged to exploit opportunities for lawmaking – arising from 'complications and emergencies' – into laws amounting to something more than a heap of Hale's 'suitable remedies and cures'.[40] But it was Adam Smith – and not Blackstone and Hale – who supplied a full-throated methodology. Smith promoted legislative competence as a goal that could be achieved by employment of his productivity analytics.[41] I turn now to challenges exposed by employment of Smith's productivity analytics.

'Men may enlist without a bounty; and if they will not, they may be drafted'

There will be times when a parliamentary assembly – in debating a bill crafted to launch a program – discovers that its lawmakers have in hand more than one acceptable means of getting the job done. In such a case an assembly will be compelled to choose between two (or more) equal-in-merit means of delivering benefits. This should not be too surprising. After all, it is likely that one of Hale's 'complications and emergencies' will give lawmakers a chance to choose between two bills, each of which promises 'suitable remedies and cures'.[42] I draw on Marshall's analysis as follows. Members of the assembly may employ Smithian productivity analytics when considering how to fill out the ranks of the nation's armed forces. (a) The Secretary of War should offer a bounty to enlistees or (b) the Secretary of War should draft men. That is, both the bounty and the draft satisfy the 'maxims' that Smith detailed in Book V, Chapter II, Part II of his *Wealth of Nations*.[43] If competing choices are possible, then it might be useful (or necessary) for an independent actor to pick one of these two courses of action. In two of his 'Friend' essays, John Marshall gave detailed attention the problem that I have outlined. I refer to essays going under the title 'Friend to the Union II' (Marshall replies to Amphictyon) and 'Friend of the Constitution I' (Marshall replies to Hampden). The following three points set up Marshall's dissection of Amphictyon's argument on the subject:

- The energy that the bill proposes to expend is too little.
- The energy that the bill proposes to expend is too much.
- The bill proposes to expend a quantum of energy that is 'just right'. Or close enough to 'just right' for everyone to stop arguing about how to get closer to an optimal quantum.

Opponents of a given bill may argue that the bill proposes to spend excess energy. On this account opponents will argue that there is some lesser quantum of energy that could/should be expended. Therefore, the bill should be amended to ratchet down the quantum of energy that the institution agent will be permitted to consume in fulfilling its mission. I tidy up Amphictyon's argument as follows. The optimal value of an independent variable (on which all else is made to depend) is that which is the 'least consumptive of energy'. This is my phrase. In Marshall's rethreading of his opponent's reasoning, Amphictyon denied that Congress should enjoy a 'choice of means'. Amphictyon restricted 'means ... in each case [to that] which is most direct and simple'.[44] Putting Amphictyon's hard and fast rule into practice, ordered discourse (on the bounty/draft issue) would play out as follows.

> Undoubtedly there are other means for raising an army. Men may enlist without a bounty; and if they will not, they may be drafted. A bounty, then, according to Amphictyon, is unconstitutional, because the power may be executed by a draft; and a draft is unconstitutional, because the power may be executed by a bounty.[45]

A majority of lawmakers in a parliamentary assembly, Marshall assumed, possessed the competence to craft semi-regimented sentences that limit institution-agent effort and, therefore, to avoid energy-wasting. Amphictyon's argument is, however, an invitation to lawmakers to waste a vast amount of *their* energy. As Marshall correctly concludes, Amphictyon's argument reduces to an 'impracticable, and consequently an erroneous rule'.[46] I note in the margin that Amphictyon channeled Zeno's paradox of motion by reviving the paradox in his (Amphictyon's) phrase 'choice of means'. Aristotle noted this paradox in his *Physics*.[47] When Amphictyon argued that 'the right of Congress to pass laws ... excludes the choice of means', he committed a parliamentary assembly to waste its energy in a search for the single 'most direct and simple' instruction that it could give to its institution agents. This instruction would guarantee that the assembly's agent will spend the least quantum of energy. Amphictyon's position on 'choice of means' choked legislative effort to the purpose of starving its agents. Marshall's 'choice of means' opened the way to methodological advance.

The reader will have noticed that if a constitution generates multiple, unique solutions to a problem – without also providing a tie-breaking function – then solutions (so generated) should be regarded as not provable in the logical system that underpins the constitution. As Amphictyon understands constitutional instruments, they can't generate more than one unique solution to problems. Every solution (statute, resolution) must trace its ancestry to a constitutional instrument. Amphictyon argues that one and only one interpretation of constitution text is valid. Put another way, a solution that a constitution generates is a *singularity* and has an exclusive claim to be *constitutionally* valid. Extending Amphictyon's reasoning: an instrument that can generate multiple and therefore competing solutions is not a constitution. Assuming Amphictyon is right about the logic underpinning constitutions, there is no need for anyone – presidents, another house of the legislature, a supreme court or voters – to review bills that a parliamentary body passes by reference to constitutional text. If there is an alternative solution that appears to possess merit equal to the bill that the legislature has adopted, then *both* solutions are invalid. Hence, 'choice of means' revives (or revisits, your choice) organic paralysis.

'The government the American people have established become an inanimate corpse, incapable of effecting any objects'

In his second series of essays, titled 'Friend of the Constitution' Marshall took aim at Hampden's attack on Marshall's exposition of the method of Congressional precedents.[48] In the remainder of this paragraph, I rely on Marshall's restatement of Hampden's points. The purpose of Marshall's method was to 'bolster up the most unconstitutional measures of the most abandoned of our rulers ... and ratify, one by one, the legislative infractions of the constitution'.[49] Moreover, 'the time may soon arrive when the constitution may be expounded without even looking into it – by merely reading the acts of a renegado congress'.[50] If Congress relied on the 'force of [its] precedents', Marshall rethreaded Hampden's attack, Congress would become 'incapable of effecting any of [the] objects' of Article I, Section 8, Clause 1.[51] That provision invoked such 'objects' as 'domestic tranquility', 'general welfare' and the 'blessings of liberty'.[52] The end result of Marshall's method, according to Hampden, would be that the 'government which the American people have ordained and established [will] become an inanimate corpse'.[53]

On this account Marshall skewered Hampden, not once, but twice. (a) Congress might be tempted to give up the ghost, so to speak, and declare itself 'incapable of effecting ... objects' such as 'promoting the general welfare'. Congress's previously enacted laws, however, supply no 'precedents' that would authorize a civil government to commit suicide. (b) On the other hand, the instinct to survive is a powerful force in political society. But it is not a force that, on its own, can guide and govern a parliamentary assembly whose immediate task is to settle on a single viable proposal, one that lawmakers select from candidates of equal merit. Here Marshall has rethreaded his argument against Amphictyon's 'choice of means' and refashioned it to the purpose of defeating Hampden. In his 'Friend of the Constitution II' essay, Marshall accepted that the 'American people' will assign the powers of the Second Republic to satisfy their tastes and interests.

> The people are as much interested, their liberty is as deeply concerned, in preventing encroachments on that government, in arresting the hands which would tear from it the powers they have conferred upon it, as in restraining it within its constitutional limits.[54]

US organic arrangements, Marshall declared, established 'that division of which its framers, and the American people, believed to be most conducive to the public happiness and to public liberty'.[55] As of 1819, Marshall argued, it was up to the American people – the framers of *Constitution II* were unavailable for tie-breaking efforts, having retired from public service or entered into mortality – to employ their collective assessments of the state of their 'public happiness' and 'public liberty' when voting in biennial elections. These assessments would reliably guide them to re-establish 'equipoise' between the federal and state governments. Marshall thereby offered an organic pedigree for the 'equipoise' that voters would reliably restore. To Marshall's way of thinking, this concept should quiet objections to Congress's employment of patterns of its past lawmaking as an aid to composing new laws.

> The equipoise thus established is as much disturbed by taking weights out of the scale containing the powers of the government, as by putting weights into it.[56]

Constitution II, Marshall argued, properly tasked voters with the kinetic effort of taking and putting 'weights [into and] out of the scale containing the powers of the government'. For example, it would be up to voters to put steamboat-safe rivers into the scales 'containing the powers of government' and remove federally-funded postal services. Marshall's two essays – 'Friend to the Union' and 'Friend of the Constitution' – concentrated attention on questions arising from allocation of 'powers of the government' between the unitary and parochial governments. Marshall argued that those participants in political society – who were the immediate and ultimate beneficiaries of *any* government's programmatic action – were best qualified to resolve disputes over allocation of powers. The arc of Marshall's trajectory – traced above – took him from inefficiency to efficiency, from deadlock to equipoise, from the work of lawmakers to the work of voters.

'Government is a contrivance of human wisdom to provide for human wants'

The experience of voting must be viewed within the framing supplied by an individual voter's experience as a consumer. I have previously referred to the following passage from Edmund Burke's *Reflections on the Revolution in France*. 'Government is a contrivance of human wisdom to provide for human wants'.[57] At the opening of Marshall's 'A Friend of the Constitution I', the Chief Justice declared that the prosperity of Americans was 'inseparable from the preservation of this government'.[58] Votarian mechanics offered the voter an opportunity to link the fortunes of his household or business with the greater goal of promoting the 'prosperity of the American people'.[59] Voting for your economic interests, in other words, promoted the long-term interests – and survival – of unitary government. The method of Congressional precedents assumed that voters could be motivated to play an essential role in three critical stages during any given two-year Congress. These stages were marked by (a) lawmaker enactment, followed by (b) voter assessment of lawmaker product at the polls, thereafter stimulating (c) lawmaker assessment of election returns.[60]

- Lawmakers assess inhabitants' needs. They devise programmatic action to fulfill service missions. The following filter operates. Lawmakers' efforts must produce semi-regimented sentences.
- Voters assess their gets and their not-gets. The following filter operates. When voters go to the polls their collective assessment must be

filtered through candidates in, candidates out and candidates back in.

- Lawmakers assess voters' wants. Lawmakers' post-election assessment is filtered through election returns.

In his article 'Government' published in the Encyclopedia Britannica (Supplement, 1820) James Mill concentrated his attention on the negative role of voters. In so doing, Mill declared a 'doctrine of checks'.[61] In the margin, I borrow from the ever-quotable Sir Lewis Namier on this point.[62] Mill tasked 'doctrine of checks' to deliver 'goodness', thereby isolating the fortunes of government from voters' bad behavior. Mill did not appreciate that a negative check might have some difficulty producing a result that qualified as 'goodness'. Nevertheless, he declared that 'all goodness of government depends [on the] right constitution of checks'. 'In the grand discovery of modern times, the system of representation, the solution of all the difficulties, both speculative and practical, will perhaps be found. If it cannot, we seem to be forced upon the extraordinary conclusion, that good government is impossible'.[63]

'Voting is another efficient way of aggregating information and more generally ideas, reflections'

Two standards measured the acceptable level of pain (insult, discomfort, pressure) that would reliably motivate voters to participate in votarian mechanics. (a) Garden variety programs reliably engaged the pocketbook interests of consumers. This type of programmatic action delivered benefits in the form of productivity gains. James Monroe warned that the government crossed a red line when it went 'too far' in its demands on the pocketbooks of households or businesses.[64] (b) In launching programmatic action government should also take care that these programs do not infringe on 'the great principles of liberty'.[65] 'If it is a doubtful question', John Marshall declared, 'one on which human reason may pause and the human judgment be suspended, in the decision of which the great principles of liberty are not concerned, but the respective powers of those who are equally the representatives of the people, are to be adjusted'.[66] I will return to the impact on the 'liberty interest' of individuals in Chapter 7, this volume.

I illustrate voter pocketbook interests via the following counter-factual. A nation's inhabitants raise no objection to the rate at which households and businesses pay taxes. They are positively inert when offered their chance to go to the polls and vote incumbents out of office. Their lazy behavior licenses inefficiencies in the operations of the government and invites lawmakers to indulge in increasing levels of corruption and apathy. 'If voters don't care about James Mills's "good government",' politicians will assume, 'then why should we care?'[67] To expand on this point, I revisit Adam Smith's family of modest means. Inhabitants 'enjoy ... the protection of the state', for which they contribute 'as nearly as possible, in proportion to their respective abilities'.[68] The working conjecture here is that voters with a stake in the stability of government are more likely to go to the polls (if they enjoy the franchise) and assess lawmakers' performance. On the other hand, lifeless behavior on the part of voters pushes the current form of representative government towards collapse. Do single issue voters, single party voters and those voting against their economic interests corrupt the operation of the votarian mechanics that have been described (in economic/kinetic terms) above?

A modern authority, Thomas Piketty, writing on wealth and income inequality, observes that 'voting is another efficient way of aggregating information (and more generally ideas, reflections, etc.)'.[69] Could the technocrats of the early Second Republic devise a role that exploited the 'talents and information possessed by millions'?

> The idea that private property and the market allow (under certain conditions) for the coordination and efficient use of the talents and information possessed by millions of individuals is a classic that one finds in the work of Adam Smith.[70]

Voter-consumers, representing the inhabitants, would be obliged, on Piketty's account, to express their hopes, wishes and fears to public officials. These voters must be assured that what they have to say is worth listening to. Put another way, the reason why voting and consuming may be merged, one into another, is that this merger enhances the probability that what voters say to the politicians matters to both the politicians and voters. First, the lens inflates. Everyone's 'ideas, reflections' matter, just as Piketty postulates. Second, the lens deflates. The filter candidates in, out and back in goes to work. This is the sieve that Marshall and Monroe put to work in their method of Congressional precedents.

If a voter cared to voice his opinion of the work of the first session of a given Congress, he would find a way to ballot his programmatic preferences *even if* these preferences were filtered through formalized choices, i.e., names of candidates logged into the county sheriff's electoral register. The double effect of these two filters made sense to those working in the public sector. Energy savings (efficiencies) could be attained if lawmakers gave careful consideration to signals that encouraged programmatic action. The working engine of votarian discipline was fueled by incentives that inspired voters to (a) rotate candidates in and out of the office *and at the same time* (b) populate tables of election returns so that (at least) officials could assess voter non-disapproval of policies adopted in the legislative assembly. This was how Congress expected to hear and respond to the inhabitants' voices, acting through voter-consumers, who were their immediate representatives. Put another way, both Congress and inhabitants exploited energy-savings measures. John Marshall and James Monroe took a comprehensive view of the dual roles of voters and lawmakers. In their view, they were mutually supporting. Legislative competence was challenged and augmented by voter-consumer participation in the system. As the Industrial Revolution unfolded, Congress effectively called on voters to respond to the more sophisticated forms of programmatic action that it was adopting. As I have described it, this reciprocal discipline encouraged voters and lawmakers to regard each other as partners in building out the Second Republic.[71]

'They forgot they were not in Westminster Hall'

My next voice is that of John Randolph of Roanoke (1773–1833). I call on Randolph to critique the acquisition and refinement of legislative and administrative competence during the Monroe administration. In the 6th Congress (1799–1801), Randolph served in both the House of Representatives and Senate. At the time of his death, Randolph was serving his 12th term in the House of Representatives.

Randolph appears in this study as the leading apologist for the superminoritarian position. Randolph wins my (grudging) respect as the majoritarians' most implacable and most articulate foe. In 1824 Randolph took aim at the bill proposing 'Surveys for Roads and Canals'. This would become known as the General Survey Act, discussed above.[72] I draw on his speech of 30 January 1824.[73] Randolph understood the challenge facing remote communities and regions. The Congressman offered himself as their champion, referring to the 'accumulated pressure' by which Congress pushed change up to the doorposts of remote businesses and households.[74] When Randolph spoke of 'the power that we are now about to exercise', as noted above, he was referring to the bill that would become the General Survey Act.[75] 'This vagrant power, (of making roads and canals)'[76] targeted those inhabitants residing 'south of Mason and Dixon's line, and east of the Alleghany mountains'.[77]

I sketch Randolph's principal arguments as follows. First, the Congressman referred to 'the original design of this Government. It grew out of the necessity, indispensable and unavoidable, in the circumstances of this country, of some general power, capable of regulating foreign commerce'.[78] Second, he appealed to the 'two distinct governments' formula.[79] 'The question for every honest man to ask himself, is, to which of these two divisions of Government does the power in contest belong ... the one general in its nature, the other internal. ... Now, sir, a government may be admirable for external, and yet execrable for internal purposes'.[80] I combine these points. A government that did more than regulate 'foreign commerce' was very likely to engage in 'execrable ... internal purposes', such as 'making roads and canals'.

'Our Government', Randolph argued, 'is not like the consolidated monarchies of the Old World'.[81] Turning to supporters of surveys for 'roads and canals' – the purpose of the General Survey Act – Randolph accused these colleagues of 'apery of foreign manner, and of foreign fashions – from a miserable attempt at the shabby genteel, which only serves to make our poverty more conspicuous'.[82] Emer de Vattel (1714–1767), a Swiss scholar, trained in international law, composed *The Law of Nations; or, Principles of the Law of Nature, applied to the Conduct and Affairs of Nations and Sovereigns* (1760).[83] Vattel's study was promptly translated from French to English. Vattel paid careful attention to the practice of governments, that is, their interactions, broken down topic by topic and surveyed accordingly. In this regard, Vattel offered a foretaste of the method of congressional precedents that Marshall and Monroe developed. Randolph took aim at 'the doctrine of the European writers on civil polity. ... When gentlemen get up and quote Vattel', Randolph continued, 'as applicable to the power of the Congress of the United States, I should as soon have expected them to quote Aristotle or the Koran'.[84] References to Vattel, quite naturally, brought Randolph's prose to the boil. 'This Government is the breath of the nostrils of the States', he argued. 'It is in the power of the States to extinguish this Government at a blow'. [85]

Randolph's speech is not pretty. Events transpiring in the last century have rendered his references to mass murder and suicide more repulsive. As victims of federal oppression, Randolph whinged, the sufferings of Southerners will oblige us 'to make up our mind to perish like so many mice in a receiver of mephitic gas, under the experiments of a set of new political chemists'.[86] Randolph's argument, on this point, reduced to the claim that self-declared victimhood released his co-adherents from norms of civilized behavior. Randolph went so far as to welcome totalitarianism, provided that the velvet glove was not employed to conceal the iron hand. 'If gentlemen will come fairly out, said Mr. R., and tell us, you have given us the power of the purse and of the sword, and these two enable us to take whatever else we may want, we shall understand them'.[87] If the federal oppressors would only throw off the Monroevian mask, Randolph argued, his appeal to victimhood might appear in a sympathetic light. Randolph rallied his co-adherents in Maryland, Virginia, North and South Carolina, Georgia and Alabama. With the admission of Missouri as the 24th state of the Union, the superminoritarians' 'Maginot Line' was now on life-support. Taken in the lens of Article V, Randolph counted only six of 24 states in the Union in the superminoritarian camp.

Randolph's ebullitions of self-pity – the soul-sibling of victimhood – were never far from his mind. 'Let them look forward to the time when such a question shall arise, and tremble with me at the thought that question is to be decided by a majority of the votes of this House, of whom not one possesses the slightest ties of common interest or of common feeling with us'.[88] In an attempt to gin up some modest claim to productivity – on behalf of inhabitants of six states – Randolph claimed that residents of these states practiced 'the industry, the simplicity, the economy, and the frugality of our ancestors'.[89] Other Americans, he argued, should 'return to those habits of labor and industry from which we have thus departed'.[90] Presumably owners and workers in Northern factories, shipyards and coal mines did not offer any species of economic accomplishment worth Randolph's mention. In the margin I refer to Capt. Rhett Butler's unsuccessful attempt to explain the concept of unevenly distributed productivity gains to cinematically-portrayed adherents of John Randolph. The discussion takes place in Ashley Wilkes's drawing room.[91] As the reader may have guessed, Randolph's principal fear is that the federal government has acquired the power to emancipate 'every slave', presumably without reparations.[92]

> If Congress possesses the power to do what is proposed by this bill [surveys of national importance for roads and canals], they may not only enact a sedition law – for there is precedent – but they may emancipate every slave in the United States – and with stronger color of reason than they can exercise the power now contended for.[93]

Randolph might have asked himself this question. If Americans living north and west of Randolph's six states were motivated by 'greediness of gain', wasn't US political society doomed? Randolph explicitly declared that 'lavish expenditure' to satisfy private 'greediness' was acceptable, provided that Congress arranged for the 'faithful discharge of the public debt'.

> Let us, then, I repeat, Mr. Chairman, pay our debts, personal and public; let us leave the profits of labor in the pockets of the people, to rid them of the private embarrassment under which they so extensively suffer, and apply every shilling of the revenue, not indispensable to the exigencies of the Government, to the faithful discharge of the public debt, before we engage in any new schemes of lavish expenditure.[94]

I expose a point that lies just below the surface of Randolph's speech. It is inconsistent with a Southerner's loyalty to his home state to support federal programmatic action in the subject matter area (transportation networks). As Randolph argued, improvements in transportation will render remote communities subject to greater 'pressure' to conform to the center's demands that inhabitants abide by the center's preferred norms of behavior.[95] When Randolph claimed that some regions suffered 'encroachments', he sought to cut the connection between political science and social science. Southern belief – sincere or feigned – in 'accumulated pressure' granted immunity to residents of his favored six states. If other Congressmen roughly handled Randolph's beliefs and those of his co-adherents, a losing record (measured in votes in the House) would not shake Southerners' convictions. Being on the wrong end of a majority vote in the House of Representatives would offer Randolph and his fellow-believers confirmation that not a single colleague in the House 'possesses the slightest ties of common interest or of common feeling with us'.[96] In this spirit Randolph concluded his speech.

> We shall keep on the windward side of treason – but we must combine to resist, and that effectually, these encroachments, or the little upon which we now barely subsist will be taken from us. With these observations, Mr. R. abandoned the question to its fate.[97]

Conclusion

John Marshall appointed Henry Wheaton as the Supreme Court's reporter of decisions at the end of 1815. Wheaton was on board for the February 1816 term.[98] Wheaton promptly expressed his gratitude in the 'Preface' he composed and published in volume 14, the first volume of the United States Reports that he brought to press. The Supreme Court's 'doctrines have been developed by the court in a masterly manner; and we may contemplate with pride and satisfaction the structure which has been built up in so short a time, and under the circumstances so unpropitious to the development of the true principles of public law'.[99] Wheaton also drew the reader's attention to the passage in Francis Bacon's *Elements of the Common Lavves of England* (1630) which I have placed in the margin.[100]

On the occasion of Congress's purchase and publication of the *Papers of James Madison*, Sen. Asher Robbins (RI) remarked that 'I consider this work of Mr. MADISON, now proposed to be given to the world under the patronage of this Government, as the most valuable one to mankind that has appeared since the days when Bacon gave to the world his *Novum Organon*. That produced that revolution in analytics, which has occasioned the immense superiority of the moderns over the ancients in the knowledge of Nature, and in the improvement of the condition of human life – the fruit of that knowledge' (18 February 1837).[101] The Senator summed up the interest that Bacon's contributions to scientific method stimulated in the 'science of free government'.[102]

> As this Organon of Bacon has been the beacon-light of mankind to guide him to true philosophy, and to the improvement of his physical condition, so will this work of MADISON, as I trust and predict, be his beacon-light to guide him to the true science of free government,

> and to the improvement of his political condition;—the science of free government; the most difficult of all the sciences, by far the most difficult, while it is the most important to mankind; of all, the slowest in growth, the latest in maturity.[103]

Francis Bacon's preliminary invocation of a method of judicial precedents will be revisited in the final chapter of this study.[104] This attempt to build out a full-featured method (1847) is one more example of the appetite of technocrats and technically-adroit officials to exploit and advance Sen. Robbins 'revolution in analytics'. Looking forwards: template-creating appeared in the work of John Adams. Looking backwards, pattern-discovering appeared in the work of Matthew Hale, Wm. Blackstone, James Monroe and John Marshall. In legislative time, Adam Smith recommended his productivity analytics to the attention of lawmakers. Thomas Bayes and Richard Price offered the contest of true and false positives to lawmakers, obliging them to recalibrate the contingent probability of the success of their efforts.

I cumulate (a) the sheer volume of statutes that the Second Republic was enacting, (b) the connections between legislative and administrative action that these enactments stimulated and (c) the reliance of households and businesses on the expansion of the Second Republic. These interconnections made it impossible for opponents to dismantle the many accomplishments that the Second Republic was rapidly gathering to its credit. The republic's ambitions equaled its pretensions. Henry Wheaton's reference to Francis Bacon must have been most pleasing to John Marshall. And if Aristotle were quoted – if only to displease John Randolph – the reference Hellenic surely cast the Second Republic in a Eurocentric perspective of even grander proportions. No public or private intervention in the pathway to international recognition – short of civil war – could overthrow the legacy of Monroe and Marshall.

Notes

1. For Fulton's inaugural steamboat voyage to Albany (1807) see text at 24. For the inaugural journey of the Mohawk & Hudson's passenger service (1831), see Albany_and_Schenectady_Railroad [last retrieved 21 August 2021].
2. See www.loc.gov/collections/samuel-morse-papers/articles-and-essays/invention-of-the-telegraph Morse's 'line was completed in time for the dramatic and spectacularly successful link between the Supreme Court chamber of the Capitol building and the railroad station in Baltimore'. *Ibid.*
3. *Statistical Abstract*; Series P 40-49, Government Elections and Politics – Bills ... and Resolutions: 1789-1945.
4. 2 Stat 18, c. 15, Act of March 17, 1800, Section 1 ['the consent of Congress ... is granted to an act of the state of Georgia ... as authorizes a duty of three pence per ton on all shipping entering the port of Savannah, to be set apart as a fund for clearing the river Savannah'.].

5. *Statistical Abstract*, Series P 89-98 'Federal Government Finances... 1789-1945. In CY 1817 federal government receipts stood at $33,099,050. Of this total 'Customs (including tonnage tax)' figured $26,283,848.
6. Aschenbrenner, *Foundings*, 158-163 ['No longer content to supply the machinery of Burke's contrivance, the systems, structures and institutions of political society might aspire to become change agents, transforming the sphere in which inhabitants lived their daily lives and went about their daily business'. At 163].
7. See Printing_press [last retrieved 23 August 2021].
8. See millercenter.org/the-presidency/presidential-speeches/january-30-1815-veto-message-national-bank
9. See text at 59.
10. See text at 43-44.
11. See text at 44, 190.
12. See text at 190.
13. See text at 59-66.
14. 3 Stat 545, c. 22, Act of March 6, 1820.
15. See text at 109.
16. 3 Stat 645, Res. I, March 2, 1821.
17. See text at 45-46.
18. See text at 85.
19. See text at 82-86.
20. See text at 44, 56n37.
21. Blackstone, *Commentaries*, IV:400.
22. *Ibid.*
23. *Ibid.*
24. *Ibid.*
25. *Ibid.*, IV:436.
26. *Ibid.*, IV:434.
27. See Titles_of_Nobility_Amendment [last retrieved 23 May 2021].
28. Author count.
29. See text at 72, 109, 121.
30. Hargrave, *Collection*, 249-289.
31. I can find no record of publication earlier than 1787, when Hale's essay appears in Hargrave's 'Collection' with other materials. One of Hargrave's annotations (for the 1787 edition of Hale's essay) begins: 'in another manuscript of lord Hale on the Amendment of the Lawes, which seems to have been his first essay on the subject ...'. Hargrave, *Collection*, 275 n. 1.
32. *Ibid.*, 251.
33. *Ibid.*, 266.
34. Hale, 'Considerations', 254.
35. *Ibid.*, 256.
36. *Ibid.*, 254.
37. See text at 256.
38. Aschenbrenner, *Foundings*, 157; see also 15, 107-109.
39. See text at 110, 111.
40. Hale, 'Considerations', 254.
41. See text at 64-75.
42. Hale, 'Considerations', 254.
43. Marshall, *Defense*, 95.
44. Marshall, *Defense*, 93. 'The right of Congress to pass laws ... excludes the choice of means'.
45. *Ibid.*
46. *Ibid.*, 95.

47. Zeno was an early exponent of the fallacious argument that Amphictyon deployed against John Marshall. Zeno claimed that reducing the quantum of energy expended – as successive trials unfolded – would defeat any experiment in the motion of bodies. Motion (legislation) was, on this account, impossible. In the *Physics*, Aristotle savaged the so-called paradoxes attributed to Zeno. He did so by restating Zeno's position as follows. The 'non-existence of motion', Aristotle declared, was established by the fact that the object 'which is in locomotion must arrive at the halfway stage before it arrives at the goal'. Aristotle, *Physics*, 239b11. Placing Aristotle's passage in the hands of Marshall, every bill that suggests a 'direct and simple' means of accomplishing a legislative end will enable other legislators to propose a competing text promising an even more 'direct and simple' means. If lawmakers were encouraged (or licensed) to browbeat each other to spend a dollar less, Zeno argues, they would never settle on spending any amount of money on a program. Text-crafting, taken kinetically, as Aristotle insists that we must, is therefore impossible.
48. See text at 62.
49. Marshall, *Defense*, 156-157.
50. *Ibid.*
51. See text at 39.
52. Marshall, *Defense*, 160.
53. Marshall, *Defense*, 160.
54. *Ibid.*, 159-160
55. *Ibid.*, 150.
56. *Ibid.*
57. Burke, *Reflections*, 70.
58. Marshall, *Defense*, 155.
59. *Ibid.*
60. See text at 49, 156.
61. Mill, 'Essay'.
62. Namier, *Avenues*, 183. '"General Elections" are the locks on the streams of British democracy, controlling the flow of the river and its traffic'. Namier's metaphor is misdirected.
63. Mill, 'Essay'.
64. See text at 138.
65. See text at 72.
66. *McCulloch*, 17 US 400, 401.
67. See text at 117-118.
68. Smith, *Wealth*, 825.
69. Piketty, *Capital*, 744 n. 56.
70. *Ibid.*
71. See text at 112-113.
72. 4 Stat 22, c. 46, Act of April 30, 1824.
73. See memory.loc.gov/ammem/amlaw/lwaclink.html; *Annals*, 18th Congress, 1st Session, 1296-1311.
74. *Ibid.*, 1311.
75. See text at 82-83.
76. *Annals*, 18th Congress, 1st Session, 1300.
77. *Ibid.*, 1310.
78. *Ibid.*, 1299.
79. *Ibid.*, 1303.
80. *Ibid.*
81. *Ibid.*

82. *Ibid.*, 1298.
83. See h2o.law.harvard.edu/text_blocks/5340/export
84. *Annals*, 18th Congress, 1st Session, 1302.
85. *Ibid.*, 1299.
86. *Ibid.*, 1310.
87. *Ibid.*, 1300.
88. *Ibid.*
89. *Ibid.*
90. *Ibid.*
91. See youtube.com/watch?v=S72nI4Ex_E0
92. *Annals*, 18th Congress, 1st Session, 1308.
93. *Ibid.*
94. *Ibid.*, 1310
95. *Ibid.*, 1311.
96. See text at 122.
97. *Annals*, 18th Congress, 1st Session, 1311.
98. White, *Marshall Court*, 388 et seq.
99. Wheaton, *Preface*, iv [United States Reports, vol. 14]
100. With a minor typographic correction, Bacon's guidance to investigators reads as follows. 'I doe not finde that by mine own travell, without the help of authority, I can in any kinde conferre so profitable an addition unto that science, as by collecting the rules and grounds, dispersed throughout the body of the same lawes: for hereby no small light will be given in new cases, wherin the authorities doe square and vary, to confirme the Law, and to make it received one way, and in cases wherin the law is cleered by authority; yet neverthelesse to see more profoundly into the reason of such judgements and ruled cases, and thereby to make more use of them for the decision of other cases more doubtfull'.
101. *Congressional Globe (Appendix)*, 24th Congress, 2nd Session, 187-188 [Remarks of Sen. Robbins].
102. *Ibid.*
103. *Ibid.*
104. See text at 159-161.

References

Primary Sources

Aristotle, *The Politics* (New York, NY, 1941; trans. B. Jowett) in *The Basic Works of Aristotle* (R. McKeon, ed. in chief). My references employ Bekker citations. These citations appear in McKeon's edition as well as in the Loeb Library edition of *The Politics* (Cambridge, MA, 1932; trans. H. Rackham). For scholarship on the manuscript tradition, I refer the reader to W. Jaeger, *Aristotle, Fundamental of the History of his Development* (Oxford, 1934; trans R. Robinson), 259–292, 'The Original *Politics*'.

Aristotle, *The Physics* (New York, NY, 1941; trans. R.P. Hardie and R.K. Gaye) in *The Basic Works of Aristotle*; R. McKeon, ed. in chief). I employ Bekker citations.

Bacon, Francis, *The Elements of the Common Lavves of England, Branched into a Double Tract: The one Containing a Collection of Some Principal Rules and Maximes of the Common Law, with their Latitude and Extent. Explicated for the more facile introduction of such as are studiously addicted to that noble profession. ...* (London, 1630; Google Books scanned the 1639 edition; the English Short Title Catalogue has 'lavves' for 'laws').

Blackstone, William, *Commentaries on the Laws of England* (Chicago, IL: University of Chicago Press, 1979; facsimile of the 1st edn published 1765–1769; 4 vols; Stanley N. Katz, ed.).

Burke, Edmund, *Reflections on the Revolution in France* (1790), in oll.libertyfund.org/title/canavan-select-works-of-edmund-burke-vol-2; HTML version used; original pagination in [] single brackets.

Hale, Matthew, 'Considerations Touching The Amendment Or Alteration of Lawes' (1690) in *A Collection of Tracts relative to the Law of England* (London, 1787; Francis Hargrave, ed.).

Harrington, James, *The Oceana and Other Works* (London, 1771); see https://oll-resources.s3.us-east-2.amazonaws.com/oll3/store/titles/916/0050_Bk.pdf

Marshall, John, 'A Friend to the Union' [and] 'A Friend of the Constitution' *in John Marshall's Defense of McCulloch v. Maryland* (Stanford, CA, 1969; Gerald Gunther, ed.).

Smith, Adam, *An Inquiry into the Nature and Causes of the Wealth of Nations* (Oxford, 1976; R.H. Campbell, A. S. Skinner and W.B. Todd, eds.; the 'Glasgow' edn). See text at 37 for details on pagination.

Secondary Sources

Aschenbrenner, Peter, *British and American Foundings of Parliamentary Science, 1774-1801* (Abingdon-on-Thames, Oxfordshire, UK, 2017).

Namier, L.B., *Avenues of History* (London, 1952).

Piketty, Thomas, *Capital in the Twenty-First Century* (Cambridge, MA, 2014).

[United States] *Historical Statistics of the United States 1789-1945, A Supplement to the Statistical Abstract of the United States* (Washington, DC, 1945). See census.gov/library/publications/time-series/statistical_abstracts.html

White, G. Edward, *The Marshall Court and Cultural Change, 1815-1835* (New York, NY, 1988).

6 'To Protect the Public Industry from Parasite Institutions'

'The proposed canal would greatly enhance the value of public lands northwest of the Ohio'

In 1806, Congress debated two bills that marked out the routes of four proposed national roads.[1] At the same time Congress rejected Kentucky's proposal to fund a bypass canal at the Rapids (or Falls) of the Ohio River at Louisville. The state legislature supported the proposal. 'Besides the general advantages which would result from the completion of the proposed canal', a Congressional committee declared, it is 'particularly interesting to the United States, inasmuch as it would greatly enhance the value of the public lands northwest of the Ohio. There can be but little doubt that, by the additional value it would give to the public lands, the United States would be more than remunerated for the aid which the Legislature of Kentucky have solicited'.[2]

In 1824, the Kentucky legislature chartered a private venture to launch the Louisville and Portland Canal. The company planned to construct the bypass canal at Louisville. As noted above, Kentucky had previously proposed this project to Congress in 1806.[3] In 1826 and 1829 the company successfully induced Congress to fund two rounds of investment. Accordingly the US Treasury purchased 2,350 shares of stock.[4] By the time that Andrew Jackson vetoed a third round of funding (1830), the stock that Congress had purchased (in the first two rounds) was worth \$290,000.[5] The House of Representatives worked until 5 am on 30 May 1829 to complete balloting on H.R. 348.[6] The bill authorized a third round of federal investment (1,000 shares) in the Louisville and Portland Canal Company and also extracted from the company a price concession (on the stock price) in favor of the US Treasury.[7] Jackson, however, refused to sign the bill. Under the 'pocket veto' rule, his non-action disapproved the bill.[8]

In his Second Annual Message in December 1830 (more than six months later),[9] Jackson explained his opposition to the Louisville and Portland project. Congress's third round of investment, Jackson declared, compounded 'the first erroneous step [that was] taken by

DOI: 10.4324/9781003019381-7

instituting a partnership between the government and private companies'.[10] Jackson's counterproposal revived the Bonus Bill formula. In 1817 Congress designed such a formula to distribute surplus federal revenues to the states as block grants. (Madison vetoed the bill.[11]) I supply further details in Appendix K: Notes on the Bonus Bill (Act of March 3, 1817) and the 1818 House Resolution (14 March 1818). Congress would make these grants 'in proportion to the number of their Representatives, to be applied by them to objects of internal improvement'.[12] I contrast Jackson's opposition to public-private 'partnerships' in road and canal projects with his willingness to subsidize 16 private railroad enterprises with federal land. Appendix B: Railroads Subsidized via Federal Land Grants details the bills Jackson approved. Making excuses for Jackson, railroad mania fired the imaginations of inhabitants in the US and UK in the 1830s. The textual wheeze – updated to 'no "railroad", no railroad' – did not materially slow infrastructure spending on this mode of transportation in the 1830s.

In Appendix C: The Political Governance and Resource Exploitation Clauses, I comment on the connections – made and missing – between the unitary and parochial governments in light of the following clauses of *Constitution II*. These are Article I, Section 8, Clause 17 *and* Article IV, Section 3, Clause 2. Delegates found that connecting the destinies of unitary and parochial governments was especially problematic. Here are two alternatives that the delegates at Philadelphia might have considered.

- Congress should *only* launch programs that are in its financial interest.
- Congress should enact laws that expend money *at the same rate* that a private business in similar circumstances would spend money.

Each of these bullet points incorporates a sliding scale approach to productivity. As to any given project or a service mission, when the material world delivered changed circumstances, the level of funding (that Congress should approve) would also vary. There were alternatives, however. (a) Economies of scale moved debate forward. Don't waste national dollars on local projects, for example. (b) Smith's feasibility analytic offered a useful opening hurdle. If it hasn't worked somewhere else on the planet, there's probably another viable course of action to take up first.[13] Under both of these approaches, Congress would match public resources available with the demands that the material world was likely to make on the project during its useful life. On this account, the two clauses (suggested above) were unnecessary.

I refer to Hans Kelsen's pure theory of law (1934). 'If a social system were to be established', he explained, 'to which the actual behaviour of human beings always and under all conditions corresponded, then its basic norm – [authorizing] at the outset all possible eventualities – would have to read, "what ought to happen is whatever actually happens", or, "you ought to do whatever you wish to do".'[14] There must always be some divergence between what a legislative body *should* do and what it *does* do. In other words, Kelsen's pure theory assumed that some instances of programmatic action would fail. A scatter graph could be constructed to display a pattern of past lawmaking. Lawmakers might, employing such a visualization, deconstruct a bill, exposing its variables (factors) and ask themselves: 'is the bill an instance of an acceptable pattern that the scatter graph reveals?' Or, 'is it an outlier with respect to such a pattern?' Kelsen would agree that, if there are (at least) some instances in which people don't get what they want, then visualization supplies a helpful tool for determining whether a proposed spending plan falls into an existing (that is, an acceptable) pattern *or* lies outside that pattern. Put another way, if a pattern were to contain all and only successful laws, there would be no failures stimulating caution in a parliamentary assembly. Lawmakers might even be tempted to attribute the success of a pattern of lawmaking to its conformity to a 'higher law' or to its equally problematic sibling, textual reasoning. A modest number of failures marks out the limits of an acceptable pattern and saves lawmakers from failing into these traps. Put in a larger perspective, giving people what they want does not maintain or augment loyalty to the current form of civil government. In other words, satisfying human needs may promote the stability of government but will not reliably secure inhabitants' loyalty. Kelsen's observations direct our attention to the detailed working of machinery distributing benefits. By convention – that is, from the seventeenth century forward – the overall responsibility for this machinery has been assigned to a parliamentary assembly.

Three points mark the operation of distribution machines. (a) I start with the expectations of communities and regions with regard to the delivery of transportation benefits. When these inhabitants are short-changed, a modest deferment of satisfaction may maintain or even augment these inhabitants' loyalty to the center's brand. Ideally, benefits deferred are randomly distributed. That is, the pattern of distribution should appear to be – in Jefferson's phrase – 'just and regular'.[15] I expand on Jefferson's insight as follows. Over time every community has an equal chance to obtain benefits from the distribution machine. (b) Benefits undelivered – in any given time-slice – do not constitute a trust violation. Targeted distribution of burdens – impacting communities of interest less able to defend their interests in the national brokerage – *is* a trust violation. For example, lawmakers may deliver benefits to stakeholders whom politicians favor, while simultaneously shifting burdens to those who lack equal political muscle. (c) Put another way, to maintain brand loyalty the center must police the foul lines against trust violations. In concrete terms, it is the job of the center to identify trust violations and launch appropriate countermeasures.

'A national domain of four hundred million acres furnishing all that is necessary for ages yet to come'

At the conclusion of 1813, the Commissioner of the General Land Office offered Congress and 'a comprehensive view of the extent and situation of the public lands'. Waxing poetic, the Commissioner informed Congress that:

> It appears from public documents in this Department that the United States, after deducting all that has been sold, leaving a sufficiency to satisfy every lawful claim, will possess a national domain of at least four hundred million acres of land, embracing a variety of soil and climate capable of furnishing all that is necessary for the supplying the wants, and affording most of the luxuries of life to man, and which, if properly managed, will secure auxiliary aids to the Government for ages yet to come.[16]

Thanks to the Treaty of Paris (1783) and Louisiana Purchase (1803) the US balance sheet acquired significant assets. I refer to this real estate as the US national patrimony. Luca Pacioli would instruct his readers 'debit real property/credit equity' (1783) and 'debit real property/credit notes payable' (1803).[17] Congress added value to these assets by slicing and dicing the bulk territories (so acquired). First, into intermediate territories, then into nascent states and finally into newly-admitted states. The rapid acquisition of these tracts – that the GLO computed at 400,000,000 acres (1813) – justified the build out of a national transportation network *if only* to move European American settlers into remote regions. The preamble to the Act of May 15, 1820 declared that the fifth national road that Congress designed (to run from Wheeling to St. Louis) would render 'lands of the United States ... more valuable'.[18] In the previous month – via the Act of April 24, 1820 – Congress authorized the General Land Office to sell public land at $1.25 per acre.[19] The minimum purchase was 80 acres.

These two statutes revealed the following bit of 'Monroevenomics'. (a) The availability of General Land Office 80-acre parcels will tend to depress the market value of the 80-acre farm I own. When I put my farm on the market, new settlers will be more likely to shop GLO's offerings of raw land before making me an offer. Moreover, the land that the government sold settlers was exempt from state and local property taxes for five years after the sale.[20] Who doesn't love a tax holiday? A private settler can't match those terms. (b) As the GLO's inventory of suitable lands declines, however, the value of my land may rise above $1.25/acre. (c) The idea that 'lands of the United States [are becoming] more valuable' (via the Act of May 15, 1820) did not mean that Congress planned to squeeze late-arriving settlers by increasing the retail price above $1.25/acre, that is, when market conditions justified a price hike. What Congress counted as 'value' was, instead, the attractiveness of 80-acre parcels to potential settlers. European Americans preferred.

I have pointed out that the motto 'expand or die' required that geophysical reality be settled, slice by slice.[21] Landowners with 400 million acres on their balance sheets have a powerful incentive to protect their holdings by encouraging settlement. Land and water must be used. Or lost to breakaway republics or aggressive foreign nations. It was in the interest of Congress to boost settler demand for resources that the US claimed as its property. In a phrase, add cash to land and water and you feed the beating heart of the 'Colossus of Roads'. That was John Randolph of Roanoke poking as much fun at the fate of parochial governments as his dignity would allow (1824).[22]

'To determine the practicability of opening an inland communication for steam navigation from Chesapeake Bay to Charleston, South Carolina'

At the conclusion of Monroe's presidency, the build out of the United States shifted into a higher gear. The 19th Congress – the first in the J.Q. Adams administration – processed 23 river and harbor projects in the Act of May 20, 1826.[23] These 23 projects may be subdivided as follows. Congress ordered surveys in 12 cases and funded construction in 11 more. These projects were located in 9 states and the Michigan Territory. The 24th Congress – the last of the Jackson administration – processed 56 river and harbor projects along with two surveys (looking forward to future projects) in the Act of March 3, 1837.[24] The surveys targeted the 'Black and White rivers' in Arkansas and 'the southern debouche of the Dismal Swamp Canal' in North Carolina. The latter project was no small potatoes affair, however. Congress sought 'to determine the practicability of opening an inland communication for steam navigation, from the Chesapeake Bay to Charleston, South Carolina'. Section 1.

I surveyed the 1826 and 1837 Acts of Congress (referenced above) to identify the 13 states and territories disappointed in 1826 Act but gaining projects in the 1837 Act. In the 'satisfied in 1826 but disappointed in 1837' category I counted New Hampshire, Vermont, New Jersey, Maryland, Illinois, Indiana, Kentucky, Tennessee, Missouri, Arkansas, Mississippi, Louisiana and the Territory of Florida. I also counted the seven states and one territory (Michigan) that got benefits in 1826 and also got benefits in 1837. These were the states of Massachusetts, Connecticut, New York, Pennsylvania, Ohio, Michigan and Alabama. Your chance of getting nothing (in 1826) and something (in 1837) was 13 of 29. Your chance of getting (at least one) river and harbor project on both occasions was 8 of 29. These figures do not suggest that Congress treated some states and territories as a permanent class of losers. There was – almost – a coin flip chance that if your state or territory didn't get a project in 1826, in 1837 you would be a winner. Moreover, fewer than one-third of states and territories were winners on both occasions. If you were a greedy state or territory – itching to win every time you bellied up to the roulette wheel in the national brokerage – the odds were against you.

Who got projects in 1837? The ratifying (original) states were New Hampshire, New Jersey and Maryland. States formed from ratifying states were Vermont, Kentucky and Tennessee. Louisiana, Indiana, Illinois, Missouri and Arkansas evolved from bulk territories; they passed through nascent statehood before Congress admitted them to the Union. Congress organized the Territory of Florida following the US acquisition of two stand-alone foreign colonies (sharing that name) from Spain in 1819.[25]

Who got projects in both 1826 and 1837? The ratifying states were Massachusetts, New York, Pennsylvania and Connecticut. The admitted states were Michigan, Ohio and Alabama. While further study is warranted, it does not appear that ratifying states feasted while Congress starved the admitted states. Moreover, the data does not indicate that benefits distributed were slanted towards one or another region of the country.

There is a larger issue that the foregoing survey discloses. *Constitution II* granted managers of bills moving through Congress the power to marginalize members objecting to maldistribution of benefits. This was accomplished by shrinking minority numbers below the critical 20% threshold. Members numbering fewer than 20% of those 'Present' in the House were constitutionally disabled from demanding a roll call vote.[26] Auction and bargaining in Congress baked deferred satisfaction into lawmaking. The optimal distribution of members (disappointed in their hopes of winning improvement projects for their districts) would avoid concentration of dissatisfied members in regions that were (more or less) contiguous. My survey in this section suggests that this did not occur when navigation projects were distributed in the interval 1826–1837.

'Alexander Hamilton touched the corpse of public credit and it sprung upon its feet'

Posterity has confirmed the laurels that Alexander Hamilton – in the cathedral of democracy – raised high and then placed upon his brow. Hamilton pushed funding programs through the 1st, 2nd and 3rd Congresses. He designed these programs to hoover up past due principal (debt that the First Republic ran up) along with accumulated interest together with a tranche of state war debt. Three bond issues totaling $64.3 million funded Hamilton's refinancing schemes.[27] Hamilton's accomplishments moved Sen. Daniel Webster to rhapsodize as follows. The Treasury Secretary 'smote the rock of the national resources, and abundant streams gushed forth' (1831). Webster then drew on the New

Testament for his next well-turned phrase. 'He touched the dead corpse of the public credit, and it sprung upon its feet'.[28]

Alexander Hamilton borrowed heavily from a fellow master of financial wizardry. I refer to the tricks that Wm. Pitt the Younger performed to dazzle *his* colleagues in the House of Commons. 26 Geo. 3, c. 31, the National Debt Reduction Act (1786), provided in Section X that 'That all monies whatever, which shall be placed from time to time to the account of the said commissioners by virtue of this act, shall be applied by them either in payments for the redemption of such redeemable publick annuities as shall be at or above par ... or to the purchase of any publick annuities below par in the manner herein-after directed'. Hamilton's counterpart handiwork appeared in the Act of May 8, 1792.[29] Section 6 of the 1792 act provided 'That the President of the Senate, the Chief Justice, the Secretary of State, the Secretary of the Treasury, and the Attorney General ... are hereby authorized, with the approbation of the President of the United States, to purchase the debt of the United States, at its market price, if not exceeding the par or true value thereof'. This was not Hamilton's maiden venture as an acolyte of Wm. Pitt the Younger. The first version of the US Sinking Fund appeared in the Act of August 12, 1790.[30] It capitalized revenue from 'duties on goods, wares and merchandise imported, and on the tonnage of ships or vessels' and then assigned this asset to the commissioners of the Sinking Fund, being 'the President of the Senate, the Chief Justice, the Secretary of State, the Secretary of the Treasury, and the Attorney General for the time being'.[31] Hamilton composed a preamble to the provisional arrangement that Congress adopted in 1790. This passage proclaimed that it was the policy of the US Treasury to conduct its financial affairs to 'be beneficial to the creditors of the United States'.

> It being desirable by all just and proper means, to effect a reduction of the amount of the public debt, and as the application of such surplus of the revenue as may remain after satisfying the purposes for which appropriations shall have been made by law, will not only contribute to that desirable end, but will be beneficial to the creditors of the United States, by raising the price of their stock, and be productive of considerable saving to the United States.[32]

Hamilton also reported to Congress that the US Treasury might require 'some time to bring the value of stock to its natural level, and to attach to it that fixed confidence, which is necessary to its quality as money' (1790).[33] Congress's success in delivering benefits (in the service missions transportation and communication) may be attributed to the ready access Congress enjoyed to 'other people's money'.[34] National financial institutions (the Treasury, the First Bank of the United States and the Sinking Fund) came on line as Congress took its first steps to fulfill communication and transportation service missions via mission specific projects. These developments were mutually supporting. Advances in transportation and communication seamed the nation into a single market. In turn, this development boosted the appetite of merchants and other business owners for affordable credit, which further enabled them to deal in the emerging nationwide single market.

Margaret Thatcher understood Hamilton's passion – on behalf of the US Treasury – to gain access to private financial resources by interlocking the fortunes of private bondholders and the public fisc. When interviewed for Thames TV's *This Week* Thatcher voiced her critique of 'socialist' governments (5 February 1976). 'They always run out of other people's money'.[35] The policy that the Iron Lady criticized was Pittite and Hamiltonian. Induce investors to buy your bonds and promise to buy them back if prices sink. Employ a system of government price supports to manage private bondholder risk and, in the bargain, you boost the nation's money supply. Cheap money stimulating inflation? Price-yield curve headed south? Dispatch the GB/UK or US Sinking Fund Commissioners with tons of public cash to shoulder private bondholder risk. What was Thomas Jefferson complaining about?[36] When the US Treasury borrowed *private* money it created tradable *public* debt instruments; according to Alexander Hamilton, quoted above, when the US Treasury printed bonds, it printed 'quality ... money'. Government bonds and price support programs, on this account, served as essential tools that enabled these magnificent men and their money machines to achieve their sublime ambitions, that is, measuring all behavior in political society by mediums of exchange. On both sides of the North Atlantic, Sinking Funds served as fiscal intermediaries to Treasury departments for the purpose of stabilizing public bond prices in 'private' markets.[37] (Notable US Sinking Fund commissioners include Thomas Jefferson and John Marshall. For 29 days, from 4 February to 4 March, 1801, Jefferson and Marshall were, ex officio, co-Commissioners of the US Sinking Fund.) In effect, the Sinking Fund commissioners fulfilled the same function that – in the post-modern era – the US Federal Reserve Bank and the Bank of England have performed via their respective quantitative easing programs. The policies (mentioned above) enabled these two governments to get their hands on plenty of 'other people's money'. Bonus feature: Thatcherites can blame 'socialists' for departing from 'capitalist' orthodoxy.

'One of the most terrible scourges ever invented to afflict a nation'

Imposition of burdens is an entirely different problem from distribution of benefits and presents difficult issues for our consideration. A lawmaker may assume a defeatist attitude, loudly proclaiming that his constituents will be, yet again, short-changed in the politics of distribution. He will discover that he has no friends to come to his aid. Better to exhibit loyalty to the distribution machine, a Congressman rapidly learns, and support your colleagues' projects in return for their support. The survival of an incumbent depends on his 'political chops'. Can the Congressman call on voters back home to support Congress in its role as broker of projects? When the lens is restricted to distribution of benefits, a Congressman's professed loyalty to the machine may be augmented (or at least maintained) if Congress delivers to his constituents *somewhat less* than the Congressman has argued (to his colleagues) that his constituency should receive.

A parliamentary assembly must be sensitive to the line between teasing loyalty from lawmakers who are getting less (yet learning to live with it) and hogging benefits, thereby driving these lawmakers and their constituents to rebellion by seriously depriving them of federal benefits. In 1820, Mainers expressed their irritation that they were not getting their fair share of infrastructure spending, according to the editor of the *Portland Gazette*.[38] Was it sufficient for Congress to vote $1,200 to build a pier 'near the harbor of Belfast', Maine in 1826? It was the first project named in the Act of May 20, 1826.[39] Did this project sufficiently reconcile Maine to the disappointment it suffered six years earlier? Put another way, getting less than all you want does not impose an intolerable burden as long as the national brokerage promises to grind out future benefits, even if delivery of *these* future benefits do not completely satisfy the expectations of voter-consumers.

'The failure of the others to bear their equal share of the public burdens'

In his 'Views' Monroe turned his attention to distribution of burdens.

> A system capable of expansion over a vast territory not only without weakening either government, but enjoying the peculiar advantage of adding thereby new strength and vigor to the faculties of both. ¶27.

This passage sets the stage for Monroe's next declaration. Left to their own devices, state governments might fail 'to bear their equal share of the public burdens'. Monroe continued: 'The several States enjoy all the rights reserved to them of separate and independent governments, and each is secured by the nature of the Federal Government, which acts directly on the people, against the failure of the others to bear their equal share of the public burdens'. ¶27. The national government, Monroe argued, should seek out those committing trust violations and initiate appropriate countermeasures. In other words, it was the job of the federal government to spring into action if and when state policy embraced burden-shirking and free-loading. In the next passage Monroe turned his attention to trust violations that members of the House of Representatives might commit.

> But should the representative act corruptly and betray his trust, or otherwise prove that he was unworthy of the confidence of his constituents, he would be equally sure to lose it and to be removed and otherwise censured, according to his deserts. ¶102.

Monroe offered this understanding of how brokerage works. 'Congress know the extent of the public engagements and the sums necessary to meet them; they know how much may be derived from each branch of revenue without pressing it too far; and, paying due regard to the interests of the people'. ¶102. Monroe argued that it was the job of lawmakers to assess how much revenue could be 'derived [from taxpayers] without pressing it too far'. One might suppose that lawmakers should be guided by a vague standard like 'moderation' when composing tax legislation. Monroe, however, employed a pocketbook standard. Voter-consumers, he assumed, could be relied upon to react when their personal autonomy was invaded to an unacceptable level. This would be the case when the center called upon voter-consumers to tender allegiance to a form of government that was taxing them 'too far'.[40] The asymmetry is worth underscoring. Learned authors and other investigators may exhort lawmakers to moderate government's appetite for tax revenue. Monroe and Marshall, however, explicitly argued that it was up to voter-consumers to draw the line when it came to government demands for revenue that taxation imposed on household and business pocketbooks.

I bring forward three more voices in the study interval (1817–1825). David Ricardo made two important contributions to the study of political economy. Best known is his study *Principles of Political Economy and Taxation*. This appeared in April 1817.[41] In a subsequent essay Ricardo shifted his attention from rent-seeking land owners (featured in the *Principles*) to bondholders. The *Encyclopedia Britannica* published Ricardo's essay 'Funding System' in one of its supplementary volumes (1820).[42] To background this point: Wm. Pitt the Younger induced the House of Commons to vest 'commissioners … for … the reduction of the national debt' with the task of serving as the Treasury's fiscal intermediary (1786).[43] David Ricardo argued in 'Funding System' that the Sinking Fund would stimulate the aggressive tendencies of ministers. In other words, easy money would encourage ministers to 'enter into a new contest [with] very little provocation'.[44] War-mongering was the focus of Ricardo's attention.

> There cannot be a greater security for the continuance of peace, than the imposing on ministers the necessity of applying to the people for

> taxes to support a war. Suffer this sinking fund to accumulate during peace to any considerable sum, and very little provocation would induce them to enter into a new contest.[45]

On this point Ricardo was not alone. 'The end answered by credit is the maintenance of distant wars, that is to say their prolongation' (1817).[46] I draw here on Jefferson's translation of Antoine Destutt de Tracy's *Treatise on Political Economy,* to be discussed later in this chapter.

Ricardo offered a programmatic solution to the challenge that maldistribution of burdens posed. He argued that popular enthusiasm to go to war would be seriously tempered if the public was made aware that consumption-based taxes would fund the munitions and manpower required. Ricardo also offered a large-scale solution, by which the burden of long-term public debt could be eliminated. By 'one great effort' the inhabitants of the United Kingdom could pay off the national debt. 'We should get rid of one of the most terrible scourges which was ever invented to afflict a nation'.[47] Manufacturers and landowners, Ricardo argued, could retire the national debt if they participated in his debt-swap scheme. Bondholders would loan cash to manufacturers and landowners. The Treasury could levy a one-time charge on this private resource and pay off the national debt. Government bondholders would switch hats, so to speak, and become holders of the private debt instruments that Ricardo's plan swapped into their portfolios.

> Manufacturers and landholders would want large sums for their payments into the Exchequer. These two parties would not fail to make an arrangement with each other, by which one party would employ their money and the other raise it. They might do this by loan, or by sale and purchase, as they might think it most conducive to their respective interests; with this the State would have nothing to do.[48]

In 1832 J.W. Goethe published Part II of his dramatic poem *Faust.*[49] Ricardo's 'Funding System' anticipated the plot device Goethe constructed for Act I of that drama. Faust and Mephistopheles time-travel back to ancient Greece. Along the way, they encounter an Emperor vexed by his Treasury Department's cash shortfalls. Mephisto assures the Emperor that it is unnecessary for his government to shovel gold out of the ground to prop up the imperial currency with newly minted coin and bullion. The ore the Empire requires to stabilize its currency, Mephistopheles helpfully explains, is safely buried within the imperial domain. To like effect, Ricardo argued that the cash the British government required to go debt-free was tucked into the pockets of its 'manufacturers and landholders'. In both fables a well-crafted statute dispatched cash and paper to whirl about and change places. Ricardo may have been inviting controversy to draw attention to his more serious work.

'It is still more desirable that government should contract no debts'

A pair of investigators, one French and one American, broke new ground in the nascent field of political economy. I refer to work published in the United States under the title *A Treatise on Political Economy* (1817).[50] Thomas Jefferson translated a work composed by Antoine Destutt de Tracy and contributed a prefatory essay to this translation. The title that Jefferson draped on de Tracy's study was a near-relation to Ricardo's *Principles of Political Economy and Taxation* which Ricardo published in London (1817). Jefferson concentrated his attention on single volume of a much larger project of de Tracy's. This was the latter's multi-volume *Éléments d'Idéologie*. I note that a modern edition (2012) obscures Jefferson's editorial efforts in a significant respect. The publisher has placed Jefferson's letter to Joseph Milligan (1818) – composed after the *Treatise* had appeared in print – following the title page and before Jefferson's six-page 'Prospectus' to de Tracy's *Treatise* (1816).[51]

What inspired Jefferson to translate and publish de Tracy's *Treatise*? Jefferson declared that de Tracy offered American readers a counterweight to Adam Smith's *Wealth of Nations*. Offering faint praise to the 'merit' of the *Wealth of Nations,* Jefferson observed that, in his opinion, Smith's work was 'prolix and tedious'.[52] Jefferson did not claim, however, that de Tracy's study replaced Smith's. De Tracy's summary of points appeared at the beginning of the *Treatise*.[53] De Tracy titled Chapter XII 'Of the Revenues and Expenses of a Government, and of its Debts'. His bullet points follow.

- As to the expenses of government they are necessary but sterile. It is desirable that they be the smallest possible.
- It is still more desirable that government should contract no debts.
- It is very unfortunate that it has the power of contracting them.
- This power, which is called *public credit*, speedily conducts all the government which use it to their ruin; has none of the advantages which are attributed to it; and rests on a false principle.
- It is to be desired that it be universally acknowledged that the acts of any legislative power whatsoever cannot bind their successors, and that it should be solemnly declared that this principal is extended to the engagements which they make with the lenders.[54]

One may give Chapter XII of de Tracy's *Treatise* a side-by-side reading with Adam Smith's essays 'Of Taxes' and 'Of Public Debts'. I refer to Smith's essays, appearing in Book V of his *Wealth of Nations*. I have noted that Smith's essay 'Of Taxes' contains his productivity analytics.[55] De Tracy's counterpoint follows: 'But is a more precise conclusion wanted? Here it is'.[56] (a) Governments should restrain their appetite for tax revenue by imposing a moderate tax burden on businesses and households. (b) The useful life of any given tax should terminate on the earlier happening of the next general election or the fall of the ministry then in power. The new administration should be at liberty to renew, modify or abandon the tax scheme. (c) From the perspective of householders or business owners – who must satisfy multiple tax demands – composers of tax policy should ensure that the burdens imposed on any given household or business harmonize one with another. In general de Tracy recommended that revenue be raised from land taxes. This would reduce reliance on point-of-sale taxes; the impact of these taxes would 'necessarily oppress principally the poor'.[57]

De Tracy's grand theme follows. A nation's inhabitants should moderate their appetite for government-delivered goods and services, especially if demand for these deliverables drives the government into debt. 'Every time a government borrows it takes a step towards its ruin'.[58] In this regard, de Tracy and Jefferson underlined the fundamental unfairness of present generations commanding benefits that future generations would be compelled to fund. Government 'remains burdened with a debt, which is so much taken from its future means'.[59] De Tracy's study did not, however, argue that bondholders – emboldened by Pittite and Hamiltonian price supports – engaged in parasitical behavior.

Drawing on letters Jefferson composed in the interval 1813–1818, I suggest that Jefferson was more inspired by his loathing for Alexander Hamilton than passion for the 'ideology' of de Tracy. And with good reason. 'It ought not to excite surprize that I have not entered into the details of political economy', de Tracy remarks, but only after baldly confessing that his 'study is not properly a treatise on political economy'.[60] Presumably Jefferson failed to notice this point before engaging himself to translate the *Treatise*. De Tracy buried this confession five pages from the end of his study.[61]

Picking and choosing topics, Jefferson was unable to deliver more than a magpie approach to the subject of political economy. I refer to his letter to John Wayles Eppes (6 November 1813).

> At the time we were funding our National debt we heard much about 'a public debt being a public blessing'; that the stock representing it was a creation of active capital for the aliment of commerce, manufactures and agriculture. This paradox was well adapted to the minds of believers in dreams, and the gulls of that size entered bonâ fide into it. but the art & mystery of banks is a wonderful improvement on that. it is established on the principle that 'private debts are a public blessing.' that the evidences of those private debts, called bank notes, become active capital and aliment the whole commerce, manufactures, & agriculture of the US. here are a set of people for

> instance who have bestowed on us the great blessing of running in our debt about 200.M. of D. without our knowing who they are, where they are, or what property they have to pay this debt when called on.[62]

'Public debts are public benefits is a position inviting to prodigality and liable to dangerous abuse'

Jefferson misquoted Hamilton. The Treasury Secretary's 'Report on Public Credit' (January 1790) stated:

> Persuaded as the Secretary is that the proper funding of the present debt will render it a national blessing, yet he is so far from acceding to the position, in the latitude in which it is sometimes laid down, that "public debts are public benefits," a position inviting to prodigality and liable to dangerous abuse.[63]

Hamilton declared that it was dangerous for the US Treasury to claim ready access to 'other people's money'. Hamilton's concern was that spending programs, if not constrained by rigorous application of Smithian productivity analytics, would induce 'prodigality and [be] liable to dangerous abuse'. Hamilton merged well-dressed spending into plain-vanilla borrowing. It wasn't a financial sin to borrow. On the other hand, government should avoid borrowing when its assessment of spending needs was undisciplined. Hamilton's 'red line' – so to speak – was 'prodigality' and 'dangerous abuse' of the government's powers to tax, spend and borrow. On this point Hamilton's views align with Thatcherite thinking.

Leaving to one side Hamilton's concern for the financial well-being of the governments' bondholders, Hamilton's solutions – creating and managing debt instruments – were in sync with economic realities. France declared war on Great Britain in 1793 and the US declared war on the UK in 1812. By the end of these conflicts – events playing out to wildly different results in the UK and US – Treasury departments offered investors (on both sides of the North Atlantic) debt instruments designed to fund the two nations' war efforts. 'During the war years up to 1815, the government financed its huge deficits principally through the sale of 3% consols at large discounts. They were sold as low as 55-57% of par to yield 5.45-5.25%, but more often at higher prices'.[64] In the spring of 1814 – during the dark days of the Second War for American Independence – American investors paid $88 for a $100 bond – with a coupon rate of 6% and an effective yield of 6.88%.[65] These rates of interest on public funded debt signaled a remarkable equivalence in investor confidence. If financial discipline means anything, a government with a longer track record of prompt repayment of its funded debt will enjoy at least a modest advantage – 5.25% to 6.88% in this case – when it solicits private purchase of government debt instruments.

Jefferson's critique of the state of public finance – as of 1813, when he composed his letter to Eppes – centered on his concern that prospective stockholders (in a soon to-be-revived version of the Bank of the United States) would gain unfair financial advantage. Implicitly, he argued, the Second Republic's organic arrangements permitted unlicensed greed. It's not that Jefferson was wrong. It was that his scholarship failed him and did so in dramatic fashion, as I have argued above. In this regard the Sixteenth Amendment delivered a measure of redemption to the shade of Thomas Jefferson. That change in organic arrangements permitted Congress to tax 'incomes, from whatever source derived' (3 February 1913).[66]

The foregoing brings up a connection between de Tracy's Treatise and Piketty's *Capital*.[67] According to de Tracy, households or businesses that did not produce tradable goods and services generated a species of economic waste. Although de Tracy declared that 'we are all proprietors … we are all consumers',[68] his grand theme did not permit him to reconcile the competing interests of classes engaging in different economic pursuits. One may, however, draw on de Tracy's *Treatise* as follows. An investigator's energy-tracking would reliably expose opportunities for energy-savings or, alternatively, opportunities to avoid energy-wasting. 'The idle rich … are absolutely good for nothing; and that their existence is an evil, inasmuch as it diminishes the number of useful labourers'.[69]

The observations of three investigator-scholars – Jefferson, Ricardo, de Tracy and the poet-scholar Goethe[70] – may be taken within a single lens. There is a serious difficulty in drawing the line between distribution of burdens and *re*distribution of assets. Put simplistically, lawmakers should not regard distribution of burdens – a necessary component of programmatic action – as an opportunity to launch 'Robin Hood' style redistribution programs. Adam Smith drew a workable line when he argued that proportionality was the most important productivity analytic. 'The subjects of every state ought to contribute towards the support of the government, as nearly as possible, in proportion to their respective abilities; that is, in proportion to the revenue which they respectively enjoy under the protection of the state'.[71] Marshall and Monroe had something to say on this point as well. Their method of Congressional precedents afforded the wealthy their opportunity to plead victim status to voter-consumers at the biennial hustings. Let the rich bribe or cajole the poor to restrain their lust for redistribution of the plutocrats' massive and unproductive wealth. There is a downside here. If compelled to compete in votarian proceedings, the super-rich may be too successful in messaging their need to protect their wealth, honestly or corruptly acquired. 'A government powerful enough to tax my second yacht is big enough to ban your dinghy from shallow waters'.

'I have little fear, knowing the bond which holds us together'

This section surveys Monroe's blind spots, including lapses, errors of emphasis or his failures to anticipate events that would transpire more than a half-century later.

First, Monroe did not come to grips with this fact of political life. If there were those in the nation who declared that they stood on the 'windward side of treason', they weren't happy.[72] Monroe did not outline a comprehensive strategy to manage relations between the center and American regions who did not want to be 'healed' or brought into a stronger 'bond' with the Union or each other. Improvements in transportation might 'cement the Union itself'. ¶117 But the 'cement' that the President and Congress offered was programmatic action funded (in the main) by federal cash and land. As to the latter, when the federal government acquired rights from native American communities the terms of these transactions were frequently one-sided. In 1946 Congress was obliged to revisit and revise these transactions.[73]

In the study interval 1817–1825 Congress accelerated delivery of roads, canals and rivers made safe for steamboats. These programs foreshadowed the arrival of railroads on the North American continent. During the Jackson administration, Congress subsidized 16 such projects.[74] By proclaiming that benefit distribution was *the* baseline output of legislative action, the triumph of transactional politics was assured. It was easy, but too easy, to argue that issues of pocketbook importance called for economic reasoning and that Adam Smith had all the answers a parliamentary assembly required. In a speech to the House of Commons, Wm. Pitt declared that Smith's treatise offered the 'best solution to every question connected with the history of commerce or with the systems of political economy' (1792).[75] That praise (1792) must be bracketed against John Randolph's 'accumulated pressure' that targeted those wishing to be left alone (1824).[76] That 'pressure' was, to Randolph's thinking, a result of Congress's appetite for power for the sake of power. Smith's productivity analytics guided a Congress – committed to spending loads of 'other people's money' – to spend money efficiently. But considerations of efficiency might not retard a new republic's appetite for power creep and this was especially the case when 'can = should' was taken as a matter of civic faith. This equivalency offered a dark side which would be exposed as soon as a strongman of violent tendencies entered the White House.

Second, Monroe's social science did not support his political science on the following points. (a) If American communities and regions were brought into closer contact, one with another, there was no certainty that an increase in geophysical intimacy would bring about an increase in mutual affection. Contact might engender loathing. Human beings don't always find their differences charming or even worth disregarding. (b) If increased contact engendered greater affection, why would this development reliably augment inhabitants' allegiance to the national government? Aristotle covered this ground in *The Politics*. This is one of his many (if frequently contradictory) observations on the role of education in allegiance-boosting efforts. 'These are programs', he remarks, 'that at present all people despise'.[77] (c) The foregoing points did not deter Monroe. He insisted that there was no downside to brokering improvement projects. Why would a majority gang up on a minority and hog available benefits?

> I have little fear of this danger, knowing well how strong the bond which holds us together is and who the people are who are thus held together; but still, it is proper to look at and to provide against it, and it is not within the compass of human wisdom to make a more effectual provision than would be made by the proposed improvements. ¶146

Third, Monroe's sunny assessment of the politics and economics of transportation and communication projects – brand loyalty boosted through programmatic action – was fact-testable. A nation with an improved transport net, Monroe and Marshall believed, could rely on the loyalty of its citizens. 'Good roads and canals' would augment inhabitants' allegiance to the center.[78] After all, the loyalty to which Monroe referred was that tendered by a 'generous, enlightened, and virtuous people'[79] who were 'devoted to our happy system of government'.[80] On the other hand, if communities and regions found that increased intimacy engendered mutual hostility, demagogic appeals might obtain a receptive hearing, offering victimhood to a community or region. Then as now, this rhetoric played on real or imagined grievances. The demagogue gins up illusions that proclaim inhabitants to be victims of centralist conspiracies. Only the demagogue can save them. Monroe was well aware how centrifugal forces might recontour the playing field. 'Ambitious men may hereafter grow up among us who may promise to themselves advancement from a change, and by practicing upon the sectional interests, feelings, and prejudices endeavor under various pretexts to promote it'. 'Views' ¶46.

> The history of the world is replete with examples of this kind – of military commanders and demagogues becoming usurpers and tyrants, and of their fellow-citizens becoming their instruments and slaves. I have little fear of this danger, knowing well how strong the bond which holds us together is and who the people are who are thus held together. 'Views' ¶146

Fourth, I offer Monroe a measure of redemption. In his 'Views', Monroe rhapsodized on the (anticipated) beneficial effects of the avalanche of improvement projects that he had green-lighted, thanks to his 'no footprint, no problem' formula. 'The facility which would thereby be afforded to the transportation of the whole of the rich productions of our country to market would alone more than amply compensate for all the labor and expense attending them'.[81] Monroe's pocketbook emphasis exposed the transactional nature of his formula. Every household and business in the US could expect that a single market would 'more than amply compensate' voter-consumers. On this account, they should regard themselves as having invested 'labor and expense' in these projects.

Monroe and Marshall assumed that household and business productivity gains could be regarded as dividends payable to preferred investors. In the largest perspective, Monroe and Marshall took full advantage of the 'wager' aspect of the metaphor. It was their task to articulate to the American people why and how the European American investment made in 1787–1789 paid off so handsomely after 1815.

Conclusion

In Appendix I: Marshall and Monroe Discuss the 'Views' I supply details of John Marshall's letter to James Monroe (13 June 1822). In this letter the Chief Justice offered the President a measure of approval to the 'Views'. Justice Joseph Story declined the opportunity to comment on Monroe's 'Views' in 1822. However, when Story published his *Commentaries on the Constitution* (1833) he did have something to say about the 'Views'. 'But perhaps the most thorough and elaborate view, which perhaps has ever been taken of the subject, will be found in the exposition of President Monroe, which accompanied his message respecting the bill for the repairs of the Cumberland Road, (4th of May 1822)'.[82]

In the next section of his *Commentaries*, Section 977, Story quotes a portion of a single paragraph in the 'Views', ¶96. Story then copied the text of Monroe's 'Views' ¶¶97 through 106, inclusive; these passages appear as his Sections 978 through 987. The reader will recall that Monroe signaled his shift from the conclusions of his 1819 essay to those of his 1822 essay by his declaration 'my mind has undergone a change'. This phrase appeared as the final sentence of ¶101. Story showcased this declaration by placing it at the mid-point of text he copied. The passage appeared in Section 982 of Story's *Commentaries*.

To sum up, Story lifted material from 11 paragraphs of Monroe's 'Views'. He drew six paragraphs of material from Monroe's 1819 essay and five paragraphs from his 1822 essay. The latter material relates Monroe's new thinking on the subject of internal improvements. Monroe died on 4 July 1831 and missed the pleasure of reading Story's assessment of his legacy in the latter's *Commentaries*. After quoting Monroe, Story offered readers his takeaway on Monroe's essays.

> Appropriations have never been limited by congress to cases falling with the specific powers enumerated in the constitution, whether those powers be construed in their broad, or their narrow sense. At 457, Sec. 988.

Take the negative energy of Story's declaration (quoted above) and construct a declaration tuned to the affirmative voice. One could be fooled into thinking that Story is working towards an overarching permission (for lawmakers) to spend money. But such a permission rethreads the obvious. Civil governments have the power to preserve themselves. Hamilton and Madison made this point to the Continental/Confederation Congress in 1780/1781.[83] It's a deadly binary. Either civil government preserves itself or it commits suicide. One can't construct a norm that authorizes a civil government to take action to preserve itself because that's what governments do *or* they collapse. Benefits distributed through programmatic action promote stability and therefore advance the goal of preserving the current form of government. 'The prosperity of the American people', Marshall argued, is 'inseparable from the preservation of this government'.[84] If there is a basic norm that authorizes programs promoting the 'prosperity of the American people', it is contentless. Such a basic norm may, on this account, be treated as a useful presupposition.[85]

Without intending this result, Monroe exposed destabilizing threats to the systems, structures and institutions of American political society. By 1861 time ran out on the Monrovian optimism that Jefferson's 'destinies ... advancing rapidly ... beyond the reach of mortal eye' would always do credit to America's self-image.[86]

Notes

1. 2 Stat 396, c. 41, Act of April 21, 1806.
2. See memory.loc.gov/ammem/amlaw/lwaclink.html; *Annals*, 9th Cong., 1st Sess., 827-828; 19 March 1806.
3. See Louisville_and_Portland_Canal [last retrieved 12 December 2021].
4. See memory.loc.gov/ammem/amlaw/lwsl.html; 4 Stat 162, c. 40, Act of May 13, 1826; 4 Stat 353, c. 33, Act of March 2, 1829.
5. See Louisville_and_Portland_Canal.
6. See memory.loc.gov/ammem/amlaw/lwhj.html; *House Journal*, 23:803-806. For the text of H.R. 348, see memory.loc.gov/cgi-bin/ampage?collId=llhb&fileName=012/llhb012.db&recNum=299
7. Relying on secondary sources, I compute the market price at over $120 a share. Via H.R. 348 Congress required that 'said shares shall not exceed the sum of one hundred dollars each'. Sec. 1.
8. Article I, Section 7, Clause 2 provides that 'If any Bill shall not be returned by the President within ten Days (Sundays excepted) after it shall have been presented to him, the Same shall be a Law ... unless the Congress by their Adjournment prevent its Return, in which Case it shall not be a Law'.

9. See millercenter.org/the-presidency/presidential-speeches/december-6-1830-second-annual-message-congress
10. *Ibid.*
11. See text at 109.
12. See Appendix K.
13. See text at 74-75.
14. Kelsen, *Legal Problems*, 60. In Sections 29 and 30 Kelsen makes clear that he views a Grundnorm/basic norm as authorizing acts of public officials, thereby conferring on their conduct the force of law. So much for the condition precedent. What happens when the government loses its 'Effektivität'? 'The validity of a legal system as a closed system of legal norms depends on the efficacy of the system'. *Legal Theory*, 62; Sec. 30(c). This is a formulation of the condition subsequent to which I have drawn attention. My favored pair of terms follow. The higher norm authorizes the lower norm. This is presupposed. The higher norm doesn't work up a sweat to accomplish this authorization. Via its encounter with the material world, however, the lower norm legitimates/justifies the higher norm by rolling up its sleeves and going to work. Hence the bracketed replacement of 'authorize' for the Paulsons's 'legitimate' in the text translated. Put another way, 'legitimacy' or justification is earned through good works; 'authority' is a gift from those on high who have the power to grant such grace.
15. See text at 14.
16. See memory.loc.gov/ammem/amlaw/lwsplink.html; *American State Papers/Public Lands*, 'State of the Public Lands', 13th Cong. 2nd Sess.; 2:736-738, Doc. No. 219; 31 December 1813.
17. Pacioli, *Details of Calculations*. There is no specific page number.
18. 3 Stat 604, c. 123, Act of May 15, 1820.
19. 3 Stat 566, c. 51, Act of April 24, 1820.
20. 2 Stat 173; c. 40, Act of April 30, 1802, Sec. 7
21. See text at 103.
22. *Annals*, 18th Congress, 1st Session, 1307.
23. 4 Stat 175, c. 78.
24. 5 Stat 187, c. 44.
25. See text at 92.
26. See text at 21-22
27. Homer and Sylla, *Interest Rates*, 293-294.
28. Webster, *Speeches*, 2:50.
29. 1 Stat 281, c. 38.
30. 1 Stat 186, c. 47.
31. *Ibid.*, Sec. 2
32. 1 Stat 186, c. 47 [preamble].
33. See founders.archives.gov/documents/Hamilton/01-06-02-0076-0002-0001; 'Report Relative to a Provision for the Support of Public Credit, 9 January 1790'.
34. See text at 70, 135-136.
35. See oxfordreference.com/view/10.1093/acref/9780191826719.001.0001/q-oro-ed4-00010826
36. See text at 131.
37. The air quotes suggest that the notions of private markets, private actors and bodies and, at the extreme, private law must be reevaluated in light of the shade cast by the Iron Lady. Unintentionally, to be sure.
38. Zeitz, 'Missouri Compromise', 480-481.
39. 4 Stat 175, c. 78.

40. See text at 138.
41. Ricardo, *Political Economy.*
42. See Ricardo, 'Funding System', 4:149.
43. 26 Geo. 3, c. 31, Sec. V. Roseveare, *Treasury*, 143-144 supplies the background.
44. Ricardo, 'Funding System', 4:196.
45. *Ibid.*
46. De Tracy, *Treatise*, 246.
47. Ricardo, 'Funding System', 4:197.
48. *Ibid.*
49. See https://www.deutschestextarchiv.de/book/show/300977 [last retrieved 13 April 2021].
50. De Tracy, *Treatise.*
51. De Tracy, *Treatise.*
52. *Ibid.*, iv.
53. *Ibid.*, xvi-xxviii.
54. *Ibid.*, xxvii.
55. Smith, *Wealth*, 825-926.
56. *Ibid.*, 231-232.
57. *Ibid.*, 229-230.
58. De Tracy, *Treatise*, 244.
59. *Ibid.*
60. *Ibid.*, 249.
61. *Ibid.* In a study of 254 pages, these remarks appear in the first paragraph of de Tracy's Chapter XIII, 'Conclusion'.].
62. See founders.archives.gov/documents/Jefferson/03-06-02-0458; 'Thomas Jefferson to John Wayles Eppes, 6 November 1813'.
63. See oll.libertyfund.org/page/1790-hamilton-first-report-on-public-credit
64. Homer and Sylla, *Interest Rates*, 190.
65. *American State Papers/Finance/*Doc. No. 422, 26 September 1814, 2:840-853.
66. See history.house.gov/Historical-Highlights/1901-1950/The-ratification-of-the-16th-Amendment/ and also law.cornell.edu/constitution-conan/amendment-16/history-and-purpose-of-the-amendment#fn1amd16
67. See text at 119-120.
68. *Ibid.*
69. *Ibid.*
70. See deutschestextarchiv.de/book/show/300977 lines 5033-5034. 'Was will das Düstre frommen? Hat etwas Wert, es muß zu Tage kommen!/ What's the point of honoring dust? Dig it up! In gold we trust!'
71. Smith, *Wealth*, 825.
72. See text at 123.
73. I refer to the Indian Claims Commission Act, Pub. L. No. 79-726, c. 959, 60 Stat. 1049, Act of August 13, 1946.
74. See text at 172-173.
75. *Parliamentary History*, vol. XXIX, pp. 834–35.
76. *Annals*, 18th Congress, 1st Session, 1311.
77. Aristotle, *Politics*, 1310a13; H. Rackham, trans.
78. 'Views', ¶107.
79. *Ibid.*, ¶27.
80. See presidency.ucsb.edu/documents/eighth-annual-message-1 [last retrieved 12 November 2020].
81. 'Views', ¶144.

82. Story, *Commentaries*, 444-445, Sec. 976.
83. Aschenbrenner, *Foundings*, 53-57.
84. Marshall, *Defense*, 155.
85. Aschenbrenner, 'Can nation-states self-stabilize?'
86. See millercenter.org/the-presidency/presidential-speeches/march-4-1801-first-inaugural-address

References

Primary Sources

Aristotle, *The Politics* (New York, NY, 1941; trans. B. Jowett) in *The Basic Works of Aristotle* (R. McKeon, ed. in chief). My references employ Bekker citations. These citations appear in McKeon's edition as well as in the Loeb Library edition of *The Politics* (Cambridge, MA, 1932; trans. H. Rackham). For scholarship on the manuscript tradition, I refer the reader to W. Jaeger, *Aristotle, Fundamental of the History of his Development* (Oxford, 1934; trans R. Robinson), 259–292, 'The Original *Politics*'.

Kelsen, Hans, *Introduction to the Problems of Legal Theory* (Oxford, 1992; trans. Bonnie Litschewski Paulson and Stanley L. Paulson; originally published as *Reine Rechtslehre*, Wien, 1934).

Pacioli, Luca, 'Particularis de Computis et Scripturis/Details of Calculations and Writings', an essay included in *Summa de arithmetica, geometria, proportioni e proportionalita/Summary of arithmetic, geometry, proportions and proportionality* (Venegia, 1494; Book 9, Tract 11). I refer readers to Particularis de Computis et Scripturis, A Contemporary Interpretation (Seattle, 1994; trans. Jeremy Cripps, Findlay University). I interviewed Dr. Cripps in preparation for this study.

Ricardo, David, *The Principles of Political Economy and Taxation* (London, 1817).

Ricardo, David, 'Funding System' (1820); see oll.libertyfund.org/title/ricardo-the-works-and-correspondence-of-david-ricardo-11-vols-sraffa-ed

Smith, Adam, *An Inquiry into the Nature and Causes of the Wealth of Nations* (Oxford, 1976; R.H. Campbell, A. S. Skinner and W.B. Todd, eds; the 'Glasgow' edn). For details on pagination, see text at 3.

Story, Joseph, *Commentaries on the Constitution* (Boston, MA, 1833; 1st edn).

De Tracy, Antoine-Louis-Claude Destutt, *A Treatise on Political Economy … Translation* Edited *by Thomas Jefferson* (Indianapolis, IN, 2012; [originally] 'Published by Joseph Milligan' 1817; 'translated from the unpublished French original').

The Writings and Speeches of Daniel Webster, '[Speech at a] 'Public Dinner at New York [March 10, 1831]' (Boston, MA, 1903).

Secondary Sources

Aschenbrenner, Peter, *British and American Foundings of Parliamentary Science, 1774-1801* (Abingdon-on-Thames, Oxfordshire, UK, 2017).

Aschenbrenner, Peter, 'Can Nation-states Self-stabilize? From Aristotle through Adam Smith to Hans Kelsen', *Journal of Parliaments, Estates & Representation* (vol. 41, no. 3, December, 2021), 259–279. doi.org/10.1080/02606755.2021.1949567.

Homer, Sidney and Sylla, Richard, *A History of Interest Rates* (Rutgers, NJ, 1996; 3rd edn rev.).
Roseveare, Henry, *The Treasury: The Evolution of a British Institution* (New York, NY, 1969).
[United States] *Historical Statistics of the United States 1789-1945, A Supplement to the Statistical Abstract of the United States* (Washington, DC, 1945). See census.gov/library/publications/time-series/statistical_abstracts.html
Zeitz, J.M., 'The Missouri Compromise Reconsidered: Antislavery Rhetoric and the Emergence of the Free Labor Synthesis', *Journal of the Early Republic* (vol. 20, no. 3, Autumn, 2000).

7 'An Important Epoch in the History of the Civilized World'

'A firm adherence to justice, moderation, temperance, industry and frugality are absolutely necessary'

During the infancy of the First Republic (1775–1787), state governments experimented with 'Declarations of Rights' or 'Bills of Rights'. In many cases, state lawmakers featured these inventories of prescriptions at the beginning of the constitutional instruments they composed. The style tended to be straightforward. 'Freedom of the press and trial by jury to remain inviolate forever', Georgia's 1777 constitution declared.[1] The New Hampshire constitution (1784) gathered 38 statements in Part I. These statements detailed the rights of inhabitants and the duties of public officials.[2] I refer to these Declarations and Bills of Rights as 'texts of political culture'.

I contrast 'texts of political culture' with 'texts of public history'. In 1813 Congress launched projects designed to compile and print the republic's public history. In the interval 1813–1861 Congress supported or sponsored 28 publishing projects. These projects included (a) compilations of public documents, (b) tables of information drawn from public documents, (c) records of action taken by public bodies or proceedings transpiring in these bodies (including debates) or (d) works of public figures deemed worthy of elevated attention. Although Congressional involvement was uneven, Congress may be credited with a total of 1,491 volumes published in the interval up to March 1861. I estimate that these volumes contain at least 100,000,000 words. This is a wildly modest guess.

- Texts of political culture sought to engage the understanding and support of inhabitants for government's stabilizing *and* allegiance-boosting efforts.
- Texts of public history sought to engage the understanding and support of inhabitants for government's allegiance-boosting efforts.

DOI: 10.4324/9781003019381-8

The Vermont constitution (1786) included 23 statements articulating the political culture of that republic. I draw on three statements; these appear at the conclusion of Vermont's 'Declaration of Rights of the Inhabitants of Vermont'.

- That all people have a natural and inherent right to emigrate from one State to another.
- That the people have a right to assemble together.
- A firm adherence to justice, moderation, temperance, industry and frugality, are absolutely necessary to preserve the blessings of liberty.[3]

That Vermont constitution (1786) also included the following provision.

> XVIII. Every man, of the full age of twenty-one years, having resided in this State for the space of one whole year, next before the election of representatives, and is of a Quiet and peaceable behaviour, and will take the following oath, (or affirmation) shall be entitled to all the privileges of a freeman of this State.
>
> You solemnly swear, (or affirm) that whenever you give your vote or suffrage, touching any matter that concerns the State of Vermont, you will do it so as in your conscience you shall judge will most conduce to the best good of the same, by the Constitution, without fear or favour of any man.[4]

The oath informed a Vermonter that he could discover the official norms (designed to guide and govern his fellow Vermonters' behavior) 'by the Constitution'. The freeman would also be obliged to cast his 'vote or suffrage [in such a manner as] will most conduce to the best good of the same, by the Constitution'.[5] In contrast Georgia's 1777 constitution called on 'every person entitled to vote [to] voluntarily and solemnly swear (or affirm, as the case may be) that I do owe true allegiance to this State, and will support the constitution thereof; so help me God'.[6]

'Every denomination demeaning themselves as good subjects of the state shall be under the protection of the law'

The Georgia constitution (1777) required that state representatives 'be chosen out of the residents in each county [and] shall be of the Protestant religion'.[7] Massachusetts (1780) offered the negative facet of this point. 'There shall be a Supreme Executive Magistrate, who shall be styled, THE GOVERNOR OF THE COMMONWEALTH OF MASSACHUSETTS ... and no person shall be eligible to this office, unless at the time of his election ... he shall declare himself to be of the christian religion'.[8]

Maryland (1776) proclaimed that it 'is the duty of every man to worship God in such manner as he thinks most acceptable to him; all persons, professing the Christian religion, are equally entitled to protection in their religious liberty'.[9] The New Hampshire (1784) constitution declared that 'every denomination of christians demeaning themselves quietly and as good subjects of the state shall be equally under the protection of the law'.[10] That declaration converted Maryland's right to protection into New Hampshire's duty to 'demean' oneself according to state-declared norms of behavior. Pennsylvania was more explicit about these norms of behavior and belief. Each 'member [of the legislature] shall make and subscribe the following declaration ... I do believe in one God, the creator and governor of the universe, the rewarder of the good and the punisher of the wicked. And I do acknowledge the Scriptures of the Old and New Testament to be given by Divine inspiration'.[11] Pennsylvania drew the line at that point. 'And no further or other religious test shall ever hereafter be required of any civil officer or magistrate in this State'.[12] South Carolina's contribution follows. 'That the Christian religion is the true religion, That the holy scriptures of the Old and New Testaments are of divine inspiration, and are the rule of faith and practice'.[13]

What do the foregoing samples demonstrate? The lesser point follows. There are serious difficulties in fusing prescription and description in a single sentence that addresses government's understanding the dominant politicial culture. The Pennsylvania constitution required its lawmakers to subscribe to the proposition that 'the holy scriptures of the Old and New Testaments [were] given by Divine inspiration'. Divine inspiration, I suggest, did not exert a uniform force. Some will remain unconvinced, while others will subscribe to competing beliefs and doctrines. Declarations of Rights and Bills of Rights did not claim divine inspiration for their composition. Instead, these instruments placed a human face on civil government's demands that inhabitants deliver norm-abiding behavior. On this account, text writers took it upon themselves to detail behavior that they determined to be worthy of incorporation into a constitutional instrument. Informing inhabitants of officially-approved political culture was essential to the fulfillment of an important task of civil government. Governments sought to inspire inhabitants to abide by these *government-articulated* norms. Some may assume that more genteel purposes inspired these text-writers. These might include recognizing (a) rights that the inhabitants enjoyed *before* the current form of civil government was organized or (b) rights that would exist even if government never articulated them. Unfortunately, civil governments don't traffic in benign, altruistic or eleemosynary purposes. Governments that declared an ascendant political culture in the First and Second Republics did so for the purpose of marginalizing dissenters and others who might dial back allegiance to the current form of government. Over time, the energy of inhabitants is sapped by internecine disputes over textual-reasoning's inability to explain what it is that government permits, prohibits and commands.

The following point is more significant. There's a lot of risk out there. Inhabitants live their lives in a material world that serves up both opportunities and challenges. The odds are overwhelming that someone living near me or with whom I do business will possess religious beliefs and practices different from those I own. Someone – me, my neighbor, my customer – is likely to get his feelings hurt in the everyday jostlings of human beings. These risks were worth the attention of composers of sonorous texts. Put another way, risk identification was a service that the civil government provided to its inhabitants. The sum of these risks, when visualized, yielded a self-portrait of a parochial government and its relationship to its inhabitants. The picture of 'who we are', 'who we should be' *and* of 'who we should not be' was embedded into constitutional instruments. These compositions were a species of bourgeois artwork. Put another way, the reader of a text invoking political culture should be swept up into a warm and fuzzy cocoon of self-congratulation. The harmonious iambs of the English language were well-suited to underscore the dramatic effect of bourgeois-complimenting prose, even if sonorous phrases were frequently spliced into lawyerly (and therefore clunky) sounding prose. 'There shall be no establishment of any one religious sect ...'. Delaware's Constitution (1776), Article 29, thereby launched its fusion of the prescriptive and the descriptive in iambic octameters.[14] The Bard said it best, in pentameter, to be sure. 'A horse, a horse, my kingdom for a horse'.[15]

This is an even larger picture at work. All of us need to know who we are. This awareness enables us to measure our differences, one from another. An enactment may favor my culture *or* the enactment may favor your culture *or* both *or* neither. My personal culture – framed by the state's declared norms of political culture – offers a touchstone that enhances my ability to assess the work of lawmakers. Put another way, Declarations of Rights leverage my personal beliefs by gently encouraging me (or aggressively compelling me) to assess the performance of the current form of civil government. Government rents my feelings by touching on my beliefs, knowing that, sooner or later, I will react to a serious divergence between my beliefs and those set forth in its latest Declaration of Rights. Put another way, a state government's Declaration of Rights ensures that I confront the following fact of political life. From the founding of the First Republic, there was no right to be let alone. I call this intended consequence 'autonomy rental'.

'The lost cannot be recovered; but let us save what remains'

To build out the human face of government Congress launched projects designed to tell the story of the Second Republic. These publication projects regarded the Second Republic as a political organism in a permanent state-of-becoming. Motivating voter-consumers to participate in votarian discipline – via the three stages previously named as enactment, assessment and reassessment – required grand drama.[16] Congress had a story of that dimension to tell. In 1813 Congress took its first steps towards compilation and publication of the republic's public history. Up to 1861 Congress supported or sponsored 28 publishing projects. I list these works by title in Appendix G: Public History, Practice and Purpose. There are alternate titles for some of the works. For example, the 'United States Reports' was originally titled 'Reports of Cases Argued and Adjudged in the Supreme Court of the United States'. By convention, reference (to cases reported in these volumes) was frequently trimmed down, citing readers to the name of the reporter of decisions. For example, from 1802 to 1815 the decisions of the United States Supreme Court appeared in 'Cranch's Reports'.

Congressional support or sponsorship (of any given project) did not always align with the date on which the first volume was published. I also note that the *Journal of the Federal Convention* – its modern title – appeared as a single volume. The title page of that volume offered the mouthful *Journal, Acts and Proceedings of the Convention, Assembled at Philadelphia, Monday, May 14, and Dissolved Monday, September 17, 1787, Which Formed the Constitution of the United States*. The remaining 27 projects were conceived as multi-volume series, that is, as 'ordered spines'. I have marked (with an asterisk) the 23 projects introduced by prefatory materials in Appendix G. The word count for these essays exceeds 42,000 words. These prefatory materials offer terra incognita to explorers.

Assembling a list of these 28 works called on multi-generational scholarly effort. This commenced with Ames's *Finding List*[17] and continued through subsequent versions of finding aids in the 1890s and 1900s. One government report listed 12 of the 'most rare and valuable' federally financed works in the study interval (1898). That report also referenced these publications as 'national treasures'.[18] The *Checklist of Public Documents* (1911) rethreaded this list. The *Checklist* is noteworthy for its ambition. It tackled the gargantuan task of supplying bibliographies, finding aids and checklists to aid scholarly reading of federally sponsored works.[19] Bassett's *Middle Group of American Historians* named 16 public history projects (1917).[20] Callcott's *History in the United States: Its Practice and Purpose* (1972) adopted these 16 as the canonical list.[21] My list expands Callcott's 16 works to 28.

Annotation, the newsletter of the National Historical Publications and Records Commission, traced the genesis of federal public history. 'The story of Federal support for publishing the documentary history of the United States dates back to the early days of the Republic, stemming from the need expressed among the states and later through historians for adequate and authentic documentation of our national history'.[22]

'But the real push', the article concludes, 'began through the work of J. Franklin Jameson and the American Historical Association, early advocates of documentary history. In the 1891 annual report of the American Historical Association, Jameson called for a commission with 'power to edit and publish not only materials in possession of the Government, but also those which are in private existence'.[23] Donald McCoy's essay, 'The Struggle to Establish a National Archives in the United States', opines that: 'while some improvements in records preservation and management were achieved randomly on the state and local levels, no significant changes were effected at the national level'.[24] To make this assessment correct, one must disregard the 1,491 volumes that appeared in the 28 projects that Congress played a role in bringing to press in the interval 1813–1861.

Inspiration for Congress's post-Ghent commitment to public history may be located in Thomas Jefferson's letter to Ebenezer Hazard (1791). Jefferson took notice of Hazard's project (which private subscriptions funded). It came to fruition under the title *Historical Collections* (1792–1794).[25]

> I learn with great satisfaction that you are about committing to the press the valuable historical and state-papers you have been so long collecting. Time and accident are committing daily havoc on the originals deposited in our public offices. The late war has done the work of centuries in this business. The lost cannot be recovered; but let us save what remains: not by vaults and locks which fence them from the public eye and use, in consigning them to the waste of time, but by such a multiplication of copies, as shall place them beyond the reach of accident.[26]

Representatives and Senators acquired the specialized knowledge involved in moving a series from conception to publication. Stages of the process include sponsoring, financing, editing, printing, distributing and (most importantly, as far as Thomas Jefferson was concerned) delivering the work to a library shelf both accessible to the reader and remote from the risk of destruction in the nation's capital city.

By the time the British expeditionary force burned Washington's public buildings (24/25 August 1814), the House of Representatives had already launched (what would become known as) the Congressional Serial Set. In December 1813 that body ordered that a continuously paginated set of documents be published. Coverage included presidential messages, executive branch 'letters and reports', 'reports of committees' and 'motions offered'. Volumes were to be 'printed in octavo folio [and] shall have their pages numbered in one continuous series of numbers, commencing and terminating with each session'.[27] This advance in the methodology of pagination may not, to post-moderns, seem significant.

Continuously paginated volumes enabled page-turning surveys of official action; in a word, 'surfing'. These surveys, in cultured eyes, exposed legislative or administrative achievements. This is another demonstration of the double-faced utility of bureaucratic agenda and bureaucratic autonomy at work.[28]

Congress – acting via a joint resolution of both Houses – also launched the federal depository library program. As to the 'public journals of the Senate and the House of Representatives and of the documents published under [their] orders ... copies shall be transmitted, to the executives of the several states and territories'. In addition, a single copy was to be distributed to 'each university and college in each state, and one copy to the Historical Society incorporated, or which shall be incorporated, in each state'.[29] I have defined this self-appointed service mission as 'enhancing public knowledge' and made it 'Job One', so to speak, in my listing of the 43 canonical service missions.[30] Public history offered Congress its opportunity to expand public knowledge of the daily work and grand accomplishments of the Second Republic.

In the opening sections of this chapter, I have compared texts of political culture and texts of political history. These offer an extreme degree of contrast, one with another. For example, the vulnerabilities expressed in texts of political culture take a negative, even pessimistic stance. This downbeat perspective is not surprising, given that any inhabitant may make the lives of others miserable. The texts of public history, on the other hand, assumed a neutral or optimistic view of the role of the inhabitant; these perspectives were on display in the prefatory essays that appeared in these works.[31]

'We do not deem it necessary to vindicate the consistency of propositions'

Following the lead of James Madison (1815, 1817),[32] John Marshall and James Monroe elaborated a method of Congressional precedents. I turn my attention to the Supreme Court's effort to construct a method of judicial precedents. I restrict my attention to the subject matter area debtor-creditor rights and remedies.[33] In 1847 the Supreme Court came face to face with Francis Bacon's challenge to judges. How difficult was it for the justices on the Taney court to see 'more profoundly into the reason of [prior] judgements'?[34] Was it feasible for these judges to follow Francis Bacon's advice 'and thereby to make more use of [prior judgments] for the decision of [future] cases more doubtfull'?[35] I refer to *Cook v. Moffat & Curtis*, 46 US (5 How.) 307 (1847) [Maryland debtor's delivery of notes in New York to his New York creditors waived protection of decree (in insolvency proceedings) obtained in Maryland].

Deciding the issues in *Cook*'s case called upon the Supreme Court to confront four tasks. (a) It was obliged to decide Cook's appeal. Judges add a single decision to a number of decisions previously handed down. This may be termed 'successive effort'. (b) The Supreme Court also weighed any proposed holding by comparing the proposed holding with the Supreme Court's previous holdings. I cite five decisions (relevant to *Cook v. Moffat*) in the margin.[36] I underscore that the Marshall court decided these cases. In line with Bacon's analysis, a judge's assessment of past holdings was a value-added effort. A judge launched that effort by invoking the cumulative function.[37] In the course of reviewing these five Marshall court holdings, judges of the Taney court were obliged to engage in pattern-discovering. This effort enabled these judges to state a proposition that embraced their vision of the pattern (of previous holdings) that they found acceptable. Thus, the immediate task of judges (in *Cook*, taken as the sixth case) was to fashion a new proposition that harmonized *both* the previous pattern (of these five holdings) *and* the rule of decision (to be announced) in the sixth case.[38] (c) The next challenge calls for an affirmative declaration of the holding that embraces both the five previous holdings and the proposed holding in the sixth case. In the margin, I reference an example of a function that calls for negative declaration.[39] (d) The Supreme Court may also confer a special status on its holding. The cue *stare decisis* signals the reader that – unless confronted in the future with an outlier to a pattern of its lawmaking – the Supreme Court assures readers that it will adhere to this pattern. That is, it is the Supreme Court's intention *today* to stand by its decisions *tomorrow*, just as *today* it is arranging *yesterday*'s decisions into a pattern that supports *today's* rule of decision, announced in the case under consideration. *Stare decisis* incorporates the cumulative function. A court can invoke the cumulative function without applying *stare decisis* to any gathering of decisions. But it can't invoke *stare decisis* without employing the cumulative function and without declaring, in the affirmative, the proposition that harmonizes the new holding with previous holdings.[40]

In *Cook v. Moffat* the Supreme Court held that a debtor's insolvency proceedings (under state law) 'could have no effect on contracts made before their enactment, or beyond their territory'. 46 US 307, 308. Grier J spoke for the Court with McLean, Daniel and Woodbury JJ concurring; Taney CJ dissented. Referring to 'the decisions heretofore given', Taney declared that 'these decisions are not in harmony with some of the principles adopted and sanctioned by this court, and therefore ought not to be followed'. At 309–310. Although concurring in the judgment, Woodbury voiced similar misgivings. 'I have the misfortune to differ as to some of the views that have been expressed in rendering it'. At 314. A proposition that embraced previous decisions, Woodbury opined, called forth an effort 'somewhat difficult to eviscerate, amidst so many conflicting and diversified views among its judges'. At 315. Writing for the majority, Grier could not avoid dealing with the troubled contours of these five Marshall court decisions. Put plainly, the Taney court inherited a dog's breakfast from the Marshall court. Nevertheless, Grier offered his best excuses for conferring *stare decisis* status on the affirmative proposition he (and the majority) declared to be *Cook*'s holding.

> We do not deem it necessary, on the present occasion, either to vindicate the consistency of the propositions ruled in that case with the reasons on which it appears to have been founded, or to discuss anew the many vexed questions mooted therein, and on which the court were so much divided. 46 US 309.

Grier's ambition was a bit out of reach. He hoped that his opinion could overcome the 'vexed questions ... on which the court were so much divided'. At 309.

> But as the questions involved in it have already received the most ample investigation by the most eminent and profound jurists, both of the bar and the bench, it may be well doubted whether further discussion will shed more light, or produce a more satisfactory or unanimous decision. At 309.

Later in the nineteenth century American *state* lawmakers rejected case-by-case judicial reasoning. The National Commissioners on Uniform State Laws – a body organized as an agent of state legislatures – set out to compose statutes marked off by subject matter area (1892). I refer to the Uniform Sales Act (1906).[41] Section by section, that statute spelled out the behavior that the National Commissioners expected of American business owners and managers.[42] On this account, the Uniform Sales Act sought to promote efficiencies in the commercial dealings of business owners and managers with their creditors and customers. 'The Uniform Law Commission (ULC, also known as the National Conference of Commissioners on Uniform State Laws) established in 1892', the online mission statement reads, 'provides states with non-partisan, well-conceived and well-drafted legislation that brings clarity and stability to critical areas of state statutory law'.[43] Put another way, 59 years after the Taney court struggled with the mess the Marshall court made of norm-crafting (in the field of debtor-creditor relations), state governments achieved a significant breakthrough by abandoning caselaw and embracing codelaw. The appetite of public bodies to promote private efficiency in business dealings by means of publicly-generated codelaw inspired these bodies to overthrow the most entrenched and well-beloved prejudices of common law reasoners. Americans had accepted, John Austin would argue, that 'a mere statement of the evils inherent in judiciary law, is amply sufficient to demonstrate (considering the question in abstract) that codification is expedient'.[44] Adam Smith would certainly be happy if efficiencies in lawmaking could be more readily achieved by codelaw than by caselaw. After all, Smith composed a lengthy essay in which he argued – in effect – that more efficient tax collection and administration were achievable by obeying his strictures and following his suggestions.[45] It's hard to see why Adam Smith would deny to the National Commissioners an equal claim to legislative competence, when it came to composing improvements in codelaw. This should be the case whether the subject matter be taxation or debtor-creditor relations. Put another way, Smith's productivity analytics are codelaw/caselaw neutral.

'We find abundant cause to felicitate ourselves in the excellence of our institutions'

From the day he took office, James Monroe shouldered the task of interpreting what the majoritarians were committed to accomplish in his presidency. In his First Inaugural Address (4 March 1817) Monroe employed the phrase 'the excellence of our institutions'.

> From the commencement of our Revolution to the present day almost forty years have elapsed, and from the establishment of this Constitution twenty-eight. Through this whole term the Government has been what may emphatically be called self-government [and] we find abundant cause to felicitate ourselves in the excellence of our institutions.[46]

On 2 December 1823 Monroe recycled this phrase into the conclusion of his Seventh Annual Message, referring to the 'excellence of our institutions' as the source of 'our blessings'. In post-Ghent America, 'blessings' served as a codeword for the achievements of the current form of civil government. Here Monroe stood on solid – and very presidential – ground.

> It is known to all that we derive them from the excellence of our institutions. Ought we not, then, to adopt every measure which may be necessary to perpetuate them?[47]

Monroe, like Marshall, elevated the geophysical perspective. A larger union, 'has eminently augmented our resources and added to our strength and respectability as a power'.[48] The 'system itself has been greatly strengthened in both its branches. Consolidation and disunion have thereby been rendered equally impracticable'.[49] 'Strength' goes off in one direction; 'respectability' in quite another. The US enjoys a strong government which exercises all the powers necessary to exploit 'resources' and take 'every measure which may be necessary to perpetuate ... our institutions'. This hints at a dark prospect. It is one thing to say that government should avoid going out of business. It is quite another thing to say that any given institution is 'excellent' and, on that account alone, is licensed to exploit 'resources', that is, any human or economic potential it can get its hands on. Marshall's observations were much to the same purpose as Monroe's. The government was licensed to take charge of available resources because it correctly anticipated that 'exigencies' were likely to challenge public and private resources. 'The exigencies of nations have been generally commensurate to their resources'.[50] I have already pointed out in Chapter 3, this volume, that, in this passage, John Marshall stands economies of scale head-on-end.[51]

In revisiting the accomplishments of *Constitution II*, Monroe looked back to constitution-writing episodes datable to 1777 and 1787. Quite naturally, he colored his prose in suitably technocratic hues. Monroe judged 'the adoption of this Constitution [as a] vast improvement made in the system itself'.[52] Monroe also noted that it was 'unnecessary' to do more than give the subject passing mention. In another very Monrovian turn of phrase, he declared that *Constitution II* was responsible for 'elevating the character and in protecting the rights of the nation as well as individuals'.[53] This assessment only made sense if the Second Republic was to be treated as an opportunity space, or, more precisely, as a political society that afforded its inhabitants diverse opportunities for personal development at varying rates. There would be little point in 'elevating the character ... of the nation' if the national government did not play a role in 'protecting the rights ... of individuals' to participate in both an evolving political society and evolving personhood. I note that Monroe's remarks on this point align him with John Marshall and the latter's attention to the 'liberty' aspect of autonomy rental.[54]

'Everything will depend on preservation of our institutions in their utmost purity'

> Monroe's final message to Congress turned on this sublime passage. Our institutions form an important epoch in the history of the civilized world. On their preservation and in their utmost purity everything will depend.[55]

The 'everything' (to which Monroe referred) included all risks taken in both civil and political society. If Monroe was right, nation-states had been competing in a world-wide race for 'respectability' since the fall of Troy, that is, throughout the 'history of the civilized world'. The United States entered the race by surviving the preliminary heats in its first and second recognition wars (1775–1783, 1812–1815). The Second Republic competed with both extinct political societies and the early nineteenth century's heavyweight nations who (at the time) dominated the world stage. The 'history of the civilized world' reminded Monroe's readers that Thucydides and Tacitus kept long-dead political societies on life support for the purpose of taunting today's political societies with the ambitions and accomplishments of Mediterranean-based governments.

The Second Republic, Monroe declared, was called upon to make good its claims that American 'institutions form an important epoch in the history of the civilized world'. Monrovian activism eagerly embraced the challenge of competitive institution-building. If 'our institutions' fail, he argued, the current form of government would be destabilized. The threat of instability offers other nations their evil opportunities for encroachment on American ambitions. In this doomsday scenario no quantum of brand loyalty would save our government, Monroe argued, if its operations were not conducted as if they were worth preserving in the 'utmost purity'. I follow up with an example of federal action that, Monroe argued, Congress launched in the 'utmost purity'. 'So far I have confined my remarks to the acts of Congress respecting the right of appropriation to such measures only as operate internally and affect the territory of the individual States'.[56] Monroe then noted two acts of Congress that 'appear to merit particular attention. These were gratuitous grants of money for the relief of foreigners in distress. The first in 1794 to the inhabitants of St. Domingo, who sought an asylum on our coast from the convulsions and calamities of the island; the second in 1812 to the people of Caracas, reduced to misery by an earthquake'. *Id.*, ¶121. In the Act of February 12, 1794 Congress voted $15,000 for relief of the 'inhabitants of Saint Domingo, resident within the United States, as shall be found in want of such support'.[57] Congress's generosity was, however, slightly undercut by that body's insistence that sums the US Treasury paid (to fund relief efforts) were to be 'charged to the debit of the French Republic'. Section 3. (Monroe neglected to mention the Act of March 7, 1794, in which Congress remitted 'foreign tonnage' tax to owners of vessels 'belonging to citizens of the French Republic' who reached US ports during the war with France.[58]) In the Act of May 8, 1812 Congress voted $50,000 for the 'relief' of victims of the earthquake in Caracas, Venezuela.[59] On this occasion, Congress directed that this 'gratuitous ... grant for the relief of foreigners in distress' was to be spent wholly in Venezuela.

During the Washington and Madison administrations, on Monroe's account, Congress purchased a measure of 'respectability' among the nations of the world by enacting the above-referenced laws. This development brought in significant consequences. By the conclusion of the Monroe administration (1825) the federal government was no longer competing with state governments. The terms 'energy and efficiency', Monroe argued, measured accomplishment at the international level.[60] 'The most despotic governments' exerted themselves with 'all the energy and efficiency' at their command.[61] As far as the Second Republic was concerned the accomplishments of these governments – after their fashion – shed a favorable light on the Second Republic's ambitions.[62] There is another aspect of competitive competence worth consideration. Should we regard superminoritarians and their leading contenders – Amphictyon (Brockenbrough) and Hampden (Roane) (1819) along with Randolph (1824) – as penny-a-punch stumblebums, fit only to buff the Second Republic into world-class fighting trim? Monroe and Marshall cut opposing Virginians down to size. And a very small size it was. Monroe and Marshall invited the Second Republic to claim its rightful and equal standing with any other government past or present, as measured by public sector competence. The 'most despotic governments' – inflicting 'oppressions and abuses' on their inhabitants – met their match when Monroe and Marshall helmed the Second Republic (1817–1825).

Conclusion

Monroe's final metaphor related his vision of seacoast fortresses protecting the American coastline. 'It is in that quarter, therefore, that we should be prepared to meet the attack. It is there that our whole force will be called into action to prevent the destruction of our towns and the desolation and pillage of the interior'.[63] Monroe's prose nails down the immense size of the seaboard that the unitary government committed itself to defend. 'Great improvements will be indispensable', he declared. 'Access to those works by every practicable communication should be made easy and, in every direction'.[64] With this dimension outlined, Monroe turned to internal improvements. 'The intercourse between every part of our union should also be promoted and facilitated by the exercise of those powers which may comport with a faithful regard to the great principles of our Constitution'.[65] I emphasize Monroe's employment of 'also' in the just-quoted passage. The equation of improvement projects with coastal fortifications permitted the reader to apply the scale of coastal forts to the dimensions that Monroe's 'great improvements' required. These improvements will be 'indispensable' to the destiny of the Second Republic.[66]

As Monroe glided from national defense to internal improvements, he deployed the following architectural metaphor. Do 'the people' serve as a foundation for the two governments? 'Resting on the people as our governments do, state and national, with well-defined powers …'.[67] No, that's not exactly what Monroe had in mind. Backtracking, he rethreaded the 'limits prescribed' to his 'two governments' formula. Monroe then declared that 'movement' between the two governments would be 'harmonious … in case of any disagreement, should any such occur'.[68] What follows is the moment that justifies your reading this volume. Monroe found a role for his – and John Marshall's – 'people'. His 'we the people' were just what the good Doctor – I refer to Adam Smith or Benjamin Franklin, reader's choice – ordered up. 'We the people' were obliged to mediate between the unitary and parochial governments. Yes, it was an oddball arrangement that Monroe and Marshall described for their readers in the almost indigestible phrase 'two governments'.[69] The risk of discordant outcomes – 'put the bridge here', 'no, over there' – was managed by the coincidence that the same voters were voting in both unitary and parochial elections. The Philadelphia convention tucked this arrangement into Article I, Section 2, Clause 1. 'The House of Representatives shall be composed of Members', the provision commences, 'chosen every second Year by the People of the several States'. That text concluded with this little-noticed sock-in-the-face: the 'Electors in each State shall have the Qualifications requisite for Electors of the most numerous Branch of the State Legislature'. It was not, on this account, the extent of the franchise that was all-important. It was the fact that *the same voters* were restoring an 'harmonious' state, that is, a measure of political equilibrium, via ballots cast at local polling stations in the course of balloting (a) for members of the federal House of Representatives and also (b) for members of their parochial House of Representatives (House of Commons, House of Delegates, Assembly). No organic arrangement posed an impediment to 'Electors' voting for candidates (for the state legislature) who might take a dim view of the desirability of federal programmatic action while, at the same time, these 'Electors' voted into Congress candidates who subscribed to the motto 'power for the sake of power'. This was the case even if the reasonings of the latter tended to 'apery of foreign manner, and of foreign fashions [and] Aristotle'.[70]

Here was a piece of votarian machinery that technocratically inclined scholars like Monroe and Marshall perfectly understood. 'A calm appeal [will] be made to the people', Monroe assured his readers. Their 'voice [will] be heard and promptly obeyed'.[71] Voters can't screw it up too badly because each individual voter possessed, every other year, *two* votes to cast in federal and state elections. Does *Constitution II* require that these two votes carry equal weight? Voters send Assemblyman Catspaw to Capital City with the mission to stand strong for 'parochial rights'. Translation, spend as little money as possible. Congressman Dogbreath will go to Washington with the mandate to spend truckloads of 'other people's money'. Translation, borrow from bondholders up to an effective yield of 6.88% per annum (the 1814 wartime benchmark) and *then* moderate your appetite for Hamilton's 'money'.[72] These facts threw into relief Monroe's appeal to the 'power of the people' in his 'Views', ¶5. The filter candidates in, out and back in enabled the 'transfer of the power of the people to representative and responsible bodies'. 'Views' ¶5. The political science of Monroe and Marshall was further backstopped by their employment of data sets designed to satisfy demands that nineteenth century social science might throw at their fact-testable propositions. The risk that 'the people' = 'the Electors' would call for *less* programmatic action from the federal government was negligible. And if it did happen, throttling back on Monroe's 'great improvements' would not subvert the legacy of Monroe's two terms as President.[73] Toss a few rocks back into a river *or* downsize an interstate expressway to a county collector and – so what? – the empire still stands. This can be put down to the mottoes that blazon the national temple. 'Expand or die *and* paralysis is death'.

Monroe's successor warmly reciprocated these sentiments. 'The roads and aqueducts of Rome have been the admiration of all after ages', J.Q. Adams declared. They 'have survived thousands of years after all her conquests have been swallowed up in despotism or become the spoil of barbarians' (4 March 1825).[74] Only a few months before – in Monroe's Eighth Annual Message to Congress – Monroe anticipated that the 'people' would save the national government's 'great improvements' from the fate of 'despotism' or the equally worse fate of destruction by 'barbarians', thereby becoming their 'spoil'.[75] Monroe concluded by acknowledging 'his great sensibility and heart felt gratitude [for] the many instances of the public confidence and the generous support which I have received from my fellow citizens in the various trusts with which I have been honored'. [76]

> Having commenced my service in early youth, and continued it since with few and short intervals, I have witnessed the great difficulties to which our union has been surmounted. From the present prosperous and happy state I derive a gratification which I can not express. That these blessings may be preserved and perpetuated will be the object of my fervent and unceasing prayers to the Supreme Ruler of the Universe.[77]

After securing today's blessings to the inhabitants of a nation, those (who bequeath their legacy to the next generation) may well ask their successors to preserve and perpetuate these gifts. Monroe's message is grounded in the second and third decades of the nineteenth century. It is also a message that echoes into the future of this the Second – or any future – Republic that offers its agency to the inhabitants of this continent.

Notes

1. See avalon.law.yale.edu/18th_century/ga02.asp; art. 56
2. See nh.gov/glance/constitution.htm
3. See avalon.law.yale.edu/18th_century/vt02.asp; Chap. I, Secs. XX, XXI, XXII.
4. See avalon.law.yale.edu/18th_century/vt02.asp; sec. 18.
5. *Ibid.*
6. See avalon.law.yale.edu/18th_century/ga02.asp; art. 41.

7. See avalon.law.yale.edu/18th_century/ga02.asp; Art. VI.
8. See law.gmu.edu/assets/files/academics/founders/Mass-Constitution.pdf; Chap. II, Sec. I, Art. II.
9. See avalon.law.yale.edu/17th_century/ma02.asp; Sec. XXXIII.
10. See en.wikisource.org/wiki/Constitution_of_New_Hampshire_(1784); Part I, Art. I, [Sec.] VI.
11. See avalon.law.yale.edu/18th_century/pa08.asp; 'Plan or Frame of Government', Sec. 10.
12. *Ibid.*
13. See avalon.law.yale.edu/18th_century/sc02.asp; [Art.] XXXVIII, [Sec.] 4th.
14. See avalon.law.yale.edu/18th_century/de02.asp Employing iambs to sonorous effect in English prose enjoys a noble pedigree. I refer to Matthew 7:19. 'The tree that does not bear good fruit/is hewèn down and cast into the fire'. If one scans the prose associated with the public life of the First and Second Republics, other examples may be found.
15. *Richard III*, Act 5 Scene 4
16. See text at 117-118.
17. Ames, *Finding List.*
18. *Report of the Superintendent of Documents*
19. *Checklist of United States Public Documents,* vii-xiii, 1668-1676.
20. Bassett, *American Historians.*
21. Callcott, *History.*
22. See archives.gov/files/nhprc/annotation/2004/fall-04.pdf
23. *Ibid.*
24. See archives.gov/files/about/history/sources/mccoy.pdf
25. Hazard, *Collections.*
26. See founders.archives.gov/documents/Jefferson/01-19-02-0059; 'Thomas Jefferson to Ebenezer Hazard, 18 February 1791'.
27. See memory.loc.gov/ammem/amlaw/lwhj.html *House Journal*, 9:166-67; 8 December 1813.
28. See text at 19.
29. See memory.loc.gov/ammem/amlaw/lwsl.html; 3 Stat 140; Res. I; 27 December 1813.
30. Aschenbrenner, *Foundings*, 173-174; Appendix B: The Forty-Three National Service Missions.
31. See text at 156, 183-184.
32. See text at 109 [Madison veto of bank recharter, 30 January 1815] and text at 130 [Madison veto of bonus bill, 3 March 1817].
33. See text at 160-161.
34. See text at 127n100.
35. See text at 127n100.
36. *Sturges v. Crowninshield*, 17 US (4 Wheat.) 122 (1819); *McMillan v. McNeill*, 17 US (4 Wheat.) 209 (1819); *Farmers and Mechanics' Bank of Pennsylvania v. Smith*, 19 US (6 Wheat.) 131 (1821); *Ogden v. Saunders*, 25 US (12 Wheat.) 213 (1827); *Boyle v. Zacharie*, 31 US (6 Pet.) 635 (1832).
37. See text at 112.
38. See text at 112, 158-159.
39. When the president is called upon to approve or disapprove a bill – Article I, Section 7, Clause 2 guides and governs this situation – he may find that the proposal is not in harmony with previous lawmaking. In that case he is obliged to state his 'Objections to that House in which it shall have originated, who shall enter the Objections at large on their Journal,

and proceed to reconsider it'. *Ibid.* Given that the president's clock for approval or disapproval is 'ten Days (Sundays excepted)' visualization of the harmony/disharmony of the bill offers a meaningful tool to the president.

40. There is another function that can be applied. A legislature may systematize (appellate court) holdings by refashioning judicially-created text into codelaw format. The Uniform and Model Acts proceed along these lines. See text at 160.
41. See source.gosupra.com/docs/statute/221
42. Staff at the Law Library (Library of Congress) has confirmed that Congress did not give its consent to state governments' organization of the National Commissioners – as a body – despite the express prohibition of Art. I, Sec. 10, Cl. 3: 'No State shall ... enter into any Agreement or Compact with another State ...'. Personal communication, 22 July 2021. Story's assessment of this clause follows. If states were at liberty to deal directly one with another, 'a foundation might thus be laid for preferences, and retaliatory systems, which would render the power of taxation, and the regulation of commerce, by the national government, utterly futile'. Story, *Commentaries*, Sec. 1349, 3:217-218. Based on Story's account (limiting the prohibition), state legislatures would not run afoul of this provision if they entered into lawmaking arrangements with other states for the purpose of replacing failed Supreme Court caselaw with codelaw of their own making. See Uniform_Law_Commission [last retrieved 23 July 2021].
43. See uniformlaws.org/home
44. Austin, *Jurisprudence*; Lecture XXXIX 'The Question of Codification', 662-666. ['I cannot see the use of all the pother about legislation', 664].
45. Smith, *Wealth*, 825-906 ['Of Taxes'].
46. See millercenter.org/the-presidency/presidential-speeches/march-4-1817-first-inaugural-address bid.
47. See millercenter.org/the-presidency/presidential-speeches/december-2-1823-seventh-annual-message-monroe-doctrine bid.
48. *Ibid.*
49. *Ibid.*
50. See text at 63, 68, 77.
51. See text at 63, 65, 77.
52. See millercenter.org/the-presidency/presidential-speeches/december-2-1823-seventh-annual-message-monroe-doctrine bid.
53. *Ibid.*
54. See text at 72.
55. See millercenter.org/the-presidency/presidential-speeches/december-7-1824-eighth-annual-message
56. See text at 56.
57. 6 Stat 13, c. 2, Sec. 1.
58. 1 Stat 342, c. 5.
59. 2 Stat 730, c. 79.
60. Views, ¶5.
61. *Ibid.*
62. *Ibid.*
63. 'Views', ¶141.
64. *Ibid.*
65. *Ibid.*
66. *Ibid.*

67. See millercenter.org/the-presidency/presidential-speeches/december-7-1824-eighth-annual-message
68. *Ibid.*
69. See text at 46-48, 179-180.
70. *Annals*, 18th Congress, 1st Session, 1298, 1302.
71. See millercenter.org/the-presidency/presidential-speeches/december-7-1824-eighth-annual-message
72. *Ibid.*
73. *Ibid.*
74. See millercenter.org/the-presidency/presidential-speeches/march-4-1825-inaugural-address
75. See millercenter.org/the-presidency/presidential-speeches/december-7-1824-eighth-annual-message
76. *Ibid.*
77. *Ibid.*

References

Primary Sources

Ames, J.G., *Finding List Showing Where in the Set of Congressional Documents the Individual Volumes of Certain Series of Government Publications are Found (1820 - 1891)* (Washington, DC, 1892).

[Ebenezer Hazard], *Historical Collections: Consisting of State Papers and Other Authentic Documents: Intended As Materials for An History of the United States of America* (Philadelphia, PA, 1792–1794).

Pacioli, Luca, 'Particularis de Computis et Scripturis/Details of Calculations and Writings' in *Summa de arithmetica, geometria, proportioni e proportionalita/Summary of arithmetic, geometry, proportions and proportionality* (Venegia, 1494; Book 9, Tract 11). I direct readers to *Particularis de Computis et Scripturis, A Contemporary Interpretation* (Seattle, 1994; trans. Jeremy Cripps, Findlay University).

Poore, B., *A Descriptive Catalogue of The Government Publications of the United States, September 5, 1774-March 4, 1881* (Washington, DC, 1885).

[United States] *Checklist of United States Public Documents, 1789-1909* (Washington, DC, 1962; 3rd edn rev. and enl.; Mary A. Hartwell, Superintendent of Documents).

[United States] *Fourth Annual Report of the Superintendent of Documents, For the Fiscal Year Ended June 30, 1898* (Washington, DC, 1899). See babel.hathitrust.org/cgi/pt?id=hvd.32044092519768&view=1up&seq=113&q1=1898

Secondary Sources

Austin, J., *Lectures on Jurisprudence or The Philosophy of Positive Law* (London, 1885; 5th edn, R. Campbell, ed., 2 vols).

Bassett, J.S., *Middle Group of American Historians* (New York, NY, 1917).

Callcott, G., *History in the United States: Its Practice and Purpose* (Baltimore, MD, 1972).

Appendix A

Survey of 1,147 Improvement Projects

I surveyed the Public Statutes at Large of the United States of America (Richard Peters, ed., first vol. published 1845). The 1st Congress wrote the first improvement project into the Public Statutes at 1 Stat 218, c. 23, Act of March 3, 1791 [Albany NY to Bennington VT designated as postal route]. The last project I surveyed was the work of the 24th Congress. I refer to 5 Stat 197, c. 52, Act of March 3, 1837 [land grant to the New Orleans and Carrolton Railroad Company 'to construct a railroad from Carrolton to the town of Bayou Sara' LA]. My definition of 'improvement projects' included postal route designations, roads, canals, railroads, navigation improvements, bridges, beach restorations, coastal surveys as well as Congress's approvals of state transportation projects involving navigable waterways. I excluded lighthouses. I included projects in the District of Columbia. I also included planning and design (which Congress sometimes termed a 'survey'), construction ('making a road' was the phrase Congress frequently employed) and resolution of claims that contractors, employees and others asserted. I explain in Chapter 1, this volume, the justification for counting projects on a state-by-state basis.[1] If a state's Congressmen were unable to settle conflicting *intrastate* demands, their colleagues would be obliged to do it for them.

I broke down institution agents into four categories: (a) the president (with or without 'commissioners' or 'engineers' that Congress assigned to carry out the project's purpose), (b) a federal agency, (c) a state agency or (d) private actors. Congress tasked these institution agents to fulfill either (a) generic service missions (transportation, communication) or (b) mission-specific instructions (remove rocks from the Big Old Nasty River, build a road from Here to There). I expand on this point as follows. Until 1855 Congress handled all monetary claims made against the US (or an agency or officer) through the legislative process. In the Act of February 24, 1855, 10 Stat 612, c. 122, Congress vested the power to investigate these claims in a newly-minted Court of Claims. Constructions claims management is a (wrongly) unheralded enterprise; *Constitution II* does not mention this service mission. Construction of transportation projects require boots on the ground. Managing claims in Congress underpinned legislative competence in design and construction. If something went wrong, it was Congress's self-appointed task – via claims management – to get its hands dirty with the necessary post mortem investigation.

I also coded the funding vehicles that Congress employed, dividing these into user fees, funds sourced to land sales (as settled in enabling acts), direct funding by appropriation, equity investment *or* land grants and water access that Congress offered as subsidies for projects.

I also divided my survey chronologically. One interval ran *from* 3 March 1791 and *up to* 4 May 1822. On 386 occasions in this interval Congress launched or curated improvements projects. These consist of 76 distinct projects appearing in 67 different Acts of Congress or Resolutions.

I supply the counts for the interval *after* 4 May 1822 and *up to and including* 3 March 1837: In this interval Congress launched or curated improvement projects on 761 occasions. These may be reduced to 163 distinct projects appearing in 123 different Acts of Congress or Resolutions.

The totals for the interval *from* 3 March 1791 and *up to and including* 3 March 1837 follow: In this interval Congress launched or curated improvements projects on 1,147 occasions. Of the grand total, I classified 501 projects as postal routes that Congress designated according to the state in which the route was located. In designing the system of postal routes, Congress named a total of 40 states or territories in the interval 1792–1837. In the same interval, Congress launched 96 different river and harbor projects along with 29 canal and five beach projects.

By type of funding, Congress appropriated funds to 150 distinct improvement projects in the 1791–1837 interval. Land sales in newly admitted states supplied funds for 12 projects. On 511 occasions Congress relied on user fees to fund project costs; 500 of these projects involved postal services. After 4 May 1822 Congress appropriated funds for improvement projects on 504 occasions. I refer to this method as 'direct appropriations'. Up to 4 May 1822 Congress had employed this method of funding on only 30 projects.

Breaking down the survey by type of institution agent: on 119 occasions Congress named the President (with or without commissioners or engineers) to fulfill the mission assigned to the President. Congress effectively deputized state and private actors on 41 and 46 occasions, respectively. However, the bulk of agents named – on 938 occasions – were federal (cabinet level) departments, agencies *or* recognizable subdivisions of these departments or agencies. The Postmaster General and the Secretary of War are two of the most familiar institution agents that Congress explicitly named.

Appendix B
Railroads Subsidized via Federal Land Grants

In Carter Goodrich's *Government Promotion of American Canals and Railroads 1800–1900* (1960) the author opens Chapter 5 with this passage: 'A new era of national action began in 1850 with an extensive grant of federal lands to aid in the construction of a system of railroads from Mobile, Alabama to northern Illinois'.[2] I surveyed federal subsidies for railroads, locating 18 instances occurring throughout the four Congresses that convened during the Jackson presidency. I refer to the work of the 21st, 22nd, 23rd and 24th Congresses. In these 18 cases Congress granted federal lands to private railroad companies. One such beneficiary was the 'Atchafalaya Railroad and Banking Company'. In some cases, Congress designated the beneficiary only by route. For example, Congress designated a project to run from the Apalachicola River to the Gulf of Mexico. Congress directed this route to intersect with that of the 'East Florida Rail-road Company'.

In the list below the single quote marks indicate that Congress referred – by name – to an organized railroad *or* rail-road company. The omission of quote marks (in the list below) indicates that Congress distributed benefits without referring to the company that the project's promoters had organized. The Baltimore and Ohio Railroad received three mentions.

- 'Baltimore and Ohio Railroad', 4 Stat 476, c. 85, Act of March 2, 1831.
- Illinois railroad project, 4 Stat 662, c. 87, Act of March 2, 1833.
- 'Baltimore and Ohio Railroad', 4 Stat 672, c. 11, Act of February 26, 1834.
- 'Winchester and Potomac Railroad Company', 4 Stat 744, Resolution III, June 25, 1834.
- 'Baltimore and Ohio Railroad', 4 Stat 757, c. 28, Act of March 3, 1835.
- Tallahassee to St. Marks railroad, 4 Stat 778, c. 45, Act of March 3, 1835.

- Pensacola to the Chatahoochee river railroad, 4 Stat 778, c. 45, Act of March 3, 1835.
- St. John's river to Suwanee river *or* to Vacasom Bay railroad, 4 Stat 778, c. 45, Sec. 4, Act of March 3, 1835.
- 'Winchester and Potomac Railroad Company', 4 Stat 792, Resolution I, January 27, 1835.
- 'Western Railroad', 5 Stat 17, c. 58, Act of April 29, 1836.
- 'New Orleans and Nashville Rail-road Company', 5 Stat 65, c. 255, Act of July 2, 1836.
- 'East Florida Rail-road Company', 5 Stat 144, c. 9, Sec. 1, Act of January 31, 1837.
- Appalachicola river to the Gulf of Mexico [to cross or intersect with the East Florida Rail-road Company to the Georgia State line to the Gulf of Mexico], 5 Stat 144, c. 9, Sec. 7, Act of January 31, 1837.
- 'Pensacola and Perdido Rail-road Company', 5 Stat 144, c. 9, Sec. 11, Act of January 31, 1837.
- 'Brunswick and Florida Rail-road Company', 5 Stat 144, c. 9, Sec. 11, Act of January 31, 1837.
- 'Lake Winnico and St. Joseph's Canal and Rail-road Company', 5 Stat 144, c. 9, Sec. 12, Act of January 31, 1837.
- 'Atchafalaya Railroad and Banking Company', 5 Stat 196, c. 49, Act of March 3, 1837.
- 'New Orleans and Carrolton Railroad Company', 5 Stat 197, c. 52, Act of March 3, 1837.

Appendix C
The Political Governance and Resource Exploitation Clauses

In Chapter 5, this volume, I explain how Congressmen and Senators acquired the technical skills they needed to build out the Second Republic. This Appendix expands on that point.

I begin with two constitutional provisions that touch on the organic relationship between the unitary and parochial governments. The first provision I term the Political Governance Clause. Scholars also term this provision the 'Enclave Clause'. Article I, Section 8, Clause 17 vests Congress with the power 'to exercise exclusive Legislation in all Cases whatsoever, over such District (not exceeding ten Miles square) as may, by Cession of particular States, and the Acceptance of Congress, become the Seat of the Government of the United States, and to exercise like Authority over all Places purchased by the Consent of the Legislature of the State in which the Same shall be, for the Erection of Forts, Magazines, Arsenals, dock-Yards, and other needful Buildings ...'. See the brief discussion at the Philadelphia convention in Farrand, *Records*, 2:510; 5 September 1787.

I term the second provision the Resource Exploitation clause. Article IV, Section 3, Clause 2 provides that: 'The Congress shall have Power to dispose of and make all needful Rules and Regulations respecting the Territory or other Property belonging to the United States; and nothing in this Constitution shall be so construed as to Prejudice any Claims of the United States, or of any particular State'. See the brief discussion at the Philadelphia convention in Farrand, *Records*, 2:466; 30 August 1787.

The delegates at Philadelphia encountered considerable difficulty in supplying norms that would guide and govern federal and state governments in resolving their differences. Delegates at Philadelphia focused on four issues in particular.

1 Land claims. Both the federal and state governments asserted land claims which, on occasion, overlapped each another. Article 2 of the Treaty of Paris (3 September 1783) described 'the boundaries of the said United States'.[3] These boundaries embraced tracts lying, more or less, outside of (what would become) the rationalized boundaries

of the 13 provinces; that is, between the Appalachian Mountains and the Mississippi River. Hence, a savings clause preserving national and state claims was in order. Delegates settled on the following: 'nothing in this Constitution shall be so construed as to Prejudice any Claims of the United States, or of any particular State'.

2 Forts. Ranks and officers were required to sign Articles of War whose purpose, in part, was to eliminate service members' access to state and federal courts for redress of in-service grievances. The Continental Congress adopted the first (permanent) Articles of War on 20 September 1776.[4] On this occasion John Adams and Thomas Jefferson copied British Articles of War.[5] The federal government required governance over the land on which a new fort would be situated. This was best accomplished by a state government ceding to Congress 'exclusive ... authority' within a tract to accommodate the dimensions of the proposed fortifications. This cession would enable Congress to establish norms of behavior in a limited and well-defined geophysical space. These cessions would satisfy the constitutional requirement that Congress 'exercise exclusive ... Authority over all Places purchased ... for the Erection of Forts'. This made vastly more sense than Congress proposing a federal footprint in such-and-such locale and discovering – thanks to the goofy co-legislation principle requiring state consents – that Congress bought a conditional state consent that was, as a practical matter, worthless.

3 The District of Columbia. If there were to be such a district, the unitary government would require 'exclusive authority' over a 'ten mile square' tract, that is, a tract embracing 6,400 acres. This acreage would supply the footprint required on which to construct a capital city. State cessions offered the best means of achieving this result. Hence, 'to exercise exclusive Legislation in all Cases whatsoever, over such District ... as may, by Cession of particular States ... become the Seat of the Government of the United States ...'. I underscore that when states go first, everything sorts itself out.

4 The national domain. I turn to the newly-won national domain or patrimony – roughly the trans-Appalachian region – that Great Britain ceded to the US in Article 2 of the Treaty of Paris (3 September 1783).[6] Congress needed to exercise both political governance and resource exploitation powers in this slice of geophysical reality. As the First War for American Independence progressed, states began to cede claims 'to the back country' to satisfy the Continental Army's need to trade land (the US didn't own at the time) to raise manpower during the First War for American Independence.[7] Hence the language (that the Philadelphia delegates crafted) ran, 'the Congress shall have Power to dispose of and make all needful Rules and Regulations respecting the Territory or other Property belonging to the United States'.[8]

Taking these points together: As of 1806 the structural relationship between the federal and state governments was experiencing rapid evolution. The key take-away here is that Congress was framing structural connections between the federal and state governments at the *mission-specific* level. An example is the road from Athens GA to New Orleans (Orleans Territory). 2 Stat 396, c. 41, Act of April 21, 1806, Sec. 7. As noted in the text, the Act of April 21, 1806 represented Congress's first attempt to batch-process national roads.[9] As of that date Congress must have realized – in my recasting – that (a) only Congress could guide and govern the fulfillment of service missions (such as transportation and communication), given the sprawling land mass that the US occupied and the crazy-quilt contours that marked off one state from another *and* that (b) it was at the mission specific level of abstraction that these structural connections could be contoured.

Differential funding also promoted Congress's acquisition of legislative competence. Take these differences in funding levels (as of 1806). Congress appropriated $30,000 to launch the Cumberland Road (from the Ohio land sales account) along with the following direct appropriations. Congress directed that $6,400 be spent on the Athens to New Orleans road, with another $6,000 to be spent on the road through northern Ohio along with and another $6,000 to be spent on the Nashville to Natchez road.[10] Planning and constructing infrastructure raised the expectations of inhabitants. Consumers of future benefits could adjust their individual and collective perceptions of the destiny of the Second Republic based on what they believed they would or should get. Purpose in doing, just as Emerson declared, reveals itself. Purpose revealed beats textual reasoning and sinews the structure required.[11]

To recap: As of the 9th Congress (1807–1809) that body did not find the Political Governance Clause and the Resource Exploitation Clauses to offer viable 'bright lines' to prevent collisions between state and federal governments. The proof of the foregoing lies in Congress's refusal to call on Jefferson to request state governments from Georgia to Ohio for permission to launch three new national road projects on 21 April 1806.[12]

Appendix D
The Cumberland Road

I surveyed the 40 statutes that launched or curated the Cumberland Road project, beginning with 2 Stat 357, c. 19, Act of March 29, 1806 (9th Congress, 1st Session) and ending with 11 Stat 7, c. 25, Act of May 9, 1856 (34th Congress, 1st Session).

I located 67 discrete instances in which Congress appropriated funds in 40 Acts of Congress. On 6 occasions Congress appropriated no amount; these statutes typically granted assents to action that a state legislature had previously taken. (Congress transferred intrastate segments of the Cumberland Road to states at the conclusion of its useful life as a national road.) I coded appropriations by type and totaled expenditures accordingly. These were $1,070,000 (Design), $2,790,000 (Construction), $1,535,069.21 (Repairs) and $623,931.89 (Claims). I note that scholars typically regard Cumberland MD as the Cumberland Road's eastern terminus, with the western terminus of the road located at Vandalia IL. Congress also planned a southerly branch from Wheeling VA to St. Louis MO. Congress appropriated a total of $6,019,001.00 on the projects I surveyed. In modern road miles the distance from Cumberland MD to Vandalia IL runs 611 miles. Based on this data, the per mile cost ran $9,851.07.

I have used the term 'batch-processing' when referring to Congressional brokerage of multiple projects (during the consideration of a single bill). In the case of the 40 Cumberland Road bills another pattern emerges. Statutes launched and curated over time (47 years) declared useful variables and assigned a variety of domains to these variables. One can disaggregate Congress's attention to the details of lawmaking by sieving variables. Statutes may be parsed

- *over* time (47 years),
- *over* space (Cumberland MD to Vandalia IL),
- *over* types of officials (i.e., superintendents tasked to build roads or repair roads),
- *over* type of effort (design, construction, repairs and claims),

- *over* tessellated segments: rights of way 80 feet wide and 10 miles long *or* undesignated,
- *as to* timber, stone, gravel and other raw materials,
- *as to* bridges, culverts and other secondary structures and
- *over* competing projects: (south to north) Wheeling VA to central Missouri, Wheeling VA to central Illinois and northern Ohio to the Mississippi River.

Appendix E
The 'Two Governments' Formula

I gathered 15 essays that James Monroe and John Marshall composed in the interval 1819–1822.[13] These 15 essays comprise 70,000 words. (I note that Monroe's 'Views' (with his Veto Message) and Marshall's 11 'Friend' essays comprise approximately 30,000 words each. Marshall's *McCulloch* opinion runs just under 10,000 words.) The 'two governments' formula appears a total of 11 times in these 15 essays. I begin with Marshall's employment of the 'two governments' formula. Marshall used the formula three times, with two follow-on recyclings of that passage.

> Whether the state of Maryland may, without violating the constitution, tax that branch? That the power of taxation is one of vital importance; that it is retained by the states; that it is not abridged by the grant of a similar power to the government of the Union; that it is to be concurrently exercised by the two governments – are truths which have never been denied. 17 US 400, 425.

Marshall recycled the phrase 'two governments' on two further occasions in his 'Friend' essays. Marshall, *Defense*, 101, 193. The eight occasions on which Monroe employed the 'two governments' formula appear in his 'Views' at ¶¶ 26, 27, 58, 64, 97, 106 114 and 123. Four representative selections follow.

> It is impossible to speak too highly of this system taken in its twofold character and in all its great principles of two governments .... ¶27
>
> I shall conclude my remarks on this part of the subject by observing that the view which has been presented of the powers and character of the two Governments is supported by the marked difference which is observable in the manner of their endowment. ¶64
>
> The Government of the United States is a limited Government, instituted for great national purposes, and for those only. Other interests are committed to the States, whose duty it is to provide for them. ... I do not think that in offices of this kind there is much danger of the two Governments mistaking their interests or their

> duties. I rather expect that they would soon have a clear and distinct understanding of them and move on in great harmony. ¶106
>
> Wherein consists the danger of giving a liberal construction to the right of Congress to raise and appropriate the public money? It has been shown that its obvious effect is to secure the rights of the States from encroachment and greater harmony in the political movement between the two governments, while it enlarges to a certain extent in the most harmless way the useful agency of the General Government for all the purposes of its institution. Is not the responsibility of the representative to his constituent in every branch of the General Government equally strong and as sensibly felt as in the State. ¶123.

Article VI, Section 3 – also known as the Supremacy Clause – plays an important role when the 'two governments' formula is closely examined. The text of that clause provides that 'all executive and judicial Officers, both of the United States and of the several States, shall be bound by Oath or Affirmation, to support this Constitution'. There is no counterpart to this clause. Federal 'executive and judicial Officers' are not bound to avoid stepping on the sensitive toes of state governments. Eli Wallach said it best in 'The Good, The Bad and The Ugly'.[14] When the urge to serve as a 'contrivance of human wisdom to provide for human wants' strikes the fancy of state governments, let them build the Erie Canal or the California Water Project. Otherwise, don't talk.[15] Marshall had a great deal to say on this point in 'Friend of the Constitution' essay no. V. *Defense*, 184–188. This point sheds light on the 'two governments' formula omission of 'equality' as a predicate that may correctly be attached to the relationship. The two governments are separate, distinct and independent in their operations but state governments are subordinate to the federal government. Marshall is rather keen to note that this will 'grate harshly on the ears of Hampden'. At 188.

Appendix F
Technical Appendix and Editorial Practices

I have posted files with content drawn from my surveys (along with other materials) at

www.parliamentary-manuals-and-treatises.com/tech.app.excellence

Readers who find errors in this publication or who wish to suggest additional postings may contact me at

aschenbrenner.historian@gmail.com.

I will consider requests by scholars for access to the underlying surveys and materials referenced in this study.

As to editorial practices, I take liberties with the initial characters in quoted passages. If my text reads 'A power to establish turnpikes', the first character in the original text may appear as an uncapitalized 'a'. And vice versa. This avoids ugly [].

I transcribe 'district', 'river' and 'lake' according to the original text. However, *my* references to the 'Mississippi River', etc. follow the modern style.

I have rearranged and deleted words from the original text to extract running chapter heads and quotes at opening of sections.

I do not mark misspellings; thus, I left Hales's 'extreams' untouched. In addition, italics or capitalized phrases – such as Blackstone's 'BRITISH LIBERTY' – appear as in the original.

The first appearance of a citation to a documentary compilation (in the end notes to a chapter) such as the Public Statutes of the United States will also contain the URL directing the reader to the resource.

United States Supreme Court cases: At the first opportunity I give the full citation (including reference to the nominative reporter) *and* the page number at which the court's opinion begins *rather than* the page number conventionally employed. Accordingly, I cite to the opening page of Marshall's opinion as

Gibbons v. Ogden, 22 US (9 Wheat.) 186 (1824).

and not as

Gibbons v. Ogden, 22 US (9 Wheat.) 1 (1824).

I explain this as follows. In the early nineteenth century it was the (nominative) reporter's practice to include a summary of the arguments of counsel. This meta-text is generally but not consistently referred to as the reporter's syllabus. Thus, vol. 22 of the United States Reports (taken from pages 1 through 186) does not contain the court's opinion. The opinion makes its appearance at p. 186. While unconventional, my format has the benefit of alerting the reader (who may not be a US-trained lawyer) as follows. When Marshall declares that he will assess the constitutionality of a national banking institution in light of 'former proceedings of the Nation respecting it', my citation to 17 US 400, 401 signals the reader that Marshall has given this declaration a prominent place at the opening of his opinion in *McCulloch*'s case.

When quoting from Monroe's 'Views', I assigned paragraph numbers to each of the 170 paragraphs. Thus, I reference his pivot:

> My mind has undergone a change'. ¶101.

This format permits the reader to gauge at point in that essay Monroe's remarks may be found *relative to* the 1819 and 1822 essays which make up his composition.

Last retrieved: I restrict that expression to websites lacking fixed content.

I employed the following online source for the text of Aristotle's *Politics*.

> classics.mit.edu/Aristotle/politics.html – Benjamin Jowett, trans.

I also supply the Bekker citation. Readers with access to the Loeb Library print editions can readily find the quoted material using that citation. For example, Aristotle, *Politics*, 1303b17.

Appendix G
Public History, Practice and Purpose

Preservation and dissemination of America's public history matured under the leadership of the 13th, 14th and 15th Congresses. These were multi-volume works, with one exception. Asterisks (below) signal that prefatory materials introduce the work. Further details may be found at parliamentary-manuals-and-treatises.com/tech.app.excellence

*Register of Officers**
*Congressional Serial Set**
*United States Reports**
*Journal of the Federal Convention**
*Elliot's Debates**
House Journal
*Senate Legislative Journal**
*Secret Journals of the Continental Congress**
*Annals of Congress**
Congressional Globe
*American State Papers**
*American Archives, Fourth Series**
American Archives, Fifth Series
*Tracts and Other Papers**
*Diplomatic Correspondence 1783–1789**
*Diplomatic Correspondence of the American Revolution**
*Register of Debates**
Senate Executive Journal
*Life of George Washington**
*Papers of James Madison**
*Public Statutes of the United States at Large**
*Works of John Adams**
*Works of Alexander Hamilton**
*Works of Daniel Webster**
*Works of John Calhoun**
*Works of William Henry Seward**

*Writings of Thomas Jefferson**
*Works of Henry Clay**

Except for the *Journal of the Federal Convention,* all projects were designed as multi-volume offerings or, in my phrase, ordered spines.

Appendix H

James W. McCulloch, John Marshall and the US Sinking Fund

I begin with the annual report of the Commissioners of the Sinking Fund dated 10 February 1818. CY 1817 was the reporting interval. My source is the *American State Papers/Financial*.[16] As a fiscal intermediary in the service of the US Treasury, the Commissioners' reports detailed holdings and transactions of the Sinking Fund in a near-modern format. Assets were assigned to a balance sheet *with* financial transactions appearing in income/expense reports. Enter James W. McCulloch, the cashier of the Baltimore Branch of the Second Bank of the United States. McCulloch's transactions in US Treasury bonds are detailed on five lines in the Sinking Fund Commissioners' report for CY 1817. McCulloch's purchases of government bonds totaled $732,978.10. Where does a bank cashier come up with that kind of money? Bray Hammond relates McCulloch's embezzlement as it unfolded in Baltimore.[17] I move forward to 5 February 1819. Commissioners reported Sinking Fund activity for CY 1818. The Chief Justice conspicuously absented himself from participation.[18] I note that the report was dated 16 days before oral argument began in *McCulloch*'s case. Had Marshall not (effectively) recused himself, the 1818 report of the Sinking Fund would display evidence of McCulloch's illegal transactions. Although McCulloch's transactions in CY 1818 were more modest than his thieving in CY 1817, it would have been odd for the Chief Justice to uphold the lawful participation of James W. McCulloch in banking transactions (that the state of Maryland challenged) while the Chief Justice was also certifying the details of his unlawful transactions with the Second Bank of the United States. Which institution, one must add, was not a party to the appeal.[19]

In Chapter Three, this volume, I raise the question: 'When did Marshall decide to pen the 11 'Friend' essays?' I conjecture as follows. The nominative reporter Henry Wheaton spread the agreement between the Second Bank and the State of Maryland over four pages of the syllabus. 17 US 316–320. Through Wheaton, it is likely that Marshall had access to the terms of this agreement before he composed his opinion for the Supreme Court. The agreement touched on three points. (a) The state of Maryland and the Second Bank asked the Supreme Court to decide the 'validity' of the Maryland statute taxing the Second Bank along with the validity of the 'act of congress' establishing the Second Bank. (b) Moreover, 'all errors in [pleadings] are hereby agreed to be mutually released'. Thus, the case could not be resolved as a matter of procedural default. For example, if the Supreme Court noted the absence of the Second Bank as a party to the appeal, the agreement conferred jurisdiction on the Supreme Court despite this glaring procedural lapse. One supposes that post-modern counsel, practicing in stratospheric heights (before the United States Supreme Court, at 100 Maryland Avenue) are green with envy. 'Why don't we just stipulate to 'cert' and don we our bespoke on the date appointed?' If Maryland won, then judgment against the Second Bank would be entered in favor of the 'plaintiffs for $2,500, and costs of suit'. The informer would, under the Maryland statute, get one-half of that recovery or $1,250.[20] I assume the reader's suspicions are now raised to the level of 'high alert'. The United States Supreme Court treated a private – that is, out-of-court – wager as binding on the Supreme Court. Marshall couldn't unravel jurisdiction 'forced' on the Supreme Court without – for a second time in a decade – avoiding resolution of the issue.[21] So there was, so to speak, no going back. On the other hand, given the collusive nature of the Second Bank's private arrangement with the state of Maryland – through its corrupt cashier – Marshall probably realized that further and solo effort on his part would be inevitable.[22] That is, if he wished posterity to make sense of *McCulloch*'s case.

Appendix I

Comparing and Contrasting Nations and Cultures in *The Federalist*

I surveyed the *Federalist* essays to test for the authors' employment of Smith's productivity analytics. These are feasibility, longevity, proportionality and diminishing returns.[23] Both Madison and Hamilton were familiar with Smith's *An Inquiry into the Nature and Causes of the Wealth of Nations*. Madison and Hamilton did not name Smith's work as a source of inspiration in the *Federalist* essays, however. One may surmise, however, that Alexander Hamilton's Essay 21 – titled 'Further defects of the present Constitution' – contains a sly clue on this point. 'The wealth of nations', Hamilton declared, 'depends upon an infinite variety of causes'.

Readers of the 85 *Federalist* essays will recall that John Jay, Alexander Hamilton and James Madison referenced political arrangements and settlements in other nations and cultures. These references enabled these authors to set up apples-to-apples comparisons and contrasts. In turn, that approach enabled them to gather support for their endorsement of *Constitution II*. Moreover, given that Jay did not attend the convention and that Hamilton's attendance was minimal – I note Farrand's survey and conjectures on this point[24] – the task of commenting on *Constitution II* was best accomplished via citations to organic arrangements and settlements in other nations and cultures. In this regard it is important to note that the Philadelphia convention sealed its official journal on 17 September 1787.[25] The best evidence of what transpired at the convention was therefore out of reach of these authors.

I count 204 raw citations that drew on arrangements and settlements assignable to other nations and cultures. I then discarded duplicates. For example, multiple references to Great Britain in a single essay counted as 1. This reduced the total to 172. I offer a Smithian sampling.

Feasibility: 'The utility of a confederacy, as well to suppress faction, and to guard the internal tranquility of states, as to increase their external force and security, is in reality not a new idea'. Essay 9.

Longevity: 'As soon as domestic manufactures are begun by the hands not called for by agriculture, the imported manufactures will decrease as the numbers of people increase. In a more remote stage, the imports may consist in a considerable part of raw materials, which will be wrought into articles for exportation, and will, therefore, require rather the encouragement of bounties, than to be loaded with discouraging duties. A system of government, meant for duration, ought to contemplate these revolutions, and be able to accommodate itself to them'. Essay 42.

Proportionality: 'The number of wars which have happened or may happen in the world, will always be found to be in proportion to the number and weight of the causes, whether *real* or *pretended,* which *provoke* or *invite* them'. Essay 3.

Diminishing returns: 'A government founded on principles more consonant to the wishes of the larger states, is not likely to be obtained from the smaller states. The only option then for the former, lies between the proposed government, and a government still more objectionable. Under this alternative, the advice of prudence must be, to embrace the lesser evil; and, instead of indulging a fruitless anticipation of the possible mischiefs which may ensue, to contemplate rather the advantageous consequences which may qualify the sacrifice'. Essay 62.

Before readers conclude that Madison, Hamilton and Jay are giving the Master of Glasgow a run for his money, I note that Adam Smith references China on 63 occasions and Africa on 36 occasions while our lads mention China on one occasion with two mentions of developments in Africa. Jay, Hamilton and Madison were, on this account, much more tethered to the Eurocentric than Smith. On the other hand, there was, at the time, a British empire and no such animal on our side of the pond.

Appendix J
Marshall and Monroe Discuss the 'Views'

I begin with Jean Edward Smith's relation of the following events in his study *John Marshall, Definer of a Nation* (New York, 1996). After sending his 'Views' to Congress (4 May 1822), Monroe dispatched copies of the 'Views' to three justices of the Supreme Court including Chief Justice Marshall. Smith, *Marshall*, 468–469. I quote from Marshall's reply to Monroe (13 June 1822). 'All however will I think admit that your views are profound, and that you have thought deeply on the subject'. Marshall's observations were circumspect in tone. 'To me', Marshall concluded, 'they appear to be most generally just'.[26] Donald G. Morgan offered further insight on this point in his study *Justice William Johnson,* a colleague of Marshall's on the Supreme Court.[27] Johnson's reply to Monroe was, Morgan opines, 'virtually an advisory opinion'. All the justices, Johnson declared, 'are of opinion that the decision on the bank question completely commits them on the subject of internal improvements as applied to post-roads and military roads'.[28] Mark R. Killenbeck, *William Johnson, The Dog that Did not Bark?* 42 Vand. L. Rev. 407, 440–442 (2019), supplies further attention to the interaction between Monroe and the justices of the Supreme Court on this subject. Killenbeck persuasively dials back several of Morgan's full-throated assessments. Further research and assessment are warranted.

Appendix K
The Bonus Bill (1817) and the 1818 House Resolution

The Act of April 10, 1816 required the Second Bank to pay the US Treasury a bonus. The relevant provision is located in Sec. 20 of that act. 'The president, directors, and company ... shall pay to the United States, out of the corporate funds thereof, the sum of one million and five hundred thousand dollars, in three equal payments'. The Bonus Bill that Madison vetoed on 3 March 1817 contained an elaborate requirement on the subject of state consents, which requirement was nested into the formula governing distribution of the bonus. Congress would be required to obtain these consents as a condition of legislating 'roads or canals or in improving the navigation of ... water courses', Sec. 2.[29] To tempt states to give these consents – and to tempt states *not* to attach conditions to their consents – the Bonus Bill distributed federal cash according to the 'ratio of representation' in the House of Representatives. The bill was silent on spending in territories. States were also permitted to trade off funding requests. For example, if the funding for improvements in a given year was likely to be small, Ohio could bargain away its allocation for that year with Maryland. Another oddity. The Bonus Bill contained no prohibition or restriction on Congress appropriating federal funds for transportation projects. In other words, as far as the national brokerage was concerned, it was business as usual.

In 1818 Congress debated four resolutions on the subject of internal improvements. Congressmen attempted to write a mini-constitution of norms guiding the behavior of all actors and bodies concerned in the process of launching improvement projects.[30] The text of these resolutions appears in the *Annals of Congress*, 15th Congress, 1st Session, 1380; 13 March 1818. Further debate transpired on 14 March 1818. *Ibid.*, 1381–1386. Only the first of the four resolutions passed the House; the vote was 90–75. The text of this resolution reads: 'Congress has power, under the Constitution, to appropriate money for the construction of post roads, military and other roads, and of canals, and for the improvement of water-courses'.

Neither that resolution (nor the other three that did not pass) mention state consents. None of the four resolutions directed that Congress employ an allocation formula that would govern distribution of federal cash to state governments. I note that Monroe's 'Views' (1822) ignored the resolution quoted above (1818). However, the text of the resolution aligns closely – but not perfectly – with the conclusions Monroe expressed in his 1822 essay.

Appendix L
Unravelling the Northwest Ordinance

My point of departure is Chief Justice Taney's (implicit) suggestion that some actor or body committed a constitutional sin when the Confederation Congress (13 July 1787) and the US Congress (6 March 1820) enacted bans on enslaved labor in US territories. Tidying up after Taney, I employ the term 'unravelling' to the process that Taney wished that his ancestors had invoked. Taney's thinking may be teased out as follows. Why didn't President George Washington disapprove the Act to 'provide for the Government of the Territory Northwest of the river Ohio'? The bill came before him on 6 August 1789.[31] If Washington considered disapproving the bill, he would not be working on a blank slate. He would have been obliged to take into consideration investments that private actors and bodies made in reliance on norms established by the Northwest Ordinance during the 25-month interval that extended from 13 July 1787 to 7 August 1789.[32] I argue that the Northwest Ordinance became an instance of an acceptable pattern of lawmaking in that interval. The president's 10-day veto clock (in this case, beginning 6 August 1789, as noted above) assumes that a deficiency will be immediately apparent to the president. In other words, visualization of patterns of lawmaking is baked into Article I, Section 7, Clause 2, guiding and governing the President's veto power.

If a given risk existed at the time the claim to ownership matured – this would be in 1834 – the buyer would be obliged to review 'restrictions that background principles of the State's law of property and nuisance already placed upon' the claim. I refer to the Court's opinion in *Lucas v. South Carolina Coastal Council*, 505 US 1003, 1029 (1992), Scalia, J. If I make an investment in 1834 that is legal in one place and illegal in another, courts should assume that I have negotiated with my seller to adjust the price according to risks I have undertaken. Acts of Congress (dating to 1820/1821) supply 'background principles' – as Justice Scalia explained – that the buyer must consult before he makes an investment. A private investor in 1834 – on Justice Scalia's account – didn't do *his* due diligence. Sandford, a white man, had no rights in the purchase he made in Missouri that a court was bound to honor. The right to make a bad investment is a private choice for which no organic arrangement or government intervention/programmatic action can (or should) deliver redress.

Notes

1. See text at 20-21.
2. Goodrich, *Promotion*, 169.
3. See avalon.law.yale.edu/18th_century/paris.asp
4. See avalon.law.yale.edu/18th_century/contcong_09-20-76.asp
5. See founders.archives.gov/documents/Adams/01-03-02-0016-0172 [Diary of John Adams; Monday August 19 1776; 'I was therefore for reporting the British Articles of War, totidem Verbis'.].
6. See text at 132.
7. Aschenbrenner, *Foundings*, 57.
8. See text at 174.
9. See text at 44.
10. See text at 42, 44.
11. 'Nature, in the main, vindicates her law. Skill to do comes of doing; knowledge comes by eyes always open, and working hands and there is no knowledge that is not power ... the men who fear no city, but by whom cities stand ...'. Ralph Waldo Emerson, *Complete Works*, 'Old Age', 7:321 (1862).
12. See text at 7, 27.
13. See text at 1-3, 38-40, 61-62.
14. See www.youtube.com/watch?v=hnFdTXtFdSE
15. Burke, *Reflections*, 70.
16. See memory.loc.gov/ammem/amlaw/lwsplink.html; *American State Papers*, 3:242-256; No. 518; 15th Cong., 1st Session, 10 February 1818.
17. Hammond, *Banks and Politics*, 260-262.
18. *American State Papers*, 3:401; No. 552; 15th Cong. 2nd Sess; 5 February 1819.
19. See text at 59.
20. See text at 60n9.
21. See text at 79n48.
22. See text at 62.
23. Smith, *Wealth*, 825-827. See text at 64.
24. Farrand, *Records*, 3:588.
25. The convention ordered its records sealed on 17 September 1787. Farrand, *Records*, 2:648. The official journal was not published until Congress ordered publication in 1818. 3 Stat 475, Res. VIII, March 27, 1818. On the first occasion that counsel cited the (now published) official journal, the Supreme Court, Marshall CJ, writing for the majority, declined to reference the journal in his opinion. *Craig v. State of Missouri*, 29 US (4 Pet.) 425 (1830).
26. Monroe Papers, Library of Congress; Reel 8, Image 360.
27. Morgan, *Johnson*, 122-125.
28. *Ibid.*
29. *House Journal*, 10:537-539; Sec. 2 [Michael Glazier reprint; Wilmington DE, 1977; the Library of Congress posting is marred by scrambled page numbers].

30. Currie, *The Jeffersonians*, 271-278 supplies details along with extensive quotations from the *Annals of Congress*.
31. *Documentary History of the First Federal Congress of the United States of America, March 4, 1789 to March 3, 1791, House of Representatives Journal* (Baltimore MD, 1977; Linda Grant De Pauw, ed.; vol. 3), 135-136, 6 August 1789 ['Mr. Speaker signed the said inrolled bills' (one of which became the 'Act to provide for the government of the territory northwest of the river Ohio') and sent these bills to the President].
32. *Continental Congress Journals*, 32:334-343, 13 July 1787; 1 Stat 50, c. 8, Act of August 7, 1789.

References

Primary Sources

Records of the Federal Convention of 1787 (New Haven, CT, 1911, ed. Max Farrand, 3 vols; rev. ed. 1937; 4 vols).

Smith, Adam, *An Inquiry into the Nature and Causes of the Wealth of Nations* (Oxford, 1976; R.H. Campbell, A. S. Skinner and W.B. Todd, eds.; the 'Glasgow' edn). For details on pagination see text at 37.

Secondary Sources

Aschenbrenner, Peter, *British and American Foundings of Parliamentary Science, 1774-1801* (Abingdon-on-Thames, Oxfordshire, UK, 2017).

Goodrich, Carter, *Government Promotion of American Canals and Railroads, 1800-1890* (New York, NY, 1960).

Hammond, Bray, *Banks and Politics in America, From the Revolution to the Civil War* (Princeton, NJ, 1957).

Morgan, Donald G., *Justice William Johnson, The First Dissenter* (New York, NY, 1954).

Index

accident 157
Adams, John 2, 9, 44, 91, 100–101, 124, 175, 189
Adams, J.Q. 9, 46, 51, 133, 136
admission to statehood 12, 21, 22, 71, 83, 86–87, 92–96, 107, 121, 132, 134, 171
African-Americans 5
Alabama 6, 92, 121, 134
Albany and Schenectady Railroad 79
Alexandria Gazette 61
allegiance 4, 14, 46, 51, 68, 70, 103, 138, 145, 153, 154
allegiance-boosting 145, 152
allegiance-building 51
Ambi-navigator 24
Amphictyon 12, 62, 73, 114–115, 126n47
Appalachicola 172, 173
Aristotle 105n50, 115, 121, 124, 145, 165, 182
Arkansas 86–87, 133–134
Arkansas River 86
Ashmun, Eli Senator 45–46
assessment 10, 13, 19, 23, 26, 63, 82, 101, 117–119, 138, 155, 182
Atchafalaya Railroad and Banking Company 172, 173
autonomy personal 67–68, 108, 138, 155

Bacon, Francis 2, 123–124, 129
Baltimore and Ohio Railroad 172
Bank of the United States v. Deveaux (1809) 79n48
Barry, W.T. Postmaster General 11, 18–19
basic norm, *see* Grundnorm
batch-process 9, 20–21, 44, 176, 177
Bayes, Thomas 28–33, 124
Bear Flag Republic, *see* California (Republic)
Beaumont, Gustave de 18
Beauvoir, François-Jean de 31
Bekker, citation format 182
Bellona 84
Bennington, VT 8, 21, 170
Berkeley, George 35n39, 53
Bickel, Alexander 61
Bioren & Duane edition US public statutes 27, 35n60
Blackstone, William 2, 110–113, 124
Bladensburg, Battle of 2–3
Bonaparte, Jerome 111
bounty-draft paradox 12, 113–114
Boyle v. Zacharie (1832) 167n36
Brockenbrough, William 62, 164
Brunswick and Florida Rail-road Company 173
Bryce, James 61
Burden-shirking 138
bureaucratic autonomy, bureaucratic agenda xiii, 19, 158
Burke, Edmund 18–19; *Reflections* 117
Burr, Aaron 95

Cairo, IL 83
California (Republic) 93, 104
California Water Project 180
Canajoharie, NY 31
canals 5, 10, 22, 38, 45, 82, 87, 129–130
caselaw 160–161
Champlain lake 31
Chastellux, Marquis de 31
Chickasaw 42, 56n39
child-entities 73

Clay, Henry 184
Clermont 24
Clinton, DeWitt 78n1
codelaw 91, 160–161
co-legislation 25, 28, 175
communication xi, xiii, 4, 8, 23–24, 69, 102, 107, 133, 136, 145, 164, 170, 176
Connecticut 133, 134
Connecticut River 101
consent Congress 168n42
consent state 7, 25–27, 42, 45, 83, 87, 124n4, 174–175
consumption 139
Cook v. Moffat & Curtis (1847) 158
Craig v. Missouri (1830) 193n25
crazy-quilt geography 92
cross-country travel i
Currie, David xiii, 194n30
custom 32, 83, 107

debtor-creditor relations 158, 160, 161
decision-makers xi, 73, 77, 78
Deseret state 93
diminishing returns 64, 74–75, 187–188
Dippel, Horst 106
Dismal Swamp Canal 133
District of Columbia, *see* Washington, City of
ditches 96–99
double duty 49, 63
Duane, James 27
Durham County 25

East Florida Rail-road Company 172, 173
Eatanswill 48
economies of scale 4, 40, 77, 98, 130, 162
Edenton, NC 19
Effektivität 148n14
efficiency 7, 13, 18, 20, 21, 23, 32, 74, 87, 99, 119, 144, 160, 163
enabling acts 27, 42, 81, 51, 53, 92, 94, 101, 109
energy-consuming 33
energy-saving 33
energy-tracking 32, 33, 95, 99
energy-wasting 115
Erie Canal 180

fact-testable propositions 5, 33, 64, 89, 145
Farmers and Mechanics' Bank of Pennsylvania v. Smith (1821) 167n36
feasibility 64, 74–75, 80n59, 82, 187
fisc 136
fiscal intermediary 60, 136, 138, 185
Florida 92, 133, 134, 172–173
founding generation ix
Franklin, Benjamin 165
free-loading 138
free-wheeling predicate-assigning 73
Fulton, Robert 25, 84–85

Galileo 29–30
Gallatin, Albert 22–26, 44
George lake 31
Germany 2
gets 47, 117
Ghent, Treaty 15n1, 14, 67, 70, 108, 161
Gibbons v. Ogden (1824) 12, 76–78, 84–92, 109–110
Goethe, Johann Wolfgang von 139–140, 143
Greenville, Treaty 42
Grundnorm 148n14, 147
Gunther, Gerald 61–62

Hale, Matthew 2, 111–113, 124,
Hamilton, Alexander 68, 85, 134–136, 141–142, 147, 183, 187–188
Hardin, Martin Senator 11
Hargrave, Francis 112
Harrington, James 48
Hatsell, John Clerk of the House of Commons 24, 82
House of Commons, United Kingdom 21–22, 50, 96, 97, 99, 135, 138, 144, 165
House of Representatives, United States 21–22, 26, 28, 33, 49–50, 53, 65, 72, 100, 118, 120, 123, 129, 130, 138, 165, 157, 190

Illinois 29, 38, 42, 53, 86, 93, 133, 134, 172, 178
Indian, native American communities 7, 27
Indiana 38, 86, 87, 93, 95–97, 133–134
Imperium in imperio x

inefficiencies 66, 69, 118
institution agents 10, 19, 26, 54, 68, 73, 107, 115, 170, 171
institution-building ix, 33, 163
investigators 33, 98, 111, 143
Italy xiii, 2

Jackson, Andrew 1, 9, 10, 48, 129–130, 133, 144, 172
James River 22, 26, 90
Jameson, J. Franklin 157
Jefferson, Thomas xi, 1, 2, 3, 7, 9, 14, 15, 25, 26, 31–33, 42, 44, 47, 95, 136, 140–143, 157, 175, 176, 184
Johnson, Chapman 75
Johnson, Wm. 189

Kelsen, Hans xiii, 130–131
Kent, James 61, 84
Kentucky 22, 86, 87, 129, 133, 134

labor-saving 49, 74, 96, 97, 98
Lake Winnico and St. Joseph's Canal and Rail-road Company 173
large-scale 112, 128
Latrobe, Benjamin Henry architect 24–25
Leutze, Emmanuel 35n40
London 18, 28, 86, 94
longevity 64, 74–75, 133, 134, 187
Louisiana 16, 42, 86, 91, 93, 132
Louisiana Purchase 6, 7, 23
Louisville and Portland Canal 129, 147n3, 147n5
Lucas v. South Carolina Coastal Council (1992) 192

Macadam, John Loudon 38, 105n53
Madison, James 1–2, 3, 9, 44, 48, 59, 109, 111, 123, 130, 147, 158, 163, 187–188, 190
Maine 22, 23, 93, 137
marginal utility 64, 74–75, 187–188
Marshall, John, Chief Justice (1801–1835): advocates method of Congressional precedents 116, 121, 123–124, 143, 180; advocates 'two governments' formula 3–4, 165, 179–180; advocates voter role in stabilizing government 116–117, 120, 138, 165; aligned with Piketty as to inflation, deflation 119; authors 'Friends' essays 61, 115, 117, authors *Gibbons* opinion (1824) 82–84; authors *McCulloch* opinion (1819) 12, 15, 60; comments on representative government 48–49, 145–146, 147; Commissioner sinking fund 136, 185–186; decisions, creditor-debtor relations 158–160; distinguishes 'liberty' interest 118, 162; discomfort during oral argument, *McCulloch* 75–76; discusses Monroe's 'Views' 189; economies of scale and national exigencies 162; hears oral argument in *McCulloch* 51; legacy 14, 77–78, 124; refounder of Second Republic 11, 164; unravels 'bounty-draft' paradox 12, 126n47
Martin, Luther 75
Maryland Falls, MD 87
Mason-Dixon line 52, 120
Massachusetts 133, 134, 154
Maysville, Washington, Paris, and Lexington Turnpike Road Company 57n52
McCulloch, James 60, 63, 185–186
McCulloch v. Maryland (1819) 15n2, 11, 51, 59–71, 85–89, 105n71, 108, 126n66, 179–180, 185
McMillan v. McNeill (1819) 167n36
Mephistopheles 139
merit-based reasoning 36n82
Mexico, *see* United Mexican States
Mill, James (1820) 118
mission-specific instructions 10, 86, 98, 107, 136, 170, 176
Missouri 121, 133, 134
Missouri Compromise 108–109, 148n38
Mitchell, Augustus S. 102–103
Mobile, AL 172
Mohawk & Hudson Railroad, *see* Albany and Schenectady Railroad
Mohawk River 31
Monroe, James career 2–3; advocates method of Congressional precedents 41–46, 89, 158–159; advocates transactional politics 144–147; approves bill to improve navigation on Mississippi-Ohio Rivers (1824) 82; approves General Survey Act (1824) 82; argues voters reestablish equilibrium (1824) 14; argues for US 'excellence of our

institutions' 161–164; distribution of burdens, comments on 137–138; efficiency in government 103; enslaves 250 persons at Highland 57n70; focus words in 'Views' 46–48; legacy 14–15, 124, 161; prefers European Americans as settlers in western county 52–54; receives Marshall's reaction to 'Views' 89, 189; refounder of Second Republic (1817–1825) 7, 60; survey of Ohio and Mississippi Rivers (1823) 88; threat of breakaway republics 94–95; trust violations by states to be policed 66; 'two governments' formula employed 67–68, 165–166, 179–180; vetoes Cumberland Road repair bill (1822) 1, 10–11, 109–110; 'Views', '1819', '1822' essays (1822) 10–11, 39–40; voter non-disapproval of Congressional action 48–51
Morris, Gouverneur 40
Morse, Samuel F.B. 107
motion 35, 50, 115, 157

Nashville 7, 27, 42, 43, 44
Nasty Old River Bridge 28–30
Natchez 7, 27, 42, 43, 176
National Pike, *see* Cumberland road
needs, inhabitants 46, 47, 52, 82, 117, 131, 142
New Hampshire 50, 105n42, 133, 134, 152, 153, 154
New Jersey 31, 85, 86, 133, 134
New Orleans 7, 8, 10, 19, 27, 42, 43, 86, 170
New Orleans and Carrolton Railroad 8, 10, 170, 173
New Orleans and Nashville Rail-road Company 173
New York city 57
New York state 3, 18, 22, 31, 50, 84, 85, 87, 89, 95, 110, 133, 134
norm-crafting 160, 148n14
North Atlantic 1, 18, 22, 23, 136, 142
North Carolina 6, 8, 10, 18, 79n42, 133
North River, see *Clermont*
not-gets, inhabitants 137

Ogden v. Saunders (1827) 167n36
Ohio 16n25, 25, 27, 44, 45, 54, 86, 87, 88, 133, 134, 176, 178, 190, 192
Ohio River 7, 12, 27, 36, 42, 43, 82, 83, 86, 87, 88, 129
Oklahoma 94
Otsego Lake 31

Pacific Ocean 62, 63
page-turning xiii, 158
Paris 2, 18, 31
Paris, KY 57n52
Paris, Treaty 91, 93, 174, 175
parliamentary-manuals-and-treatises.com technical appendix 181
pattern-discovering 111, 113, 124, 159
Peach Bottom, PA 87
Pennsylvania 7, 12, 23, 26, 44, 87, 133, 134, 154
Pensacola and Perdido Rail-road Company 173
Pensacola to Chatahoochee railroad 173
Philadelphia Union 61
Philadelphia Wardens of the Port 10
Piketty, Thomas 119–120, 143
Piranesi, Giovanni Battista 35n40
Pitt, Wm. (the Younger) 36n82, 136
political culture 52, 152–158
political science 5, 48, 144, 165
Pollard's Lessee v. Hagan (1845) 83
Portland Gazette 137
Post Office Department 10, 16, 18–20, 31–33, 107
practice x, xii, 41, 55, 71–72, 89–90, 109, 111, 114, 154, 156, 182–184
Price, Richard 28–31
principal-agent 89
probability 28–29, 79n52, 119, 124
problem-solving 101, 114, 98
procedure-based reasoning 30, 36n82
process 32, 53, 71, 92, 94, 98–99, 157, 170, 176, 190, 192
productivity 13, 84, 122, 130
productivity analytics 55n33, 54, 64, 74, 75, 86, 113, 114, 124, 140, 142, 143, 161, 187
productivity gains 23, 33, 43, 55n33, 84, 118, 122, 146
prone-to-wander republics 92
proportionality 64, 74–75, 187–188

quantum, energy 33, 114–115, 126n47, 163
Quasi-War with France *see* War with France

railroads, rail-roads 10, 29, 107, 124, 130, 170, 172–173
Randolph, John Representative 6, 13, 120–124, 133, 164
random, random-like, randomly generated values 97, 131, 157
rate of change 110, 111
rational xi, 69
reassessment Congressional 49, 108, 156
reciprocal discipline 33, 120
Republic (French) 163
Republic (US, First) 5, 68, 91, 100, 134, 152, 154, 155, 167n14
Republic (US, Second) 1, 4, 5, 7, 10, 11, 12–15, 33, 44, 50, 51, 54, 60, 62, 70, 72, 77, 84, 92, 102, 107, 110, 111, 116, 119, 120, 124, 143, 154, 155, 156, 158, 162, 163, 164, 166, 167n14, 174, 176
republic breakaway 94
republics ix, x, xi, 19, 51, 62–63, 92, 95, 102, 110, 133, 144
Representatives state legislators 153, 157, 165
Rhode Island 20, 69–70
Ricardo, David 14, 138, 139–143
road-building 87, 91, 100
road-making 4–5, 27, 99, 100
Roane, Spencer 62, 164
rock-strewn 70

Sayre, PA 87
Senate United States 1, 2, 22, 27, 29, 46, 71, 112, 120, 135, 158, 183
single market 107, 136, 146
sinking fund 60, 185–186
Slumkey 48
Smith, Adam 2, 19, 32–33, 41, 54, 63–64, 65, 73, 75, 84, 86, 99, 113–114, 119, 130, 140, 142–144, 160–161, 164, 167, 187, 188, 189
Smithville, NC 19
social science 53, 89, 123, 144, 165
state-making 12, 92–94
Statutes, Federal Congress: 1 Stat 1, Act of June 1, 1789 (oaths) xiii; 1 Stat 50, Act of August 7, 1789 (Northwest Ordinance confirmed) 101, 192; 1 Stat 69, Act of September 16, 1789 (tax on NC and RI imports) 70; 1 Stat 70, Act of September 22, 1789 (temporary delegation, postal system) 20; 1 Stat 96, Act of September 29, 1789 (time fixed for next session, Congress) 50; 1 Stat 125; 1 Stat 178, Act of August 4, 1790 (temporary delegation, postal system) 20; 1 Stat 186, Act of August 12, 1790 (public debt, management) 135; 1 Stat 191, Act of February 25, 1791 (First Bank, charter) 59, 72, 135; 1 Stat 218, Act of March 3, 1791 (temporary delegation, postal system) 20; 1 Stat 232, Act of February 20, 1792 (nationwide postal routes) 20, 21, 44; 1 Stat 281, Act of May 8, 1792 (public debt, management) 135; 1 Stat 305, Act of February 18, 1793 (regulation of coastal shipping) 85; 1 Stat 342, Act of March 7, 1794 (relief, Hispaniola) 163; 2 Stat 18, Act of March 17, 1800 (assent of Congress) 44; 2 Stat 125, Act of March 3, 1801 (nationwide postal routes) 44; 2 Stat 152, Act of April 14, 1802 (assent of Congress) 90; 2 Stat 173, Act of April 30, 1802 (enabling act, Ohio) 132; 2 Stat 269, Act of March 16, 1804 (assent of Congress) 26; 2 Stat 353, Act of February 28, 1806 (assent of Congress) 26; 2 Stat 357, Act of March 29, 1806 (Cumberland Road) 4, 7, 25, 26–27, 42, 43, 44, 45, 129, 176, 177–178; 2 Stat 396, Act of April 21, 1806 (three national roads) 4, 7, 27, 42, 44, 129, 176; 2 Stat 444, Act of March 3, 1807 (rerouting national road) 27; 2 Stat 484, Act of April 16, 1808 (assent of Congress) 21, 90; 2 Stat 491, Act of April 23, 1808 (post roads) 21; 2 Stat 517, Act of February 16, 1809 (DC canal) 38; 2 Stat 570, Act of April 20, 1810 (DC turnpike) 38; 2 Stat 661, Act of March 3, 1811 (Cumberland Road) 25; 2 Stat 668, Act of December 12, 1811 (treaty road) 42; 2 Stat 670, Act of January 8, 1812 (treaty road) 42; 2 Stat 730, Act of May 8, 1812 (Cumberland Road) 163; 3 Stat 140, Res. I,

December 27, 1813 (journals, distribution) 152; 3 Stat 125, Act of April 16, 1814 (assent of Congress) 90; 3 Stat 129, Act of April 18, 1814 (statutes, publication) 42; 3 Stat 206, Act of February 14, 1815 (Cumberland Road) 38; 3 Stat 257, Act of March 19, 1816 (Congress, pay rise) 43; 3 Stat 266, Act of April 10, 1816 (Second Bank, charter) 59; 3 Stat 289, Act of April 19, 1816 (enabling act, Indiana) 38; 3 Stat 301, Act of April 26, 1816 (assent of Congress) 90; 3 Stat 315, Act of April 27, 1816 (road repairs) 42; 3 Stat 318, Act of April 27, 1816 (road, Illinois) 42; 3 Stat 345, Act of February 6, 1817 (repeal, pay rise) 44; 3 Stat 377, Act of March 3, 1817 (road, Reynoldsburgh Natchez) 42; 3 Stat 475, Res. VIII, March 27, 1818 (journal, Philadelphia convention, publication) 187; 3 Stat 426, Act of April 14, 1818 (Cumberland Road) 38; 3 Stat 428, Act of April 18, 1818 (enabling act, Illinois) 38; 3 Stat 433, Act of April 18, 1818 (time fixed for next session, Congress) 49; 3 Stat 545, Act of March 6, 1820 (enabling act, Missouri) 109; 3 Stat 562, Act of April 14, 1820 (survey, Ohio River) 88; 3 Stat 566, Act of April 24, 1820 (sale, public lands) 132; 3 Stat 604, Act of May 15, 1820 (Cumberland Road, southerly route) 43, 132; 3 Stat 645, Res. I, March 2, 1821 (admission, Missouri) 109; 3 Stat 665, Act of April 20, 1822 (assent of Congress) 90; 3 Stat 728, Act of February 28, 1823 (Cumberland Road, repair) 45; 4 Stat 22, Act of April 30, 1824 (General Survey Act) 82, 120; 4 Stat 32, Act of May 24, 1824 (survey, Ohio Mississippi Rivers) 82–83; 4 Stat 162, Act of May 13, 1826 (canal, stock subscription) 129; 4 Stat 175, Act of May 20, 1826 (navigation projects) 133; 4 Stat 241, Act of March 3, 1827 (improvements, Ohio River) 88; 4 Stat 288, Act of May 23, 1828 (navigation projects) 83; 4 Stat 353, Act of March 2, 1829 (canal, stock subscription) 129; 4 Stat 476, Act of March 2, 1831(railroad) 172; 4 Stat 662, Act of March 2, 1833 (railroad) 172; 4 Stat 672, Act of February 26, 1834 (railroad) 172; 4 Stat 744, Res. III, June 25, 1834 (railroad) 172; 4 Stat 757, Act of March 3, 1835 (railroad) 172n; 4 Stat 778, Act of March 3, 1835 (railroad) 172; 4 Stat 792, Res. I, January 27, 1835 (railroad) 173; 5 Stat 17, Act of April 29, 1836 (railroad) 173; 5 Stat 65, Act of July 2, 1836 (railroad) 173; 5 Stat 144, Act of January 31, 1837 (railroad) 173; 5 Stat 187, Act of March 3, 1837 (navigation projects) 133–134, 171; 5 Stat 196, Act of March 3, 1837 (railroad) 173; 5 Stat 197, Act of March 3, 1837 (railroad) 8, 173; 6 Stat 13, [Private] Act of February 12, 1794 (relief, Santa Domingo) 163; 7 Stat 49 [Treaty of] August 3, 1795 (Greeneville) 27; 10 Stat 612, Act of February 24, 1855 (Court of Claims) 170–171; 11 Stat 7, Act of May 9, 1856 (Cumberland Road) 170; 17 Stat 28, Act of February 2, 1872 (elections, House of Representatives, date) 49; 30 Stat 1151, Act of March 3, 1899 (Rivers and Harbors Act) 91–92; 60 Stat. 1049, P.L. 79–726, Act of August 13, 1946 (Indian Claims Commission Act) 144; 67 Stat 29, P.L. 83–31, Act of May 22, 1953 (Submerged Lands Act) 83; 67 Stat 407, P.L. 83–204, Act of August 7, 1953 (admission, Ohio) 94

Statutes, Great Britain: 5 & 6 Will & Mary c. 20 (Bank of England Act/Tonnage Act (1694) 78n6; 13 Geo. 3 c. 78 (Public Highways Act) 96–100; 26 Geo. 3 c. 31 (National Debt Reduction Act/sinking fund) 135, 149n43

Statutes, United States Continental Congress: Bank of North America, Congress establishes (1781) 59–60; land grants to veterans, Congress

promises (1776) 86; western cessions, Congress urges 4, 86
Statutes, United States Confederation Congress: Northwest Ordinance, Congress adopts (1787) 101–102, 192–193; Congressional election arrangements, Congress orders (1788) 49–50; sets 'time ... for commencing proceedings' under *Constitution II*, 57n57
Statutes, US States, Indiana highways (1819) 95–100; Maryland tax on Second Bank operations (1818) 60–66, 109; New York steamboat monopoly (1807) 84–86
Steele, John Representative 11, 19–20
Stephens, Alexander H. 75–76
Stockton and Darlington Railway 25
Story, Joseph 11, 40–41, 43, 75–76, 146–147
Stoudinger 84
Sturges v. Crowninshield (1819) 167n36
superminoritiarians x, xii, 6, 7, 46, 52, 70, 71, 120–121, 164
Susquehanna River 22, 31, 86, 87
Suwanee St. John's Vacasom Bay railroad 173
systemic 28–29

Tallahassee to St. Marks railroad 172
Taney, Roger B. 98, 158–160, 192–194
task-fulfilling 88
technocrat, technocratic 24, 32, 33, 60, 85, 119, 124, 165
Tees river 25
telegraph 107, 124n2
template 5, 41, 54, 96–97, 99, 124
Tennessee 42, 44, 86, 133, 134
texts of political culture 152–158
texts of public history 152, 156–158, 183
Thatcher, Margaret 136, 142
Thayer, James Bradley 61
Tocqueville, Alexis de 18
Tracy, Antoine-Louis-Claude Destutt de 141–143
Trans-Appalachia 175
Trans-Atlantic 2
transportation i, xi, xiii, 4, 6, 8, 11, 12, 14, 19, 21–25, 28, 38, 43, 44, 52, 63, 69–71, 82–84, 86, 87, 90, 91, 95, 102, 107, 122, 130, 131, 132, 135, 136, 144–146, 170–171, 176, 190
Trenton, NJ 2
turnpikes 23, 38
two governments x, 3–14, 46, 51, 66–69, 103, 136, 164–165, 179–180

United Kingdom 2, 25, 139
United Mexican States 93
United Netherlands 1
United States v. Carolene Products Company (1938) 65–66
United States *Constitution I:* crises in governance (1781–1784) 16n20; ratified (1781) 7
United States *Constitution II:* admission offered to 37 states, allocation of representatives, initial (1787) 20; amendment (1804) Twelfth Amendment 6; Americans, constitution elevates the character, 162; annual meeting of Congress 49; biennial election cycle 49–50; endows voters with two votes 165; *Federalist* draws support from other nations and cultures 187; framers 116; inserts biennial election between sessions of Congress 49–50; late ratifications, North Carolina 79n42, Rhode Island 69–70; Necessary and Proper Clause 61; original states invited to ratify 92; Political Governance clause 130; power over claims management, absence 170; power to launch internal improvements 39; power over navigable waters, absence 12, 26, 76; powers listed 5; presidential election procedures 6; quorum rule 21; ratification debates 2, 75–76; ratification 66; Resource Exploitation Clause 130; unratified amendment, Titles of Nobility 111; voter participation as tie-breaking function 117; yeas and nays in Congress to be recorded 21–22, 134
Universität Wien, Rechtswissenschaftliche Fakultät xiii
unpredictable 60
useful life 64, 74–75, 187

Vacasom Bay railroad 173
Van Buren, Martin 9, 21, 31, 84
variables 28–30, 32–33, 54, 114
Vattel 121
Vermont 92, 95, 101, 153
Vermont v. New Hampshire (1933) 105n42
Vice President, Vice-President 71, 75
'Views' *see* Monroe
Virginia 2, 6, 7, 12, 13, 25, 26, 61, 76, 83, 86–87, 90, 92, 121, 164
votarian discipline 47, 66, 108, 113, 119, 156

War, Articles of 175
War Civil English 112
War Civil US xii
War for American Independence (1775–1783) First 2, 17n58, 52, 157
War for American Independence (1812–1815) Second 1, 17n58, 26, 142
War with France, Quasi-War 2, 17n58
War with Mexico 93
Wars of the Coalitions 15, 142, 163, 175
Warren, Charles 61
Washington, City of 1, 11, 19, 38, 45, 70
Washington, George 1, 2, 3, 9, 10, 31–33, 44, 93, 163, 165, 183, 192
Washington, NC 19
Washington state 103
Washington Turnpike Road Company 57n52
Webster, Daniel 134, 183
West Virginia 83, 90, 82
Western Railroad 173
White, G. Edward 75
Wilmington, NC 19
Winchester and Potomac Railroad Company 172
Wirtschaftsuniversität Wien, Institut für Wirtschafts- und Sozialgeschichte xiii
Wisconsin 93
Witton Park Colliery 25
wants, inhabitants 47, 108, 118, 132, 180

Zeno 126n47

Kolibri 360 GmbH
Ferdinand-Jühlke-Straße 7
99095 Erfurt, Deutschland
produktsicherheit@kolibri360.de